United States

of

AMERICA

St. Peter Ev. Lutheran School
2400 Oxford Way
Lodi, CA 95242

Scale of Miles, 120 to an Inch.

St. Peter Ev. Lutheran School
2400 Oxford Way
Lodi, CA 95242

THE
AMERICAN
FRONTIER
PIONEERS, SETTLERS & COWBOYS 1800-1899

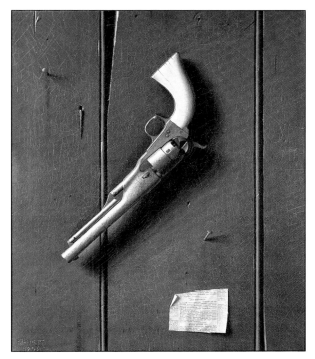

William M. Harnett, 1848-92,
'The Faithful Colt', 1890

Photograph: *Bear River City, Wyoming, 1868, a town built on false hopes. The railroad bypassed it.*

THE
AMERICAN FRONTIER
PIONEERS, SETTLERS & COWBOYS 1800-1899

WILLIAM C. DAVIS
TECHNICAL ADVISOR: RUSS A. PRITCHARD
WITH ARTIFACTS FROM THE BUFFALO BILL
HISTORICAL CENTER, CODY, WYOMING

BCA
LONDON · NEW YORK · SYDNEY · TORONTO

A SALAMANDER BOOK

This edition published in 1992 by SMITHMARK
Publishers Inc.,
16 East 32nd Street, New York, NY 10016

SMITHMARK books are available for bulk
purchase for sales promotion and premium use.
For details write or call the manager of special
sales, SMITHMARK Publishers Inc., 16 East 32nd
Street, New York, NY 10016
(212) 532-6600

© Salamander Books Ltd 1992

ISBN 0 8317 1825 0

All rights reserved. No part of this book may be
reproduced, stored in a retrieval system or
transmitted in any form or by any means,
electronic, mechanical, photocopying, recording, or
otherwise, without prior permission of Salamander
Books Ltd.

All correspondence concerning the content of this
volume should be addressed to Salamander Books
Ltd, 129-137 York Way, London N7 9LG, England

CREDITS

Editor: Richard Collins
Designer: Mark Holt
Color photography: Don Eiler, Richmond, Virginia
© Salamander Books Ltd
Color artwork: Jeffrey Burn
© Salamander Books Ltd
Line artwork: Kevin Jones Associates
© Salamander Books Ltd
Maps: Janos Marffy
© Salamander Books Ltd
Filmset: SX Composing Ltd, England
Color reproduction: Bantam Litho Ltd, England
Printed in Italy

ACKNOWLEDGMENTS

Salamander Books owe a debt of gratitude to the
Buffalo Bill Historical Center, Cody, Wyoming, for
throwing its doors open so willingly in 1991 for the
photography and research undertaken for this
book. With three exceptions, the color spreads
showing grouped artifacts, individual items and
reconstructions of settings come from its
collections. In acknowledging the contribution of
all personnel at the BBHC, the editor would
particularly like to thank the following for the
parts they played in making this book a reality:

Peter Hassrick (Director, BBHC), Dr Paul Fees
(Senior Curator, BBHC), Frances Clymer
(Curatorial Assistant, Cody Firearms Museum),
Elizabeth Holmes (Assistant Registrar), Connie
Marie Vunk (Collections Manager), Gary L. Miller
(Collections Technician), Kelly Jensen-Webster
(Grants Manager), Beverly Perkins (Conservator),
Sarah E. Boehme (Curator, Whitney Gallery of
Western Art), Christina Stopka (Librarian/
Archivist), Joan Murra (Library Clerk). Devendra
Shrikhande (Photographer) generously gave his
time and, ultimately, his studio space for the
duration of the shoot; Faith Bad Bear (Intern,
Plains Indian Museum) not only wrote on the
Crow, Sioux and Cheyenne Indians on pages 10-11,
104-105, 110-111, 116-117, but also helped to select
and identify all the artifacts shown in these plates.
She also advised on the Plains Indians firearms
accouterments on pages 122-123 and was the
inspiration behind Eagle Who Walks.

Photograph: *Cowboys eating lunch, by C. A. Kendrick.*

CONTENTS

I

OPENING THE WEST

Below: *W.H. Jackson's photograph of Frémont's Peak in the Wind River Mountains, Wyoming: a small part of the vast canvas.*

THERE WERE THOSE who maintained that had the Almighty been a painter, the American West would have been his canvas. The sheer vastness of it invited the brush of a great master, and who but a god could work on such a scale? It would take European adventurers, opportunists, settlers, empire builders, more than a century to come to terms with, and even to begin to understand, this massive living landscape. Even then, they never really dominated this Old Master. Rather, the two co-existed, and not always peacefully. Such is the nature of art. Certainly such is the nature of the American West.

Typically, no one then or later could ever completely define what was meant by the term 'the West'. For the first settlers, of course, the distant ancestors of the Indians who migrated from Siberia across the land bridge that once connected Siberia with Alaska, all the country before them was quite literally 'the East'. Thousands of years later the Europeans came from another direction, and from the moment they first landed on the shores of future North Carolina and Florida, the whole continent was the West.

It was a fluid concept, this idea of the West. From the very first step on the Atlantic beaches, it meant opportunity and promise limited only, it seemed, by the boundaries of daring and imagination. That, at least, remained constant. But the physical definition changed with each westward step these Europeans took. Quite literally, the farther west they moved, the smaller 'the West' became. Through the 1600s, any land more than 100 miles from the Eastern seaboard was the West. Anything beyond the Appalachians was 'terra incognita'. During the next century, however, they crossed that barrier and pushed their outposts to the majestic Mississippi. Even into the early 1800s, however, men still spoke of the sparsely settled regions of Kentucky, Tennessee, Illinois, and Mississippi, as 'the West', and

men born there, like Abraham Lincoln and Jefferson Davis, would be known all their lives as 'western' men.

But once white men crossed that great river, all definitions changed. Beyond it lay almost two and one-half million square miles of wilderness, and European eyes had never seen more than a speck of it. There were mountains higher than any had ever seen, ranges whose vastness dwarfed the Alps. Not even the arid plains of Spain could match the vast deserts that lay ahead here. There were wonders and terrors such as the Old World had never seen. Truly this region before them *was* a New World that defied adequate description, and

here the evolution of definitions had to stop. This West was a West of the mind and imagination, one whose impact upon those who set forth into it was so forceful that it precluded any further refinement of the meaning of mere words. This was *the* West, and so it would remain.

The Mississippi almost completely cut the country in two, dividing the settled part of the future United States in 1800, from the two-thirds of it yet to be that stretched westward to the Pacific. The great river ran from New Orleans on the Gulf of Mexico, almost straight north, past old French and Spanish outpost settlements in Louisiana and Missouri, until it

sliced through unorganized and hardly explored territories to terminate near the future Canadian border. Major tributaries flowed out of those unknown lands to feed the Father of Waters. The Red River brought water from 700 miles west, across the flat, arid reaches of what would one day be Texas and Oklahoma, to flow into the Mississippi 100 miles upriver from New Orleans. Further north half a dozen others, the Canadian, Cimarron, Arkansas, Verdigris, and more, brought headwaters formed in the distant mountains across what would be Kansas, Oklahoma, and into Arkansas, to swell the Mississippi's flow. The principal tributary, however, was the Missouri, even

First westward probes of the expanding empire investigated the new Louisiana Purchase territory and sought a safe and practical route to the Pacific and its presumed riches in furs and trade. Following the Missouri from St Louis,

Lewis and Clark moved northwesterly across the Great Plains, into the Rockies, across future Idaho to reach the Columbia and follow its course to the Pacific. Succeeding westward routes would evolve from their trails. Most of

PIONEERS & EARLY SURVEYS

these routes – the Oregon and Santa Fe trails – would depart from Independence then take a more southerly route than Lewis and Clark's, across Kansas Territory and through

future Colorado and Wyoming, or south from Colorado into New Mexico. Jedediah Smith extended the southern route to California along the Old Spanish Trail, then up the Pacific coast

to Oregon. At first the pioneers came for furs and trade, but as war with Mexico approached in 1846 the trailblazing took on a new impetus as military men used them – and blazed new ones – as pathways of invasion and conquest in the South-

west, fear of which had always kept Spanish and Mexicans on arm's-length terms with the Anglos in the territories. Already the whites had left their names on the land as they sent their paths of settlement forward. The flood would follow.

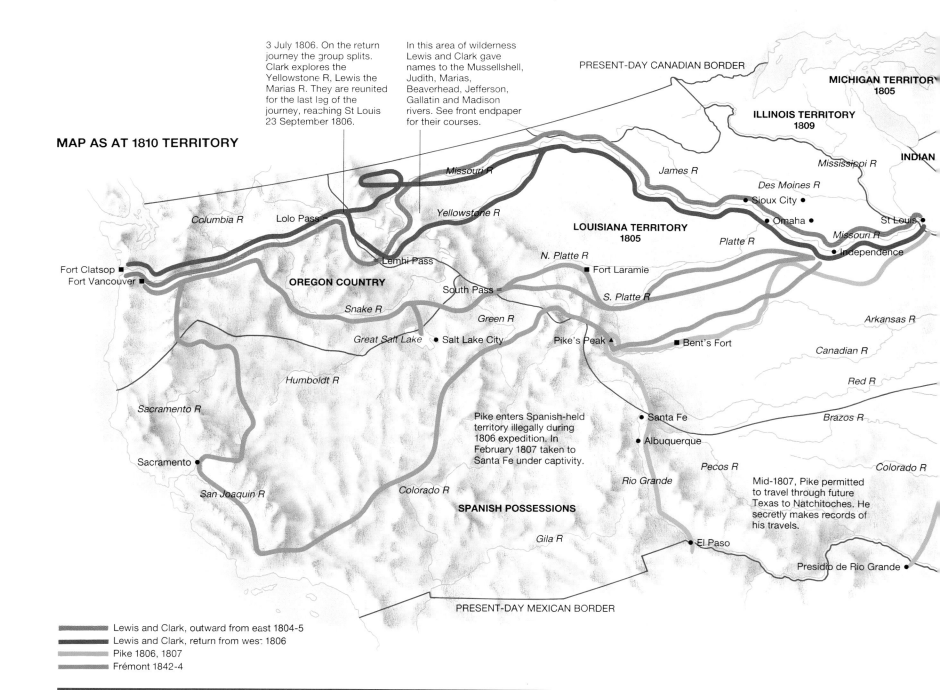

MAP AS AT 1810 TERRITORY

3 July 1806. On the return journey the group splits. Clark explores the Yellowstone R, Lewis the Marias R. They are reunited for the last leg of the journey, reaching St Louis 23 September 1806.

In this area of wilderness Lewis and Clark gave names to the Mussellshell, Judith, Marias, Beaverhead, Jefferson, Gallatin and Madison rivers. See front endpaper for their courses.

PRESENT-DAY CANADIAN BORDER

MICHIGAN TERRITORY 1805

ILLINOIS TERRITORY 1809

INDIAN

Missouri R

James R

Mississippi R

Des Moines R

Sioux City

Columbia R   Lolo Pass

Yellowstone R

LOUISIANA TERRITORY 1805

Omaha

St Louis

Platte R

Missouri R

Lemhi Pass

N. Platte R

Independence

Fort Clatsop
Fort Vancouver

OREGON COUNTRY

South Pass

Fort Laramie

S. Platte R

Snake R

Green R

Great Salt Lake   Salt Lake City

Pike's Peak

Bent's Fort

Arkansas R

Canadian R

Humboldt R

Red R

Sacramento R

Pike enters Spanish-held territory illegally during 1806 expedition. In February 1807 taken to Santa Fe under captivity.

Santa Fe

Brazos R

Sacramento

Albuquerque

Pecos R

Colorado R

San Joaquin R

Colorado R

Rio Grande

Mid-1807, Pike permitted to travel through future Texas to Natchitoches. He secretly makes records of his travels.

SPANISH POSSESSIONS

Gila R

El Paso

Presidio de Rio Grande

PRESENT-DAY MEXICAN BORDER

Lewis and Clark, outward from east 1804-5
Lewis and Clark, return from west 1806
Pike 1806, 1807
Frémont 1842-4

longer than the Mississippi, extending from the frontier settlement at St Louis, in a north-westerly track for almost 1,500 miles and half-way across the continent. It was, in turn, fed by a host of smaller streams – the Platte, the Yellowstone, and more. And north of St Louis, even more streams added their water to the great river's incalculable volume.

Once across the Mississippi, the eyes beheld the beginnings of almost 700 miles of plains, prairies, and near-deserts, from the low hills and limestone outcroppings of future Missouri, across the endless flatness of what would be Kansas and Nebraska, Texas and Oklahoma, Iowa, Minnesota, and the Dako-

tas. It was a region of terrific storms, horrific droughts, and unforgiving heat. It was also the land of the Mandan and Blackfeet, the Crows and Arikara and Sioux, of the Pawnee and Cheyenne, the Kiowa, the Comanche, and a host of other tribes.

If those arid plains and those intimidating inhabitants were not enough to give pause to a man with a westering urge, then there was what lay beyond. Stretching from the Rio Grande in what was then Spanish held territory, straight north in a line paralleling that of the Mississippi, the Rocky Mountains stretched to the future Canadian border and beyond. Moreover, the Rockies were not just a

single range of mountains, but a series of ranges, one behind the other, extending in places as much as 400 miles across impassable peaks, broken only by a precious few passes. Here lay the continental divide, from which all waters flowed either eastward to the Mississippi, or west to the Pacific. In the few lower river valleys that interrupted the chains of mountains lived yet more native tribes, the Flathead and Kalispel in the north, the Shoshoni and Bannock, Ute, Arapaho, and more, in the central regions, and the Navajo and Apache far to the south.

Even more challenges awaited beyond the great mountain barrier. Then came the track-

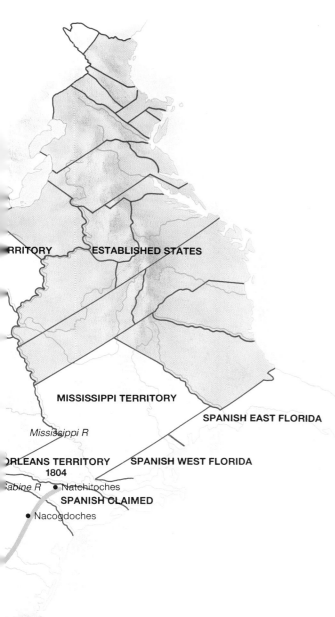

Above: *W.H. Jackson's photograph of Teapot Rock, near Green River Station, Sweetwater County, Wyoming. Jackson recorded the landscape decades after Lewis and Clark first pushed into the interior.*

Below: *The Bannock Indians lived close to their neighbors the Northern Shoshoni in the northern Great Basin area. Like other groups, they lived as foragers, wresting a living from a hostile environment.*

CROW

The Crow, also called Absaroka, were a noble but fierce people who in the 1800s followed the migrating herds across the Great Plains. In their nomadic ways they encountered other native peoples who subsequently became their grave enemies – the Cheyenne, Blackfeet, Flathead and Sioux to name a few. The Crow were known to be great fighters who fearlessly went into battle with a protector who only their enemies could see. This vision was enough at times to deter their enemies. The Crow were sought after by their enemies but in the same right they were also revered for their medicine. The tribe consisted of about ten warrior societies and every man in the tribe belonged to one or more. The young men had to prove their self-worth before acceptance was assured. Counting coup was the main rite for entering a warrior society. There were four or so important coups: the striking of an enemy with a riding quirt or weapon; the stealing of an enemy's horse from outside his tipi; the taking of an enemy's weapon during battle; and the riding down of an enemy. Upon completion of these coups warriors marked or placed different symbols on their person and their belongings – horse, tipi etc – to show tribal members their great feats in battle. Only men were allowed in these societies and in the event of a member's death a replacement was sought. The western Crow, rather than those who migrated to the plains, would encounter the mountain men who followed Lewis and Clark.

1 Saddle: wooden frame, rawhide stretched over it with canvas and buckskin.

2 Brown horsehair rope.

3 Buckskin crupper, small circular rawhide pieces decorated with beaten spoons (trade items).

4 Horse's chest decoration of buckskin and canvas and red tradecloth embellished with seed beads.

5 Headdress of eagle feathers. (Feathers were even numbered and, symbolically important, divisible by four.)

6 Peace medal given to Chief Plenty Coups by Rodman Wanamaker.

7 Beaded pipe bag, with buckskin tassels.

8 Keyhole-shaped rawhide pendant, with metal bit and chainmail-like decoration hanging below horse's mouth.

9 False saddlebags, red and navy blue trade wool

10 Buffalo horned headdress of buffalo skin and rawhide. Long feathers are eagle, shorter are from prairie chicken.

11, 12 Stone-headed war clubs.

13 Pair of green tradecloth leggings, decorated with beads.

14 Carved spiral pipestem, with separate bowl of red catlinite, lead inlay.

15 Hand-drum of raw deerskin, with two drumsticks.

less deserts of Nevada and Utah, the Great Salt Lake, and the barren soil of New Mexico and Arizona. A traveler could face 400 miles of unrelenting rocks and sand, broken only by cactus and rattlesnakes, from the Rockies westward until he reached yet another barrier. Though not as deep as the Rockies, the Sierra Nevada Mountains extended along almost the full length of what would be the eastern border of California, and were just as high and impenetrable. Above them, the Cascade Range stretched northward into Canada, and in these two ranges stood the highest peaks of all, with only a few streams like the Columbia and the Sacramento to interrupt their majesty.

If a man survived everything else to get this far, and if he could drag his aching feet through the frozen passes of the Sierra, or get past the Nez Perce Indians along the waters of the Columbia, he would come at last to a true promised land. Just the other side lay the most beautiful and fertile valleys on the continent, the Willamette west of the Cascades, and the San Joaquin beyond the Sierra. And from either there was little more than fifty miles to go across gentler coastal ranges to reach, at last, the roaring surf of the Pacific. Truly it was a continental mass of epic proportion.

Just as surely, it took an epic journey in those early days to cross it all, but at least, by 1800, the very few who might have made it – none did – would have found not only the scenic wonder of California awaiting, but also a guarded welcome from Europeans. The

Below: *Also inhabitants of the Great Basin, most of which is in present-day Nevada and Utah, were the Utes. Their lands were to be crossed and recrossed by whites seeking the California goldfields.*

Spanish had come here decades before, extending their conquest and settlement northward from Mexico. In 1769 they had founded San Diego around a small presidio and a mission, San Diego de Alcala. With bible and sword the padres and conquistadores moved northward along the coastline, establishing more outposts, and a chain of missions reaching all the way to the peninsula that formed the great bay they named San Francisco. At every mission in between, each placed to be about a day's journey from the next, small settlements grew: San Gabriel, San Juan Capistrano, Los Angeles, Monterey, and more. And to connect them, the Spaniards

Above: *Meriwether Lewis (1774-1809) was sent by Jefferson in 1804 to explore the lands bought in the Louisiana Purchase. Lewis was also instructed to strengthen U.S. claims to the fur-rich Oregon country.*

anticipated the great need that would dominate the West for the next century. They made a road, 'El Camino Real', 'the King's Highway'. Thus they set the pattern: acquisition, exploration, and then the making of the arteries for more to follow.

While the Americans back east of the Mississippi were not completely unaware of the Spanish in California and the very sparsely settled lands along the Rio Grande, the Gila, and the Colorado rivers, at the northern edge of Mexico, they had almost no communication with them directly other than some sporadic trading at the settlements along the Mississippi, and especially New Orleans. But then in one gigantic swoop, these Americans took advantage of the continual political turmoil in Europe, and acquired at a stroke fully one half of the West, virtually doubling the territory of the fledgling United States.

It wouldn't have happened but for Napoleon. Ironically, it was French explorers who first claimed a vast tract of land west of the Mississippi for their king, Louis. It stretched from New Orleans all the way to Canada, and as far west as the Rockies, where it bordered on the Spanish claims. To the northwest it extended even farther, spilling over the continental divide into the ill-defined borders of the Oregon Territory claimed by Great Britain. The French established only a few settlements along the lower Mississippi, extending up to St Genevieve in what would become Missouri. But then they ceded all of the territory they called Louisiana to Spain in the Treaty of Paris in 1763, ending the Seven Years' War. It was a humiliating loss for France, and one not forgotten when a newer, stronger nation emerged from its revolution in 1789 and a great leader, Napoleon, began to

make for himself a continental European empire. An alliance with Spain – dictated, in fact, by force – led to the return of Louisiana in 1800. But then he turned around and offered the whole territory to President Thomas Jefferson. Napoleon needed money. Worse, he knew that when war with Britain commenced once more, as surely it would, his enemy would move out of Canada and take possession of the scarcely defended territory. Selling it to the Americans would remove the liability of having to try to hold on to Louisiana, and at the same time raise cash for his armies in Europe. Napoleon demanded $23 million for the enormous tract of land, and Jefferson happily paid up. Acquisition.

In fact, Jefferson had anticipated much the same course of events. Months before he was approached about making what came to be known as the Louisiana Purchase, he had already issued preliminary instructions to Captain Meriwether Lewis, his private secretary, to prepare to lead an expedition clear across the territory, and through the Oregon lands to the Pacific Ocean. This 'Corps of Discovery of the Northwest' was to move up the Missouri River to its headwaters, explore its tributaries, and look for a connection with the Columbia leading to the ocean to the west. Exploration.

Jefferson's instructions left no doubt as to his ultimate aim. Lewis and his partner William Clark were to look for whatever 'may offer the most direct & practicable water communication across this continent for the purposes of commerce'.[1] This was to be a West of opportunity, and that required, in Jefferson's word, 'communication' – routes for settlement and exploitation, and streams for shipping.

Lewis and Clark never found what Jefferson hoped they would locate – a non-existent direct water route linking the Atlantic with the Pacific, the fabled 'Northwest Passage' – but they found everything else. 'Discovery', of course, is a relative term when applied to the American West. After all, the Indians had lived there for thousands of years, and they were the true discoveries. But with the ethnocentrism typical of the age, Lewis and Clark and all of the explorers who followed regarded themselves as the discoverers of these new lands.

It was an epic journey that began on 14 May 1804. These were not mere adventurers. Re-

Above: *As his second-in-command Lewis appointed an army friend, William Clark (1770-1838), a better woodsman and more outgoing than Lewis. Clark skillfully handled most negotiations with Indians.*

flecting the passion of Jefferson himself for knowledge of the physical and natural world, the fifty or so men who started up the Missouri River from near St Louis that day carried with them scientific instruments, reference books, materials for keeping botanical samples, and bales of trading goods for the tribes they expected to meet and befriend. Interpreters, artisans, soldiers, frontiersmen, and more, made up the complement, which also included Clark's servant York, without doubt the first black ever to see, or be seen on, this frontier.

Slowly they progressed up the Missouri in their two long canoes and even longer river keelboat. Others had covered some of this ground before them, Spaniards and isolated trappers working for the Canadian fur companies. But they were the first to come to make maps and extensive study. All through that summer they pressed on, leaving behind them a legacy of names. Of course, the land already had Indian names, but again these Europeans were discovering a new continent for themselves, and must leave their own titles upon it. They also met with their first native Americans, giving out their trade goods and telling of the great leader in the great city to the east, who now ruled them all, a concept that caused most Indians only to smile with bemusement. On a bluff overlooking the river, in what is now Iowa, they met with leaders of the Oto and Missouri Indians. When they departed early in August, they left behind the name Council Bluffs.

So it went until late that fall, when they stopped for the winter in the land of the Mandan and Hidatsa, in what is now North Dakota, barely 150 miles from the Canadian border. At the time, however, they were barely twenty miles from the boundaries

THE EXPLORERS

The Louisiana Purchase in 1803 opened some two million square miles of vast wilderness west of the Mississippi River to explorers, hunters and soldiers. President Thomas Jefferson was cognizant of the opportunities that lay west and were now available for exploitation. He lost no time in dispatching an expedition, the Corps of Discovery, headed by Captain Meriwether Lewis and William Clark. After reaching the Pacific Ocean, this group returned to St Louis, which was then the frontier, in 1806 with reports and documentation of what lay west. Soon after, adventurous trappers and hunters began to venture into the wilderness in search of furs. Joseph Walker was one of the most prominent of these early explorers in the 1830s and was followed by such men as John C. Frémont, the 'Great Pathfinder'. After initial surveys and mapping, the West lay open to all those of brave heart and strong body willing to trade danger for opportunity.

1 Hudson's Bay multi-colored four point trade blanket.
2 Beaver pelt of type traded by Indians to early explorers.
3 Iron-bound leather trunk decorated with red and blue trade cloth.
4 English manufactured flintlock trade musket, about .50 caliber.
5 Various beads used as trade items: includes multi-colored chevron beads; amber; bone hair pipes; wire-wound beads; assorted glass beads, mostly Venetian 1700/1800.
6 Odometer with tin container used to measure distances on the march.
7 Leather case for above.
8 Single breasted tanned buckskin coat with fringed cuffs and cape, fur collar, bone buttons.
9 Flintlock swivel barrel rifle, maker unknown, about 1820-30, brass mounted with plain brass

patch box. .45 caliber.

10 Powder horn carved in geometric design with carved neck.

11 Post ledger of Fort Bridger, Utah Terr., written by Judge W.A. Carter, 1858.

12 Journal of the Yellowstone Expedition, written by William Raynolds.

13 Wrought iron trade axe head and strike-a-light.

14 Sketchbook of Henry Lewis illustrating Voyage on the

Mississippi River by Fort Snelling, MN, to Eagle Bluffs, Northwest Terr., 1848.

15 MS field map, ink on linen, drawn by Samuel B. Reed, chief engineer of the U.P. Railroad, depicting South Pass to the Great Salt Lake, Wyoming and Utah Terrs, 1864-65.

16 Harpers Ferry Model 1803 flintlock rifle, .54 caliber, one of the very few extant specimens dated 1803, the type of

longarm carried by some members of the Lewis and Clark expedition.

17 Powder horn with turned wood plug and carved neck.

18 Air rifle made by Jacob Kuntz of Philadelphia. (Air reservoir contained in hollow metal butt; the false flint cock actuated the release of air, firing the arm.) This type of firearm was taken on Lewis and Clark's expedition.

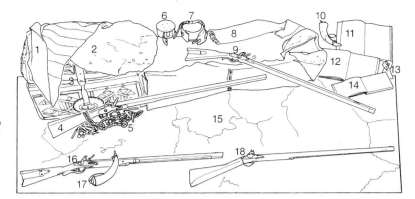

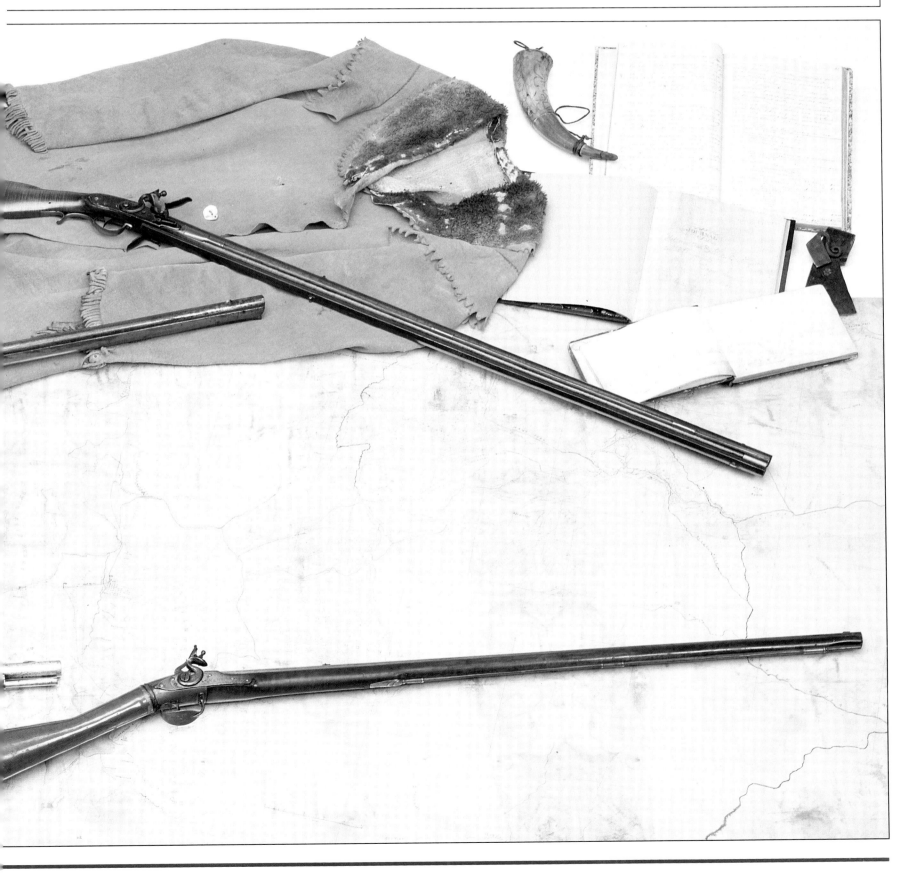

claimed by the British in North America. Here they built log huts close to the friendly Indian villages, and here they spent the coming months of cold studying their neighbors, and learning from them what they could of the 'road' ahead. Here, too, they met a French-Canadian *voyageur* named Toussaint Charbonneau and his Shoshoni wife Sacajawea. Charbonneau had been west of the Mandan villages as far as the Rockies, or so he said, and he warned the explorers of what might be ahead. For one thing, he disspelled any notions of finding a water route to the Pacific. They would have to make a long portage over the continental divide, and that would require horses, which they did not have.

The Shoshonis did have horses, however. Neither horse nor mule was native to the hemisphere. The first came with the conquistadores in the sixteenth century. As these fell into native hands, they spread rapidly northward out of Mexico, their numbers augmented by more that filtered eastward from California. By 1800 most of the Indians of the plains were mounted nations, some, like the Cheyenne, masterful horsemen. It is significant of what Lewis and Clark expected to find on their journey, that they did not take such animals with them. They planned on riding their boats all the way to the Pacific. When they accepted the reality that there would not be a direct water route to their goal, they passed a major milestone in Western history. Important as boats of many kinds would be in the days ahead, as well as other means of transportation, the 'winning' of the West would be done first and foremost on the backs of animals.

Lewis and Clark would have to get their horses from the Shoshonis, which made Charbonneau's wife Sacajawea a desirable asset. To obtain her influence with her people, the explorers hired her husband as an interpreter. Meanwhile, as the winter passed, the Americans busied themselves building smaller canoes for the spring journey, and erecting Fort Mandan beside the river. When the spring thaw arrived, many of the original party returned downriver to St Louis. Lewis, Clark, Charbonneau and Sacajawea and their infant son 'Pomp', along with twenty-seven others, set forth for the Shoshoni country.

The Missouri led them almost due west now, across what would one day become Montana. They passed the mouth of the as yet unexplored Yellowstone, then the Mussellshell, then two more that they named for female relatives, the Judith and the Marias. Then the river took a disturbing turn southward. After they portaged around Great Falls, the river kept going south, while the explorers expected – and wanted – it to go due west. They named this south-bearing main branch of the Missouri the Jefferson, and christened two more tributaries the Gallatin and the Madison, after other leading statesmen in the East. They could do nothing but continue to follow the river. Finally, now on a branch they called the Beaverhead, they approached the continental divide at longitude 113° 30′ west. On either side during the last several days, the mountains had been high, and the going became ever more difficult as the stream became more shallow and narrow. It was July 1805 now, and though they saw snow atop the mountains and the water beneath them was icy, the intense summer heat withered the men day after day.

Still there was no sign of the Shoshoni. But then on 8 August Sacajawea saw in the distance a rock outcropping that her people called 'the beaver's head', and from which the stream took its name. At last she was on familiar ground. The next day Lewis and a few others found an Indian pathway that led alongside the river, and this cheered them. They continued until the Beaverhead split in

two, and took the western fork, Horse Prairie Creek. It was impossible for the canoes to proceed further, so the men set out on foot to cover the last miles to the continental divide. Soon the landscape opened up before them somewhat. On 12 August they saw undeniable Indian prints in the ground before them, and followed. Later that day the prints led them to Lemhi Pass, the doorway through the continental divide. The next day they finally met the Shoshonis.

In fact, they had the good fortune to encounter a chief who was Sacajawea's brother. He sold them horses and gave them what lore he could of the country ahead. It would be a long and difficult portage to get the boats and gear from the Beaverhead up through the pass and down to the headwaters of the Lemhi River on the other side. Lewis decided to remain behind and supervise the task, while Clark and eleven others went on before him down the Lemhi and then into the Salmon River – all of which they mistakenly thought to be the Columbia. There they would begin building new canoes. But Clark's reconnaissance down the Salmon revealed that it was impassable. Other Indians told the travelers of another route, down the Bitterroot, which flowed northward for several days before

flowing into what they would later call Clark Fork.

Thus they went on, until they stopped at the mouth of the Bitterroot. There they stopped for several days, dubbing their campsite Travelers Rest. On 11 September they started overland to the west, and after two hard days' travel crossed through Lolo Pass. A week later, after a nightmarish passage through mountains, tangled forests, and boulder-strewn hillsides, they finally saw the Clearwater River ahead of them. It was navigable, and it flowed into the Snake, and that in turn flowed into the Columbia at last. By now they were cold and almost starving, so much that Lewis named one tributary 'Hungery Creek as at that we had nothing to eate'.[2] The next day they met a band of the Nez Perce, who gave them food. Here the explorers would leave their horses and once more take to the water in newly built canoes. By 16 October, they at last reached the Columbia, 3,714 miles from their starting point.

Thereafter it was a swift passage down the Columbia, though not an easy one. Falls had to be portaged, rapids run. But everywhere they saw growing evidence that their journey's goal was almost attained. These were different Indians now, with strange totem poles erected

in their villages, and canoes distinctly different from those east of the divide. They saw a man wearing a British naval jacket, obviously traded from some Canadian post to the north. Then after portaging the Columbia Cascades, they noticed that the river level rose and fell. That meant that it was affected by tides, and the ocean could not be far. On 7 November they finally sighted Gray's Bay, the estuary linking the Columbia with the Pacific, and in days ahead actually stood on the shore looking out into the Pacific, having traveled over 4,000 miles to get there.

That is how it began. Lewis and Clark did not find a Northwest Passage, no water route to the western sea and the riches of trade with the Orient. They found rivers and Indian trails and mountain passes, portages, campsites, native villages. They built small log forts in a token attempt to establish and protect their trails, and where they did not find existing routes, they blazed new ones. They set out with specific intentions, met insuperable obstacles, and adapted and improvised, living off the difficult land, to achieve their ends. It was a story that became the very soul of the West.

But the achievement of Lewis and Clark in their two-year exploration did not automatically open the vast new territory to settlement and exploitation. They had seen and mapped only a tiny fraction of the new Louisiana Territory. Even while they were making their way back from the mouth of the Columbia in 1806, others were setting out to discover. Lieutenant Zebulon Pike mapped the upper reaches of the Mississippi, looking for its source, then in 1806 set out on an epic trek that took him from St Louis westward along the Missouri, then the Osage Rivers, into the heart of Pawnee country, then south to the Arkansas, and west along it to the foothills of the Rockies. There he saw, but could not climb, a snow-capped summit that others later named Pike's Peak. It took him more than a year, including a period in Spanish captivity, before he returned to safety.

Left: *The Nez Perce were mentioned by Lewis and Clark in 1805. By the time of this much later photograph (1860) of members of the Dreamer cult, so much of their land had been usurped by whites.*

Above: *Of those tribes who early inhabited the plains, the Pawnee were probably one of the first. Lewis and Clark saw the earth lodges of the Pawnee on the banks of the Platte River.*

Below: *'Pike's Peak or Bust', 1860. Others named it later – and painted it on their wagons – after Zebulon Pike who saw but could not climb a snow-capped summit in the Rockies.*

Neither Lewis and Clark, nor Pike, effectively opened the West, and after their adventures concluded, Jefferson was not able to finance further official exploration. War with Great Britain in 1812-15 further distracted Washington's attention from the vast unknown, while political events following the conflict prevented any further explorations until 1820. In the interim, however, the idea of the West did not let go. Lewis and Clark's report, when made public, fired the imaginations of Americans. 'It satisfied desire and it created desire,' said Bernard DeVoto, 'the desire of the westering nation.'[3]

The first to follow that desire were private entrepreneurs, opportunists who saw their fortune 'out there'. Indians and *voyageurs* alike brought back stories of the rivers and valleys teeming with beaver and other potentially profitable fur-bearing animals. The Hudson's Bay Company had already been exploiting North American species in Canada. Now men from Kentucky and Illinois and Missouri set out on their own to find the furred fortunes awaiting in the Rockies. They were the first of the mountain men, a distinctive breed such as America never saw again, rugged, individualistic, solitary. They came not to settle, but to exploit, yet in the process they found new trails, sent back stories, and lured others to follow. For the most part, they followed the water routes at first. Led by John Coulter, the first to extensively trap the Rockies, they con-

centrated on the headwaters of the Yellowstone, on the fringes of mountains the *voyageurs* called the Grand Tetons. They left place names of their own, like Coulter's Hell and Jackson's Hole, in what is now Wyoming.

At the same time other trappers went over the ground first trod by Pike, looking not so much for furs as for an efficient route for getting them back to markets. A terrible depression had hit the United States, but one in which the price of furs did not fall with everything else, making them all the more lucrative. Thus across a front several hundred miles in length, enterprising men were repeatedly traveling and refining routes that took them

deep into the heart of the West. It only remained for someone to repeat Lewis and Clark's feat by reaching the Pacific across the southern part of the country, a route made more practical by the 1819 Adams-Onis Treaty in which Spain ceded to the United States any claim on most of what later became Oklahoma. Yet this still meant that explorers going beyond that territory would have to risk arrest by Spanish officials in the southwest.

It started in 1821, with the Independence of Mexico from Spain. With the Old World power out of the equation at last, traders were anxious to open a route to Santa Fe to capitalize both on its market for their wares, and for the goods that could be purchased for return and resale in the East. Robert McKnight first blazed the trail, leading from Independence, in the western part of the new state of Missouri, southwestward to the Arkansas, and then west along it to the confluence with the Purgatoire. McKnight, and William Beckwith who later that year more permanently marked the route, then moved along the eastern fringe of the Rockies to San Miguel, a small Spanish – now Mexican – settlement, and from there a few miles northwest to Santa Fe.

Before long a flourishing trade developed, the traders traveling in large caravans to provide defence against the raiding parties of Cheyenne, Kiowa, and Comanche. It was an experience never to be forgotten. The bands of merchants gathered at Council Grove when

Below: *Some of the first to follow the lead of Lewis and Clark were* voyageurs. *This later group (1860) at Fort William, Ontario, typified a breed of independent toughs who exploited the wilderness.*

Left: *The Comanche of the southern plains were outstanding horsemen and savage raiders. They were to resist invaders, and the creation of Texas, until 1875 when the might of the whites overcame all.*

FRENCH VOYAGEUR

Canoeing and portaging their way westward in pursuit of the fur-bearing beaver in a trade where none but the hardiest could survive, the spirited *voyageurs*, together with the enterprising Scots who led them, opened up the Canadian interior. Their employers were the powerful Hudson's Bay and Northwest companies. Living in a world defined by the canoe and French language, they maintained their own hierarchy within the freight canoes, the *milieux* (paddlers) being the lowest rank. The preferred garb was the *capot* or hooded coat, but the *ceinture flechée*, a long woven sash as shown here, was their most distinctive trademark.

the word went out that another caravan was to make the trek. Weeks might go by as more and more arrived, until in the end there might be fifty wagons and more than 200 men. They organized themselves for defence, selected leaders, and set out. The whole journey of some 800 miles or more might take fully two months, a pace of not more than fifteen miles a day. Every night they formed their wagons into a hollow square, both to keep their animals safely inside, and marauding Indians out. It could be nerve-shaking standing a watch through up to half the night, staring into the grim solitude of the plains and listening to nothing but the night winds and the faraway cries of prairie animals that were hoped to be four-footed and not two.[4]

In 1825 trappers opened a short parallel extension of the trail through Taos, north of Santa Fe, selling and buying their wares there instead of going on to the original destination. And from Santa Fe, they could move farther west thanks to what they called the Old Spanish Trail, a winding, circuitous route used by the conquistadores for communication between the region and its outposts at Los Angeles and San Diego. If this could be used and refined, then it and the Santa Fe Trail combined would provide the first 'direct' route from the East to California.

The man who did it was Jedediah Smith, a 26-year-old trapper who had already spent a few years trapping in the Rockies. At the annual trappers rendezvous at Bear Lake in 1826, Smith decided to take a party of men southwest to see what opportunity might await his traps in California. It was a gruelling trek, past the Great Salt Lake, south along the Wasatch Range until they struck the Old Spanish Trail near the Virgin River in what is now southwestern Utah. Pressing almost straight south, and starving from lack of provisions, they left the Spanish Trail in what is now Arizona, and soon struck the Colorado at the edge of the massive Grand Canyon. The river

PIONEER TRAILS

The war with Mexico over, land- and adventure-hungry Americans set out to find new opportunity in the vast reaches of the 'new' West. Most of them took the Oregon Trail from Independence, across Kansas and Nebraska, through Indian lands to first passes through the Rockies. Thereafter, an arduous trek took them through freezing mountain gaps, across the arid Great Basin north of Salt Lake, before finally following the Snake toward the Columbia and the fertile Willamette. The Mormons cut their own trail to the Deseret (Utah) waste that would be their haven, largely to avoid persecution. Others wanted only to reach gold-rich streambeds of northern California. They cut their California Trail as a spur off the Oregon route, roughly along a path traveled by Jedediah Smith two decades before. Their trail took them across the Nevada desert, through the passes of the Sierra Nevada, where hundreds perished. California also beckoned to the south, leading the Old Spanish Trail across New Mexico, parts of Utah and Arizona, to lure thousands more to the tiny settlements at Los Angeles and San Diego. Across the trails a new nation moved, most of them wanting land; behind them their rude trails started to become the roads of future empire.

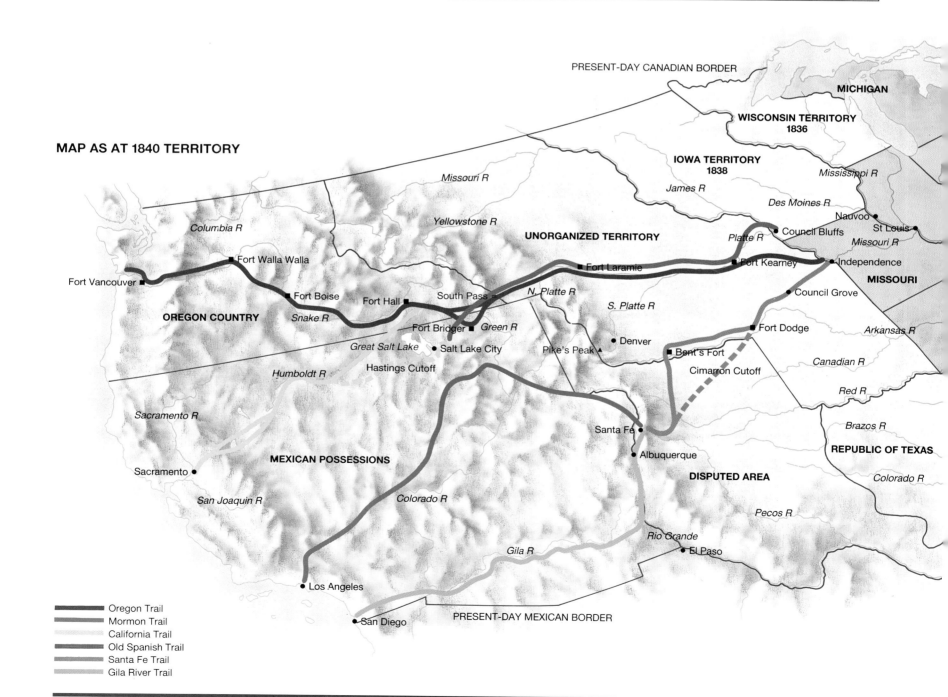

MAP AS AT 1840 TERRITORY

PRESENT-DAY CANADIAN BORDER

MICHIGAN

WISCONSIN TERRITORY 1836

IOWA TERRITORY 1838

Mississippi R

James R

Des Moines R

Nauvoo

Missouri R

Yellowstone R

UNORGANIZED TERRITORY

Platte R

Council Bluffs

St Louis

Missouri R

Columbia R

Fort Walla Walla

Fort Laramie

Fort Kearney

Independence

Fort Vancouver

MISSOURI

Fort Boise

South Pass

N. Platte R

S. Platte R

Council Grove

OREGON COUNTRY

Snake R

Fort Hall

Fort Bridger

Green R

Fort Dodge

Arkansas R

Great Salt Lake

Salt Lake City

Pike's Peak

Denver

Canadian R

Hastings Cutoff

Bent's Fort

Cimarron Cutoff

Humboldt R

Red R

Sacramento R

Santa Fe

Brazos R

MEXICAN POSSESSIONS

Albuquerque

REPUBLIC OF TEXAS

Sacramento

DISPUTED AREA

Colorado R

San Joaquin R

Colorado R

Pecos R

Gila R

Rio Grande

El Paso

Los Angeles

San Diego

PRESENT-DAY MEXICAN BORDER

—— Oregon Trail
—— Mormon Trail
—— California Trail
—— Old Spanish Trail
—— Santa Fe Trail
—— Gila River Trail

took them to peaceful Mohave Indian villages, where they fed and rested before pushing straight west through the San Bernardino Mountains. They skirted the vicious Mohave Desert, saw the San Gabriel hills ahead of them, and finally reached Mission San Gabriel. From there, Smith followed the coastline south to San Diego.

The Mexican officials did not react approvingly to the appearance of this Anglo, and Smith soon left, but in doing so he explored straight north through the fertile San Joaquin almost to San Francisco before turning east again and trekking across the Sierra and the deserts and salt flats of future Nevada and

Utah to arrive once more at Bear Lake, almost a year after his departure. Instead of resting, he told friends of the riches he had seen, of the furs he had taken but left behind in California, and immediately put together another expedition to return. He followed his original path to California, and then up the San Joaquin and beyond, all the way along the coast to Fort Vancouver on the Columbia, where the British had a trading outpost. It was a miserable trip, Indians repeatedly attacking and killing almost all of the party but for Smith and three others. They lost all of their pelts as well, and when Smith finally returned to the next rendezvous, he came almost empty handed.

But not quite. He had found a practical way to reach California overland. The Mexicans there might not be too friendly, but California might not be theirs forever, and already promoters and politicians in the East were calling for westward expansion all the way to the Pacific. Moreover, from his second trip Smith also brought back reports that the British appeared intent on occupying all of Oregon for themselves, even though a recent treaty provided for joint occupancy by the United States and Great Britain. Furthermore, he had seen the lush Willamette Valley for himself. This was land for Americans to settle and farm, a place for their own outpost of empire.

Above: *Geographical surveys of the 1870s would record a land little changed from when Jedediah Smith trekked past the Great Salt Lake and along the Wasatch Range, shown here in Jackson's photograph.*

Below: *The Mission San Gabriel, shown in an 1832 oil painting by Ferdinand Deppe, hinted of the promised land. It was still a Spanish settlement when Smith arrived in California in the 1820s.*

Smith's stories of Oregon reached anxious ears, and so did the tale of a subsequent exploit in which he and others took wagons all the way from Independence to the divide, in present-day Wyoming, confidently asserting that he could have taken them further, to the Columbia itself. Smith was killed by Comanche in 1831, but others continued the searches for speedier, easier, and safer routes to the far West, refining the trails he had first established to California, and the wagon route that he half used and half predicted to Oregon.

The flood that would follow those trails commenced with a trickle just the year after Smith's death when Nathaniel Wyeth took a small party of men west from Independence to the trappers' rendezvous, this year in the Tetons. From there they went on, and by October 1832 they had reached the Columbia, and Fort Vancouver. Two years later he would still be trying to capitalize on what he had done. It came to nothing, but along the way he had built what he called Fort Hall on the Snake River, as a trading post. Behind him, in future Wyoming, others built Fort Laramie, and ahead of him the Hudson's Bay people had constructed Fort Boise where the river of that name flowed into the Snake. Thus the forts that anchored the Oregon Trail were in place. The influx of immigrants would only now be a matter of time.

Below: *Horse- or oxen-drawn covered wagons flooded the trails west, from the 1840s onwards, heading across the plains and mountains for California and Oregon. These are post-1850s.*

Above: *Pioneers camped near the Hogbacks, on the Front Range of the Colorado Rockies. The bared wagon (right) shows the naked structure of the vehicle. Many took household furniture with them.*

Right: *An unidentified pioneer family with their covered wagon at Hailey, Idaho. While the whole family might travel in the wagon, in general most people cooked, ate and slept outside it.*

The explosion came soon thereafter as first missionaries and merchants, and then land-hungry settlers, moved west. They brought animals, seed, money, and – most important – they brought women, Narcissa Whitman being the first to reach Oregon overland in 1836. Women meant wives and children for the trappers and explorers, and that meant stability, the beginnings of permanence. Independence remained what they called the 'jumping off place' for these first emigrant trails. From that thriving frontier community, the Oregon Trail followed the Kansas River westward, then turned northward until it struck the Platte, where in 1848 the U.S. Army

would establish Fort Kearney. Then the wagons rolled west along the Platte to Fort Laramie, past it to the Sweetwater River, and to its headwaters. There they crossed the divide at South Pass in the Wind River Range, and finally reached Black's Fork on the Green River, where a new trading post went up in 1842 called Fort Bridger. From there the trail led over the ground traveled by Smith and Wyeth and a host of the mountain men to Fort Hall, then along the Snake to Fort Boise. From there it led overland to Fort Walla Walla at the confluence of the Snake with the Columbia, and finally along that great river westward to Fort William, where Portland stands today.

For those with California in their sights, the trail branched at Fort Hall and turned southeast, past the Great Salt Lake until it found the Humboldt River. Wagons could follow it across latter-day Nevada to the Sierras, and thence through dangerous high mountain passes like the Donner, to emerge at last at Swiss entrepreneur John Suter's (more commonly Sutter, and hereafter used) fort just north of future Sacramento.

Thus the overland routes, the first 'transcontinental highways', were marked on the landscape. Actually, they were not so much marked as simply 'known' by those who led trains over them, but in a few short years the wagon wheels and animal hooves would wear away a wide path which can still be seen today in places.

But the nation had been on the move West even before the overland routes began to rumble under the wagon wheels. Lewis and Clark had presaged another way to get to much of the new land when they, of necessity, wedded themselves to the Missouri through its entire length. The Louisiana Territory, and more land to follow, struck the American imagination almost at the same time as another new passion arose – steamboats.

In fact, of course, water transportation was an old story on this continent so penetrated by mighty rivers. Canoes, flatboats, and later keelboats, were already plying the Mississippi between St Louis and New Orleans. In just one winter season, more than 1,000 of them came down the Ohio to the Mississippi, filled with people who would settle both banks of the great river, or laboriously travel upstream to

AMERICAN GUN-MAKING SHOP

The earliest known depiction of an American firearms manufactory dates to about 1820. The reconstructed colonial gunshop here depicted may be somewhat earlier (probably 1800-10) and is typical of a three- or four-man operation where there was a distinct division of labor and specialized crafts. An individual had a specific talent, be it as a lock maker, barrel forger, stock maker or gun fitter. Each practised his trade, turning over his finished product to the master for final fitting and assembly. There was no such concept as interchangability at this time, each firearm being an individually crafted piece. Not only would such a shop manufacture new and improved pattern arms but it would also do a thriving business repairing and upgrading obsolete arms such as the flintlock pistol of about 1800-20, the Model 1777 and Model 1795 flint muskets, all shown in the window area of this illustration. Note also the stock blanks and rough cast brass trigger guards ready for future production, and the complete absence of any mechanical power. All the arms used by early explorers and pioneers were hand crafted in the east in just such cottage industry shops by unknown and long-forgotten gunsmiths. Recognizable products of these early shops are great rarities today, most of them having been long destroyed by hard use and abuse even before the middle of the nineteenth century. As pioneers crossed the Allegheny Mountains into what is now western Pennsylvania, Ohio,

Kentucky, and Tennessee, immigrant gunmakers soon followed. New and up-to-date technology did not always accompany colonists or reach settlers. The colonists' governments were generally unwilling to offer the latest in arms technologies on what might be risky or unsuccessful forays into the unknown; settlements therefore quite often served as dumping grounds for obsolete military arms or were equipped with inexpensive and unsophisticated sporting pieces. But as technology improved so did the arms the gunmakers produced. Rifled firearms received early recognition and acceptance in the colonies and later on the frontier as it pushed ever westward. Their superior accuracy when compared to the smoothbore musket made such arms the obvious choice of one whose own survival depended on the proficiency of his arms. As the flintlock era gave way to the percussion ignition system, firearms makers along the Mississippi River kept up with this advance in technology. A great gunsmithing center evolved in St Louis, Missouri, one of the primary jumping-off points for the west. The shops of Hawken and Gemmer produced some of the great rifles that crossed the plains. Military development also played a dominant role in the evolution of firearms with the adoption of a reduced bore rifled musket in 1855. With the acceptance of the rimfire metallic cartridge, the age of modern firearms had arrived. Much of this development can be traced back to the need for improvement established by westward mobilization.

the Missouri, against the current, propelling themselves with sails, ropes towed by animals ashore, or pushing themselves through the less turbulent shallows by shoving long poles against the river bottom and 'walking' the poles from bow to stern. But no matter how propelled, they were slow, and inevitably vessel and occupants were always subject to the whims of the river. Most simply floated downstream, and were broken up for lumber or sold as firewood when the destination was reached. Any return journey was afoot.

Consequently, only limited exploitation of the upper reaches of the Missouri, the Arkansas, the Red, and other western feeders of the Mississippi, was possible, and then usually for fur trading companies. But then came Robert Fulton and Robert Livingston, fathers of steam navigation in America. With their help, another entrepreneur, Nicholas Roosevelt, designed and built the first steamboat west of the Alleghenies. When he christened it *New Orleans* in 1811, his intent was clear, and that same year he set off down the Ohio from Pittsburgh, Pennsylvania. It was a hair-raising experience, from floods, a comet, an eclipse, to the epochal New Madrid earthquake, which sent tidal waves flowing up the river and changed the course of the Mississippi. Still, Roosevelt finally reached New Orleans in 1812, and the rush to exploit steam navigation on the western rivers was on. Within three years steamboats were able to steam back upriver against the current. In 1817 the first one pulled in to shore at St Louis, and by the end of the decade they were venturing up the Missouri as far as Independence, and up almost the full length of the Mississippi.

They were ungainly craft, not the sleek, stately riverboats of later decades. They drew only a few feet of water in their bows, to avoid the snags and shallows that filled these waters. Their decks sat low, barely above the water, and freight, livestock, passengers, and operating machinery all shared much the same space.

There was always a danger in this, for these craft used a high-pressure steam engine developed in America. If the boiler were punctured or broke a seam, scalding steam could kill dozens, and an explosion of a boiler could send boat and passengers to the bottom, sometimes in a blazing inferno. Nearly a third of these boats went down in accidents of one kind or another, and a lore soon developed around the people who piloted them. In 1844 one proud steamboatman boasted that 'it takes a man to ride one of these half alligator boats, head on a snag, high pressure, valve sodered [*sic*] down, 600 souls on board & in danger of going to the devil'.[5]

The trappers went up the Missouri, carrying their traps and trade goods with them, and came back down again with their pelts. Often, too, these journeys presaged the development of frontier communities, for on each voyage the passengers became their own law as they steamed through lands with no other law at all. Everyone mixed irrespective of wealth or station, for space was too cramped to allow distinctions of class. They also decided punishments for offenders like thieves and pickpockets, and the will of the majority ruled. It was frontier society in microcosm.

As the decades passed, more and more vessels plied the rivers, stretching ever farther

Above: *Before the days of the railroad, steamboats carried freight and passengers across the country on rivers such as the Missouri. The* Mary McDonald *seen in 1867 eventually caught fire off-shore.*

Below: *In a country crisscrossed by many rivers, water transportation was crucial. Nascent towns such as this one on the banks of the Kaw in Kansas state might rely on a rough ferry to carry its people.*

west until, by the 1870s, there were even steamboats on the Yellowstone, almost within sight of the continental divide. Meanwhile, on the Pacific side of the divide, steam was eventually brought around Cape Horn to San Francisco Bay, and from there the boats plied the Sacramento River and the San Joaquin, though only to support settlement already in place. Still, between the overland trails and the riverborne routes, the network of travel and communications across the West expanded rapidly from the 1850s onward.

But it was still terribly slow. An overland journey could take five months. In the early days, a journey upstream from New Orleans to St Louis could require nearly a month. Imaginative men looked for ever-faster means, both for travel, and communication. One man invented a 'wind wagon' or 'prairie ship', little more than an overland wagon equipped with a huge sail! It did not work, of course. More imaginative yet was the founder of the distinguished magazine *Scientific American*, who proposed in 1849 that he could get 200 people to San Francisco in just three days! Rufus Porter designed a 1,000-foot-long hot air balloon, to be powered by steam-driven propellers. It presaged the flights of invention of Jules Verne, but it never flew.[6]

For several decades, instead, the emigrant wagon train would have to do for passengers and settlers. But as America expanded in the days leading to the Civil War, and especially after California became a state in 1852, rapid communication of information became essential. Washington could not wait months for vessels to sail from the East coast down past South America, around the Horn, and then up to California, and back. As usual, there were visionary men waiting to match problems with solutions.

Clipper ships, linked with a railroad across the Isthmus of Panama, could carry mail from New York to San Francisco in a month by the mid-1850s, but still that was not fast enough.

Above: *The stern-wheeled* Rosebud *would have plied the Missouri River in the 1880s. Built for shallow water and muddy going, it could carry both freight and passengers through waist-high water.*

Below: *The levee at St Louis in the 1850s, lined with paddle-wheeled steam boats. They played their part in developing the vital network of travel and communication as the century advanced.*

TRANSPORTATION: FREIGHT & EXPRESS

Names synonymous with the frontier are Pony Express and Wells Fargo and Company. These two companies carried a major portion of the mail and valuable cargo in a short period of time and captured the imagination of the world, a highly romanticized image which is still prevalent today. Less glamorous were the plodding ox and mule teams of many smaller companies that pulled the heavy freight – bars, mirrors and pianos for saloons, cast-iron stoves, nails and equipment for hardware stores, and plows and other tools for farmers, miners and tradesmen. Every commodity other than raw materials had to be shipped west. The east, hungry for raw materials from the frontier, saw the West as a vast consumer of manufactured goods. Transportation, like other endeavors in the West, was perilous. Cargo had to be hauled hundreds of miles through inhospitable terrain, sometimes through rapidly changing climates, and the drivers had to contend with hostile Indians and whites in a hostile environment. It was hard physical work and could be appallingly tedious, but loss of one's team for any reason signaled loss of valuable cargo and sometimes the driver's life. The individuals who brought material things to the West played no small part in the establishment of civilization and their exploits, against quite considerable odds, are largely unsung. William H. Russell may be considered one of the great freightmen of the period.

1 Wooden yoke for oxen, and ox bow, one of two on each yoke.
2 Driver's bullwhip.
3 Wooden grease or lubricant bucket for wagon wheels and axles.
4 Wood iron-bound strong box painted with logo, 'Wells Fargo'.
5 Breech-loading side hammer double-barrel shotgun made by J.B. Clabrough and Bro., London, 12 gauge.
6 Sharps new Model 1859 carbine with special order 15 inch barrel, .52 caliber, for Wells Fargo, for protection of coaches.
7 Breech-loading side hammer double-barrel shotgun with short barrels made by Rhode Island Field Gun Company 12 gauge. Stock marked 'Adams Express Co., No. 10, Denver, Colo'.
8 Two brass base shot shells for 12-gauge shotgun.
9 Iron and wood wagon jack.
10 Iron mule shoes.
11 Painted canvas saddle bags used by Wells Fargo & Company Overland Pony Express.
12 Whitney Navy revolver, .36 caliber, in open top 'Slim Jim' holster.
13 Pony Express saddle with *mochila*, which fitted over the saddle and had four locked compartments integral to body.
14 Metal advertisement sign for Pony Express.

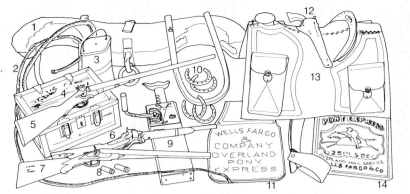

Mail traveling overland had to go by mule-driven wagon to Santa Fe, or else from Independence to Salt Lake City, and then on to San Francisco, but the journeys were only made once a month, and schedules were honored mostly in the breach.

Then came the enterprising partnership of Russell, Majors, and Waddell. Driven by guiding light William H. Russell, the partners announced on 27 January 1860 the inauguration of their Pony Express. Telegraph lines now connected the East with Missouri as far west as St Joseph, on the Missouri River north of Independence. For $2.45 for each ten words, a message could be telegraphed to 'St Joe', and there be transcribed on to special lightweight paper, and sealed in an envelope. Stuffed into special leather pouches carried on either side of the saddle, the treasured correspondence was then to be taken on a hair-raising ride clear across the continent. Riders rode in relays between stations spaced all across the country, with food, fresh mounts, and replacement riders spaced at intervals. If all went well, ten days later the pouch rode into Sacramento, where the telegrams were sent by wire to their final destination in San Francisco.

It was a daring, and quickly doomed, enterprise. The first rider set out in April, and for the next eighteen months he and the others risked Indians, droughts, blizzards, and everything else the elements could throw at them, to get the mail through. Many a future luminary of the post-Civil War 'Wild West' made his first mark as a Pony Express rider, including William F. Cody, James Butler Hickok, and more. Most got through on a route that followed the emigrant trail along the Platte and then passed over the Rockies south of Fort Laramie on a direct line to Fort Bridger. From there they rode straight on to Salt Lake City, and then on a direct line to the Humboldt, across the Sierras, and into Sacramento. Politics and progress killed the Pony Express

Above: *The short-lived Pony Express, inaugurated in January 1860, finished by 1862, attracted young men such as Richard Egan. Despite the hazards of the service, he for one survived beyond youth.*

Below: *The advance of technology in 1868: Union Pacific surveyors at the site of a former Pony Express station, Echo Canyon, Utah. As the railroad advanced, so too did the transcontinental telegraph.*

THE PONY EXPRESS

As the nation of America grew, so did the express companies. For many years this mode of transportation and communication was a private enterprise exerting major influence well before the Civil War. The Pony Express transported mail and governmental documents between 1860 and 1861 from the Missouri to California in just ten days. The riders might carry a pair of Colt's army pistols and sheath knife; the saddle was as light as possible. Mail was carried in a pair of saddle bags with four pockets (*mochila*), or *cantinas*, as shown here. Towards the end of 1861, telegraph lines had spanned the continent and suddenly the fabled Pony Express had no role to play.

THE STAGE STOP

When stage lines were established it was essential for sites for stage stops to be selected in advance. Requirements were usually a convenient source of water and wood, topography conducive to defense and an adjacent area suitable for a corral for spare teams of horses. Security and sustinance were primary prerequisites. Availability of game for food was another consideration. After site selection, stage line employees were sent out to improve the site by building a shelter for stop staff and corral for the stock they would tend. Eventually these individuals would become the staff of that particular stop on the route. Stage lines covered vast areas of desolate wilderness, so these outposts had to be established and functioning before the first stage could make its run. Therefore, considerable investment of time and money was made before the stage owners ever hoped to see a return on their capital. Stage stop personnel were, by necessity, an independent lot, used to living rough without much comfort in primitive surroundings for long periods of time. Stops were manned year round by one or two individuals who tended the teams not in use, and hooked and unhooked teams as stages stopped for new teams and left almost immediately. Stops in remote areas, miles from any vestige of civilization and devoid of any real amenities, were little more than rude shacks that offered shelter (usually dirty), liquid refreshment (oft-times bad), and food of varying quality. Any furniture

was hand made, crude and utilitarian. Roofs were often sod: it did not burn. Floors were swept dirt when dry, mud when wet. In most cases these shelters could become defensive positions if need be in perilous times. Stage line employees managing the stop were well armed for their own protection and the gathering of game to feed themselves and passengers.

The interior of this late nineteenth-century stop is much the same as it would have been fifty years earlier, with the exception of a modern marvel, the Kellogg wall telephone, made in Chicago. There are no closets: there was no need for them. Staff only had the clothes on their back and possibly a change of underwear. Sanitation was non-existent in remote areas and little better elsewhere. Life was a real hand to mouth proposition. The stop crew ate, lived and slept in such a structure week in and week out. Along with a bucket for water and an axe for securing wood, the firearm was an essential tool for survival – providing food for the table and protection for the individual. Arms here include a Colt Lightning slide action large frame rifle on the left, a Model 1899 Marlin lever action rifle hanging on the wall, and single and double barreled shotguns propped against the far wall. A popular and warm buffalo hide coat also hangs against the far wall. Like most things on the frontier, the stage stop was simple and efficient. There was little need for foolish luxuries and non-essentials in this rough lifestyle.

before the end of 1861, when Congress refused to grant it a subsidy for carrying the mail, and when an even faster and more efficient (and considerably less dangerous) means of transmitting communications became available.[7]

Ever since the commercial practicability of the telegraph had been demonstrated in the 1830s, men had dreamed of spanning the continent with a wire that would link East with West almost instantaneously. By the 1850s, the wire had reached St Joseph. In 1858 the line from San Francisco to Sacramento was extended even farther to Genoa on the Utah Territory border near what is now Nevada, and its owner was lobbying Congress for money to extend the wire to St Joseph. By 1860, even as Russell, Majors and Waddell were sending their riders across the plains, work parties were out stringing mile after mile of wire along exactly the same road, the so-called central stage route. Working from opposite ends of the gap in the wires, the parties finally met at Salt Lake City on 24 October 1861. From that day forward, except for the occasional break in what the Indians came to call the 'singing wire', messages from the Atlantic could reach the Pacific in a single day. It ended the Pony Express abruptly, and it ended forever the millennia-long isolation of East from West.

Quite perceptibly the country was growing 'smaller'. Three years before the Pony Express commenced, other mail schemes were attempted to link California with the East. Congress put out a contract for carrying mail and passengers via a circuitous southern route that would also link Missouri with the newly acquired New Mexico Territory taken from Mexico by war in 1848, and augmented by the Gadsden Purchase in 1853. John Butterfield

Below: *John Butterfield's Overland Mail Company had carried most of the transcontinental mail since 1858. After the demise of the Pony Express, his company utilized some of the remote stations.*

won the contract, and using military roads already being constructed between El Paso and Fort Yuma, on the border with California, he inaugurated the Butterfield Overland Mail. It started in Tipton, Missouri, moved almost straight south to Fort Smith, Arkansas, then swung deep into and across Texas to El Paso, thereafter skirting the border with Mexico until it turned upward again to terminate in Los Angeles or go on to San Francisco.

To compete with Butterfield, Russell and John S. Jones started their own more central line connecting Leavenworth, Kansas, and Denver, in what would later be Colorado. The Leavenworth & Pike's Peak Express Company stumbled almost immediately, and was soon re-organized by Russell, Majors, and Waddell, into the Central Overland California & Pike's Peak, merging it with other floundering lines. It was over their stage route, stretching as far as Salt Lake City, that the later Pony Express riders rode, using the same relay stations already set up for the overland coaches. Then cruel irony stepped in to take a hand. In 1861, with Southern states including Texas and Arkansas seceding from the Union, Butterfield's route was clearly out of the question, for now fully half of it ran through hostile Confederate territory. Russell and his partners appeared to be riding high. But Russell himself had offended many, and embarrassed his partners with questionable financial dealings and what appeared to be outright embezzlement in order to keep the Pony Express going. Congress could not swallow that. In the end, they offered the lucrative mail contract and huge subsidy – amounting to hundreds of thousands of dollars – to Butterfield, if he would switch his operation to the Central's route.

Left: *Four St Joseph Pony Express riders. Johnny Fry (top right) rode the first leg of the first westbound run. He later joined the Union army but did not see the end of the Civil War.*

Above: *Ben Holladay was the sole owner of his eponymously named stagecoach company. Between 1862 and 1866 he enjoyed a virtual monopoly on the eastern part of the central overland route.*

Below: *The Rock Creek stagecoach station in 1861. By then, the stage was the most popular means of carrying people, mail and valuables across the West. Stations offered food and change of horses.*

THE HEAVY CONCORD STAGECOACH

The most familiar vehicular mode of transport in the West was the stagecoach, romanticized in countless wide screen epics, particularly John Ford's classic movie 'Stagecoach' which launched the career of the then unknown John Wayne, countless B grade Saturday afternoon action adventures and good and not so good art. The stagecoach has been the focal point of television programs and the original film has been recast and remade in the last twenty years for another generation of theater goers. In reality, this rough and sturdy means of transport was neither romantic nor comfortable, although it did have some advantages over walking. This type of transportation evolved slowly from the stage wagons of England, springless open wagons with backless benches, which appeared during the sixteenth century. By the time this conveyance appeared on the American continent it was already enclosed. The first public stage line on the North American continent opened in 1732 and ran between Burlington and Amboy in what is now New Jersey. A New York to Philadelphia line was in operation by 1756 and it took three days of traveling eighteen hours a day to complete the journey, now made by rail in one hour and fifteen minutes. The heavy Concord stagecoach was first manufactured in Concord, New Hampshire, by the Abbot, Downing Company in 1827. It was so well received that many other manufacturers soon joined the ranks. Made of wood and

iron with leather 'springs' and weighing over two thousand pounds empty, these vehicles cost over $1,500 to construct in a time when such a sum was considered a small fortune. To offset such expense some eighteen to twenty hapless souls were carried within and about the coach with a crew of two or three, a driver and one or two guards riding shotgun, a term still used today to describe front seat passengers. The vehicle and mob of passengers was pulled by a team of six to eight horses, harnessed in pairs, depending upon the terrain to be traversed and the weather to be encountered. A ticket for a trip from a stage depot on the Mississippi River to a destination in California might cost some $200 per person and the journey could be made in three weeks in the mid-nineteenth century . . . if there were no mishaps. A fully loaded stage might average about eight miles per hour over reasonable terrain. Tired teams had to be changed at remote stage stations every twelve to fifteen miles and there was usually a short break every forty to fifty miles at a more comfortable stage stop where crew and passengers could dismount, eat and drink if lucky or physically still able and attend to the call of nature with some semblance of privacy. In any event, passengers paid for the trip in more ways than one. Stages were used in the West in less accessible locations as late as 1910 when they were replaced by the automobile. Train travel, which began in the east in the 1840s, with heated cars, even full of smoke and cinders was a great and welcome improvement . . .

It was Butterfield's salvation. He happily agreed, Russell and his partners' overland operation was ruined, and wound up letting out its services and equipment to Butterfield, and the completion of the transcontinental telegraph effectively finished them. By this time, a number of smaller refinements to the overland routes had been effected as well, but the coming of Civil War effectively punctuated what was already becoming evident anyhow – that the central route across the Kansas and Nebraska Territories, thence into the Utah Territory – later Colorado, southern Wyoming, and Utah – was the most direct and effective route to Salt Lake and California.

No sooner did the Civil War come to an end than the eyes of Americans, North and South, were redirected westward once more, and more and more trails began to slice into as yet undeveloped regions. In 1865 John Bozeman started from Julesburg, in the northeastern corner of new Colorado Territory, and a stop on the Central Overland road, and explored northwestward across Wyoming Territory into the southern reaches of the Montana Territory, heading for Virginia City. Precious ores had been found there, and would-be miners needed a road to get them there, while cattlemen were anxious to have a safe route to drive herds to the hungry mouths of the Virgi-

nia City miners. The Army built forts along the Bozeman Trail to provide protection for both – Forts Fetterman, Phil Kearny, Reno, and more – and even though the influx of exploiters violated treaty promises made to the Lakotan (Sioux) tribes, the whites were not to be stopped. John Mullan had already pushed a road 600 miles from Fort Walla Walla eastward across the Idaho Territory to reach Fort Benton, deep in northern Montana, on the Missouri River. There he met steamboats, now full partners in the work of frontier transportation and conquest. Mullan's Road, like the Bozeman Trail, opened a vast new region to exploitation.

By the 1850s, the arms of transportation, communication and commerce were stretching in the wake of the pioneers. Early on, mail went with the wagon trains and had haphazard schedules. By the time of the Gold Rush, the statehood of California in 1850, and the stretch of the United States from coast to coast, such methods were no longer acceptable. John Butterfield's Overland Mail route from central Missouri cut deeply across Arkansas and Texas, hugging the

STAGE ROUTES & RAILROAD SURVEYS

Mexican border all the way to California and up the coast to San Francisco. Both the rival San Diego and San Antonio mail route traveled almost exactly the same ground, seeking to avoid mountains and Indians. To the north, the Central Overland, California and Pike's Peak Express took regularly scheduled mail and passenger stages along the line of the Oregon and California trails while the Leavenworth and Pike's Peak took care of the burgeoning Denver and Rocky Mountain communities. The Pony Express operated on the Central Overland route between St Joseph and Sacramento. Meanwhile, other entrepreneurs were already planning a new advance. Four railroad routes were surveyed in the 1850s, and by 1860 the Judah-Dodge route had been laid, the first destined to be realized.

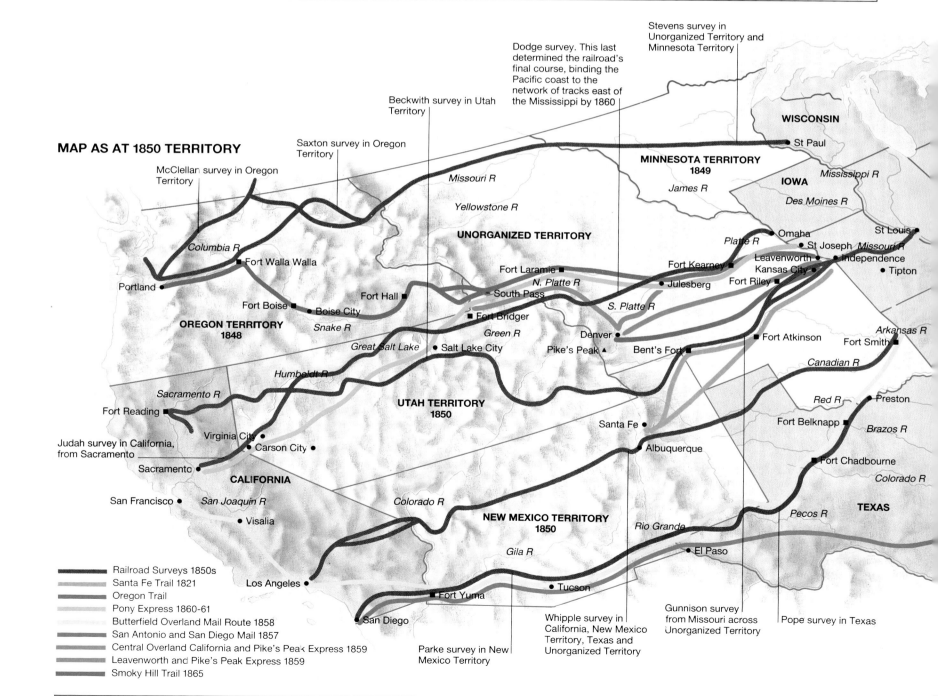

MAP AS AT 1850 TERRITORY

Railroad Surveys 1850s
Santa Fe Trail 1821
Oregon Trail
Pony Express 1860-61
Butterfield Overland Mail Route 1858
San Antonio and San Diego Mail 1857
Central Overland California and Pike's Peak Express 1859
Leavenworth and Pike's Peak Express 1859
Smoky Hill Trail 1865

But it would remain for one more road to bind the Pacific to the East, and this one did it with ties of iron. The idea of a transcontinental railroad dated back almost as far as railroading itself in America. By the 1840s rail lines linked the Mississippi with the eastern seaboard, and visionaries were already scuffling among themselves to predict the best route for a line extending on to the Pacific. It would be faster

Right: *Officers of the 6th Cavalry relax under a tree bower near Fort Fetterman, Wyoming. As a vital line of communication and an important Army presence in Sioux country, such activities were a luxury.*

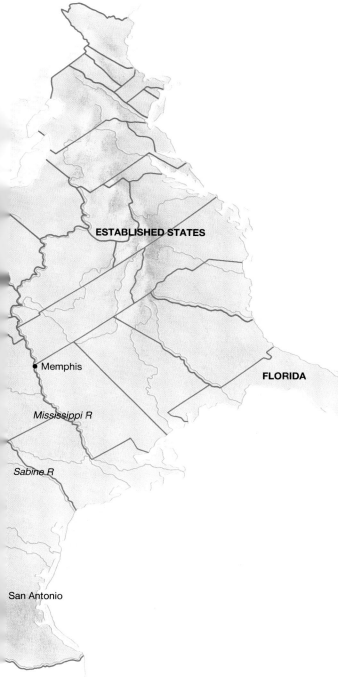

ESTABLISHED STATES

Memphis

FLORIDA

Mississippi R

Sabine R

San Antonio

Above: *Stagecoach at the Branco stage station about 5 miles below Silver City, Idaho. Concord stages, drawn by four to six horses, could carry about twenty passengers, including those on the roof.*

Below: *After the Civil War, railway survey crews were much in evidence: members of the Union Pacific, Eastern Division, in west Kansas here protected by troops from Co. I 38th U.S. Infantry.*

than the overland routes, could carry far more than any Pony Express rider, and would be sturdier and more dependable – if slower – than the telegraph. As early as 1840 speculators were buying property in Missouri in anticipation of its being an eastern terminus of the rail line west. The war with Mexico stalled serious discussion of the idea for a time, but afterward, with the acquisition and then admission of California as a state, the race and the debate were on.

Like every other debate in the 1850s, it took sectional lines. Leading Southern politicians, most notably Jefferson Davis of Mississippi, argued for a southern route to the Pacific, commencing at New Orleans or Memphis. Northerners, especially Stephen Douglas of Illinois, pushed for a northern route linking with the East at Chicago, then a tiny town that would see its growth and fortunes derive exclusively from the railroad. The arguments grew vitriolic, and extremely self-serving. Even after the secession of the South left the decision securely in the hands of central or northern proponents, removing entirely the southern option, the argument raged. No one would favor a particular route, cracked one Congressman, 'unless it starts in the corner of every man's farm and runs through all his neighbor's plantations'.[8]

As the Civil War raged, the debate went on, finally coming to two alternatives, one with an eastern terminus at Omaha, Nebraska, that would then link through Iowa with Chicago, and another ending at fledgling Kansas City, near Independence, going on to link at St Louis with the East. At last government contracts and subsidies, including vast sums and virtual empires of right of way land on either

Above: *Well-organized teams of laborers laying tracks in Montana in 1887. The railroads cut great swathes through country which, only twenty years earlier, had seemed a limitless frontier.*

Below: *Section hands such as these near Atchison on the Santa Fe line followed early construction of Kansas' railroads to straighten and ballast the line, then continued to maintain the roadbed.*

side of the proposed routes, went to two firms. The Central Pacific, owned by California entrepreneurs like Charles Crocker, Mark Hopkins, Leland Stanford, and Collis Huntington, would build eastward from San Francisco. Meanwhile, the Union Pacific, backed by Eastern financial interests, would build westward from Omaha. Precisely where the two lines would meet, no one predicted with accuracy, and in any event, so little money actually reached the firms that by the end of the Civil War, neither had laid more than a few score miles of track.

But the coming of peacetime meant the race was on as the whole nation looked West. A spirited, and not always gentlemanly, competition began between the two firms. The Central line bought precious miles of rails out from under the Union line's purchasing agents. An army of Chinese coolies was imported to do the dangerous and back-breaking work of chiseling a roadbed out of the mountainsides of the Sierras. At the same time, the Union Pacific, though not contending with such mountains, still had to deal with the Plains Indians, and with the fact that it was starting from Omaha . . . without any eastern link to that city. In fact, it did not see completion until 1867, and prior to then all of the line's materials had to be sent to Omaha by steamboat up the Missouri.

Still, the Union Pacific almost roared westward, covering 266 miles in 1866, and increasing the pace the next year. It passed through Nebraska, bypassed Denver to head straight on through southern Wyoming Territory, and by early 1869 had edged into Utah, just as the Central Pacific had conquered the Sierras and raced across Nevada. Washington finally

Above: *The Chinese were an indispensable part of a railroad's labor force. At work here for the Central Pacific, they were fearless, inexhaustible, tough, probably the backbone of the whole enterprise.*

Below: *Pushing into the wilderness, Green River, 1868, the Union Pacific might build temporary wooden bridges which would be replaced by masonry, as here, when government grants came through.*

RAILROAD WORKERS

Although some doubt existed that railroad technology could cope with the challenges of the American West, the Pacific Railroad Act was nevertheless passed by the Senate in 1862. Two railroads were to be constructed, one from mid-continent, the other from the West coast to join somewhere in between. The backbreaking work was carried out by men who were probably among the most cosmopolitan in American history. Tracks were laid at the rate of between two to five miles a day, the rails being taken up to the front by carts. Vital clothing was heavy leather gloves and boots, with low crown hats for protection from the elements on the windswept plains.

decreed that Promontory Point, Utah, north of Great Salt Lake, should be the point toward which both lines should head, and there, on 10 May 1869, they finally met. It was a festive occasion, despite the bleak location. Leland Stanford was there to drive the last, golden, spike linking a rail to a tie that bound East and West. He missed the spike at his first swing with the maul, just as so many before him had missed with their initial attempts to bridge the continent and open the West. But like them as well, he swung again, and this time he hit the mark, driving the spike, and with it cementing the bond that girdled the continent at last.

In the wake of that historic moment, more railroads sprouted. The Kansas Pacific shoved westward from Kansas City across Kansas, then turned north to Denver, and on to Cheyenne to link with the Union Pacific. The Atchison, Topeka, & Santa Fe, struck southward from Topeka, Kansas, crossing into southern Colorado, then south to Santa Fe, and on to El Paso. The Southern Pacific in time realized Jefferson Davis' dream of a southern route, linking New Orleans with Los Angeles, then turning northward to extend all the way to Seattle, Washington. From there the new Northern Pacific and Great Northern ran parallel to the Canadian border all the way to Duluth, Minnesota, connecting with Minneapolis. As the end of the century approached, branch lines and spurs extended like barbs to anchor the main lines' hold on the land.

Below: *At Promontory Point, Utah, in May 1869, the symbolic last spike was driven, linking the Union Pacific with the Central Pacific and cementing the bond that girdled the continent at last.*

Above: *End of track on the Atchison, Topeka & Santa Fe railroad, near Hutchison, Kansas, in 1872. Taken by the city's founder, he for one would enjoy the proximity of town to railroad.*

Thus, by 1900 the great, once impenetrable, American West had been conquered by transportation, bridged by overland trails that had become roads, crossed by wires that dwarfed its great distances with the wizardry of science, and forever nailed to the iron rails that brought with them not only the settlers who would tame the land, but also, inevitably, the end of the frontier.

Thus it was that Jefferson's prophecy was fulfilled, to find a 'direct & practicable . . . communication across this continent for the purposes of commerce'. It was not by water, as he had hoped and expected, and some of the trade he had anticipated had died by the time the overland routes opened. But new riches undreamed replaced the furs, and new expectations unthought of in 1804, made of the American West an even more enticing lure to the American mind. And all the while that the explorers and travelers and road builders were doing their work of spanning the great domain, others followed in their shadow, the men and women who came not to discover, but to stay, to exploit, to make their fortunes.

REFERENCES

1 John Logan Allen, *Passage Through the Garden* (Chicago, 1975), p. xix.
2 *Ibid.*, pp. 290-92.
3 Bernard DeVoto, ed., *The Journals of Lewis and Clark* (Boston, 1953), p. lii.
4 Daniel Boorstin, *The Americans: The National Experience* (New York, 1965), p. 54.
5 *Ibid.*, pp. 100-101.
6 John D. Unruh Jr., *The Plains Across*, pp. 100-101.
7 David Lavender, *The Great West* (New York, 1965), p. 296.
8 Boorstin, *The Americans*, p. 256.

II
THE OPPORTUNISTS

Below: *Armed pioneers in Lawrence, Kansas, 1856. Most early eastern Kansas homes were built entirely of logs. That was to change.*

WHEN HERNANDO CORTES first landed his small band of conquistadores on the shores of Mexico, the Aztec ruler Monteczuma thought to deter him from coming further by giving him lavish gifts and telling him to go home. Instead, the presentations of gold and jewels gave the Spaniards a broad hint of the fabulous riches there for the taking, and only spurred them on in their quest for gold and glory. Again and again as the adventurers advanced deeper into the Mexican heartland, Monteczuma sent more and more bribes, each time hoping that the last gifts would be enough, yet all the while sealing his own doom and that of his people.

It is one of the perverse ironies of American history that the Indian helped to bring his own downfall in much the same way. Exploration and colonization were inevitable in any case, but after the first white explorers from the East had passed through the lush landscape rich in animal and mineral wealth for the taking, they left behind tantalizing hints for the Indian as well. The white man had brought trade goods, pretty cloth, better knives and blankets, liquor, and even guns. All were things much desired and prized by the native Americans, and they were somewhat startled to find that the whites would give them in return for furs and beaver pelts. The Indian had never man-

aged to trap the beaver on any sort of efficient basis, and simply took what furs he could when opportunity afforded. Yet the whites seemed positively hungry for them. Consequently, many Indians, chiefly the Nez Perce of today's Oregon country, began taking what pelts they could and bringing them to white traders in exchange for goods.

It did not take long for enterprising whites to see that behind this trickle of fur coming to them there must lie an untold wealth in the multitude of animals inhabiting the mountains and streams of the interior. Nor did it take long for them to realize that the best way to tap that resource was to go in after it themselves.

MOUNTAIN MAN

The mountain men were the first to exploit the beaver-rich areas in the West in the first half of the 19th century. They trapped throughout the winter, caching the dried pelts, then in spring rendezvousing at the headwaters of the Missouri, Green or Columbia rivers to trade and relax. The trade was the product of a demand for the beaver hat, a fashionable status symbol in European society. By the mid-19th century the fashion changed from beaver to silk and the day of the mountain man was over. This man wears practical, tough buckskin clothing tastefully embellished, reflecting the various tribal groups he would have encountered during his travels.

Several daring individuals began to penetrate the interior on their own in order to bring back pelts, but none of them was organized or systematic. Soon a few enterprising companies formed to take the matter more in hand, though most still relied chiefly on trade with the Indians. But William Ashley and Andrew Henry broke with tradition. They would set up a company solely for the purpose of trapping, and do so on a large scale, hoping to employ fully 100 men in the enterprise. At first thought it would have seemed to be an impossibly expensive enterprise, for they would have to pay a trapper anywhere up to $400 for the full year he would have to stay in the interior working the streams. That would have meant as much as $40,000 in outlay before the pelts ever hit the eastern markets.

Instead, the partners hit on the novel – and blatantly self-serving – expedient of taking on trappers in the manner of latter-day sharecroppers. The company offered to furnish the volunteer all the traps, provisions, and other necessary gear, take him up the Missouri to the jumping off place for the beaver country, pick him up again at a rendezvous at the end of the year, and then split the profit from the pelts evenly between trapper and employers. Unrevealed to the trappers was Ashley and Henry's idea that at the rendezvous they would bring a quantity of trade goods with which they hoped to trade at inequitable rates for the trapper's half as well.

On 20 March 1822 the partners placed an advertisement in the St Louis *Missouri Gazette*, addressed 'To Enterprising Young Men', and inviting 'ONE HUNDRED MEN, to ascend the Missouri to its source, there to be employed for one, two or three years.' Daring young men like Jedediah Smith answered the call, and that fall the first keelboats loaded with trappers and supplies crawled slowly up the Missouri to the confluence of the Yellowstone. From here the trappers proceeded up the tributary to the hunting grounds on what would be, for those who survived, a three-year odyssey of danger, excitement, and discovery. Arikaras and Blackfeet Indians killed several. Hardship, freezing winters and summer starvation took more. Men like Smith went far beyond the territory Ashley and Henry had envisioned, crossing the Rocky Mountains into completely unknown lands beyond. It all became too much for Henry, who backed out of the partnership, but Ashley was stimulated by the challenge. When hostiles all but closed safe passage up the Missouri, he decided to lead an overland pack train across the plains along the Platte River, and into the Rockies to Henry's Fork of the Green River. Word went out ahead of him that his trappers were to rendezvous in July 1825 at the foot of the Uinta Mountains along the later Utah-Wyoming border.

Ashley's own trek was a Homeric enterprise, covering almost 1,200 miles across the center of the continent from St Louis, but by April 1825 he had reached the Green, and three months later arrived at the rendezvous. Incredibly, many of the trappers, after three years in the wilderness, were there to greet him. So were other independent trappers who took advantage of the encampment to trade their pelts as well, and to enjoy a little rough society after the years of solitude. Ashley soon had 120 of these new 'mountain men' playing and brawling, and yielding up what turned out to be ninety packs of beaver pelts in return for Ashley's trade goods.

Ashley had started more than he realized at first. For the next dozen or more years an annual bonanza of animal wealth came down out of the mountains, of which a natural by-product was an increasing store of information on the still mysterious interior of the continent. Beaver streams tended to play out rather quickly, so year after year Ashley's trappers had to roam farther into the interior, up ever-smaller and narrower streams, to set their trap lines. Along the way such men became the first whites to see the Yellowstone geysers, previously unknown breaks in the mountain chain forming the continental divide, and more and more practical – if difficult – routes to reach the other side of the continent.

For the trappers themselves there ensued a life like no other lived by white men before them. Survival required bravery, resilience, ingenuity, and certainly luck. For those who possessed the requisites, the rewards could be great. Few Americans have ever known the independence, the sense of discovery, and

Below: *Bigger game, such as bears, were hunted by the trappers. This old deadfall trap was used in Colorado. It was hoisted at one end and set with a trigger fixed to the bait inside. Apparently it worked.*

TRAPPERS

The trappers came hard on the heels of the early explorers. Their livelihood was the earliest form of entrepreneurial effort on the frontier. These hardy souls lived off nature and usually managed to co-exist with the Indian because he lived much as they did. Some trappers lived with Indian tribes and took Indian women as wives, building a strong bond with this relationship. Their primary motivation was money, earned by securing fine furs for sale to the lucrative eastern markets. Some trappers ran their own trap lines but many traded fancy goods with local Indians for cured pelts. Their life was certainly one of loneliness, danger and sometimes death. While Indians were always a threat, accident and illness killed far more trappers. A broken leg or infected wound usually caused a solitary, slow death in the high mountains or vast prairies and plain dysentery was a common killer. The rendezvous was the high point of the year for these people. This was the gathering of the trappers at which they sold their pelts harvested for almost a year, were paid for their labor, outfitted for the year ahead and spent what was left in one great debauch. A highly romanticized picture now exists of these rugged individualists, but in reality they were almost without exception filthy, dirty men with little notion of personal hygiene. Today their great Hawken rifles are eagerly sought by western collectors, as well as other primitive memorabilia of these early Americans.

1 Bear claw necklace.
2 Heavy buckskin single breasted coat with fringed neck, chest and sleeve ornamentation.
3 Leather haversack.
4 Elk skin leggings with fringed leg decoration.
5 Spear point side knife with shaped wooden hilt.
6 Pair of lined bearskin gloves.
7,8 Metal traps with anchor chain, for small game.
9 Large metal bear trap.
10 Iron bound whiskey barrel, with handle.
11 Ash frame snowshoes.
12 Metal trap with anchor chain, for small game.
13 Tanned black bear skin.
14 Metal trap with anchor chain, for trapping medium size game.
15 U.S. North Model 1819 single-shot pistol, altered to percussion.
16 Brass-mounted, half-stocked plains rifle made by Sam Hawken, St Louis, Missouri.
17 Horn handled, iron bladed knife used for scraping hides.
18 Iron mounted, half-stocked plains rifle by Sam Hawken, with brass tack decoration.
19 Utility knife with double loop leather sheath and brass stud decoration.
20 Powder horn with carved spout and wooden plug, with iron staple for shoulder strap.
21 Brass double cavity bullet mold.
22 Iron single cavity scissors bullet mold.

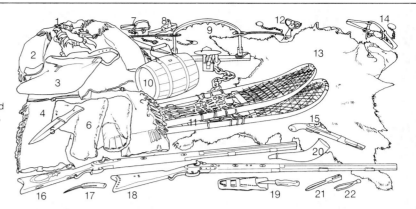

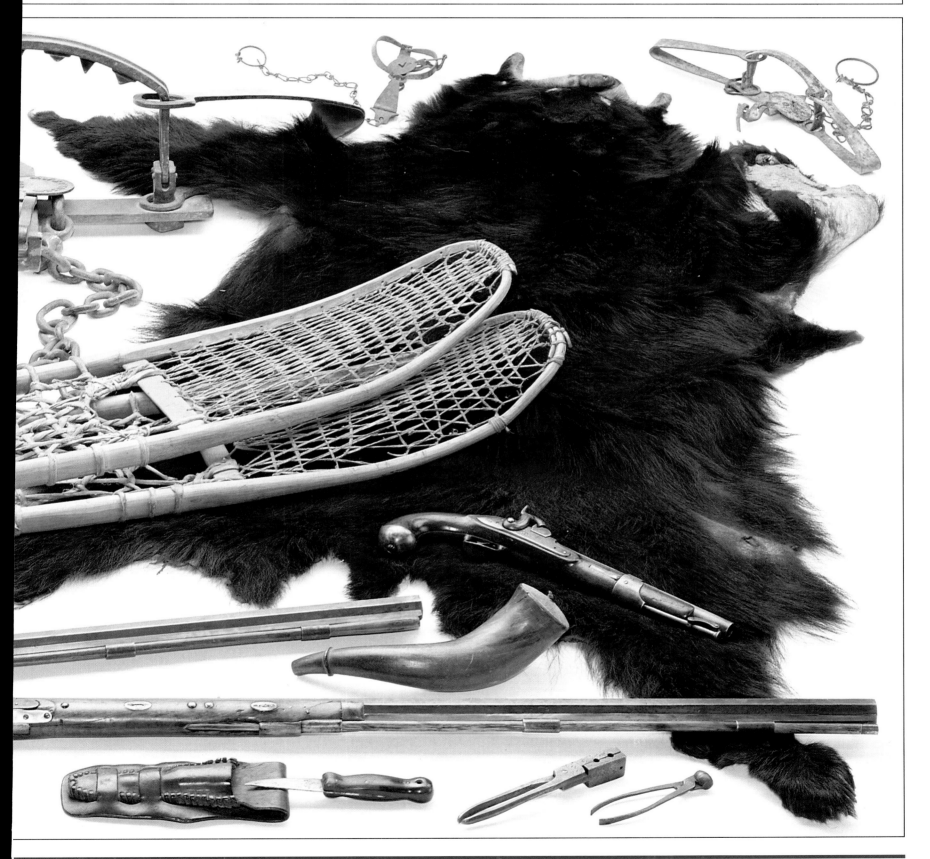

sometimes wonder, that the mountain men enjoyed during their brief reign as masters of the mountains. Some operated entirely alone. More worked in small groups, sometimes called 'brigades', led by an organizer like William Sublette or David Jackson, or Smith. Some took native Indian women as informal wives, occasionally out of affection, more often from baser needs, and just as frequently as a means of securing amity and protection from the woman's tribe, who might otherwise pose a threat. Establishing a base camp somewhere in the mountains, the brigades built small villages, and then set off up the streams to lay their traps.

The hardships, especially for those who moved alone, could be daunting. Baking in summer, freezing in winter snows, men were known to drink buffalo blood to stay alive, and to cut open an animal and crawl inside on freezing nights in the open in order to be saved by the beast's body heat. A man could be mauled by a giant grizzly bear, as Hugh Glass was, and so obviously unsavable that com-

Below: *When the fur trade had been exploited out of existence, drifters such as this man encamped on the Plains with his Indian wife and half-breed children, became a more common sight.*

panions would abandon him. A man could break a leg as Thomas Smith did, with the knowledge that inevitable gangrene would mean a lingering death.

Yet if a man was made of sufficient will, he could survive. Hugh Glass did, crawling almost 100 miles before reaching Fort Kiowa and assistance. So did Thomas Smith, who took his own knife and without anaesthetic cut through the flesh of his broken leg, snapped off the remaining bone, and then thrust the stump into the flames of a fire to cauterise the wound. Ever after he would be known as 'Pegleg' Smith from the wooden stump he used for walking. It was a sign of the brittle toughness

Above: *Jim Beckwourth became something of a legend in fur-trade circles up until the 1840s. A mulatto, when he gave up the lonely life of a mountain man it was to become a chief of the Crow Indians.*

Above: *'Liver-Eating' Johnson had a fearsome reputation. To revenge his murdered Flathead wife, he is said to have hunted, killed and eaten the livers of the finest Crow warriors sent against him.*

of the men, one that also showed in their social behavior. Freed from all of society's restraints, all too many descended the human scale toward their more base instincts. Liquor, women, and brawling, were almost their only entertainments for leisure hours, and life became cheap, indeed, especially that of Indians, and occasionally fellow trappers as the growing scarcity of pelts made competition the more keen in the 1830s.

One thing that virtually none of them got out of their epic-making experience was wealth. For all that they brought out of the mountains to the annual rendezvous, the only real profits went into the pockets of men like Ashley. The only mountain men to make much of anything were Jim Bridger, Sublette, and a few others, and then only when they emulated Ashley and formed the Rocky Mountain Fur Company, exploiting their former comrades just as they had once been exploited themselves. Still they all gathered memories that those who survived would tell and re-tell, usually with considerable exaggeration.

Most of all they remembered the annual rendezvous with its almost carnival-like atmosphere, the revelry with liquor, women Indian and white, the horse races and gambling, the exchanging of tales with trappers from other parts. It could last for weeks in the summer, the location changing from year to year and tending generally northward from Ashley's first site, to follow the remaining stock of beaver. Every few years the rendezvous came south again, but not after 1834, and five of the last six were held on the Green River in southern Wyoming. As early as 1830 men like Jedediah Smith could see that the beaver population was thinning out. Each succeeding year there were fewer pelts, and the men had to go farther to find them. By 1840 all the streams had been found and trapped, and the beaver, while far from extinct, simply no longer survived in numbers that allowed a

Above: *Jim Bridger, King of the Mountain Men, crossed the plains at eighteen, and did not return from the wilderness for seventeen years. He claimed not to have tasted white bread during that time.*

Above: *William Bent gave his name to Bent's Fort, built by himself and his brother on the Arkansas River in 1833. The Bents chose to trade there to avoid the all-powerful American Fur Company.*

BENT'S FORT

This plate shows a reconstruction of the trading post on the mountain branch of the Santa Fe Trail known as Bent's Fort, after Charles and William Bent, founders, with Ceran St Vrain, of the Bent, St Vrain Company. It was probably built around 1829-30 and certainly completed by 1833. Standing on the north side of the Arkansas River in today's southeastern Colorado, it was architecturally unique to the mountains-plains region because it was

built of adobe – sun-dried mud bricks – showing a Spanish-Mexican influence and probably owing something to St Vrain.

The backgrounds of all three men offer pointers. Charles and William Bent were the grandsons of Silas Bent, who had led the bogus Indians in the Boston Tea Party incident during the American Revolution; their father was a prominent judge who was appointed surveyor-general of the new Louisiana Territory in 1806. As young men, both worked in St Louis for the fur traders Manuel Lisa and Joshua Pilcher.

Ceran St Vrain was born in Missouri, the son of an aristocratic French family displaced from Europe by the French Revolution of 1891. His uncle had been lieutenant-governor of Louisiana under both French and Spanish rule; St Vrain was a civilized, educated man, fluent in Spanish, a naturalized Mexican citizen and highly regarded in Santa Fe. When the company was formed in 1833, Charles handled freighting and buying and the management of affairs in St Louis and Santa Fe; William (who took a Cheyenne

wife) worked closely with the plains Indians and trappers and oversaw construction and maintenance of the trading post; and St Vrain concentrated on trade in the southwest, especially Santa Fe and Taos, where goods of American and plains Indian origin could be traded for gold, silver and Mexican and Navajo wares.

Bent's Fort came to exist for a simple reason. Lewis and Clark's exploration of the Louisiana Purchase territories from 1803 exposed, unwittingly, a new world to be exploited for its natural resources. Where the Indians had once trapped productively but unsystematically, now the regions of the Upper Missouri became the haunt of the mountain man, either the individual working for himself or those employed by bigger concerns such as the Hudson's Bay or the American Fur companies. In the early 1830s, the American Fur Company built a number of trading posts in the Upper Missouri area; forts Union on the Yellowstone, Cass on the Bighorn and Piegan on the Marias were all intended to ensure a position of strength in the Rockies. So it was that, with the beaver gone from the Missouri, increasing trade opposition in the north and much of the emphasis on trade itself returning to the Indians, the Bent, St Vrain Company turned its attention to the lucrative potential of the Santa Fe Trail and all points southwest. It would survive for nearly twenty years until events in the emerging nation – the war with Mexico, increasing conflict with the Indians among others – sounded its death knell.

profit. That was the year of the last rendezvous, and the virtual end of a brief explosion of exploitation that made fortunes for a few.[1]

Meanwhile another fur trade had flourished to the south of the Rockies, centered on the old community of Taos, in latter-day New Mexico. Its origins went back 300 years before Ashley's last rendezvous, and successively Spanish, Mexican, French, and American trappers operated a thriving business, especially after Mexico's independence from Spain in 1821 removed bans on immigrants. Here future legends like Christopher 'Kit' Carson, 'Old Bill' Williams, and more, including Pegleg Smith, flourished, and largely on their own, for the Ashley-style companies never operated successfully in the region. Here, too, trappers blazed trails across the unknown, chiefly heading west toward California, hard on the heels of Jedediah Smith's first journey. Immigrant groups soon moved along their new trails, while the trappers themselves continuously explored new areas of the southern Rockies. In the end, when their beaver streams played out, too, many would follow their trails to settle along the Pacific coast. By 1834, the Taos trade, too, started to decline, in part from shortage of beaver, and also because the fashion that drove the market – gentlemen's beaver hats in the East and Europe – was changing. Some trappers turned to hunting buffalo, which were far more plentiful, and for whose hides a new market had arisen. Others remained to eke out a living on the streams until 1846, when the outbreak of the war with Mexico virtually ended the trade, and an era.[2]

Indeed, the so-called Mexican War of 1846-8 put a hold on exploitation of the new

Above: *Kit Carson was the* beau idéal *of the scout. Showing the sincerest form of flattery, an actor who called himself Kit Carson Jr played frontier scouts in the border dramas of the 1870s and 1880s.*

Below: *When beaver hats were no longer* de rigueur *in the East, some trappers turned their attention and their guns onto the buffalo on the plains. After the Civil War, the wanton destruction really began.*

West generally. But the check could not but be temporary and, in fact, the results of that sad conflict led indirectly to a renewed boom of opportunity that would dwarf the fur trade by comparison. At its height there were never more than 500-600 trappers operating between the Yellowstone and Taos. An isolated event in 1848, just two years after the death of the fur trade, would bring tens of thousands to seek their fortunes.

In fact, as evidence of the inevitability of the march of opportunity, it happened just nine days before Mexico signed the Treaty of Guadalupe Hidalgo, ending the war. One of the territories that Mexico lost in the conflict was California, which the Mexicans had unwisely allowed groups of Anglo settlers to infiltrate for the past two decades. Once there they formed an enemy in the rear that quickly wrested California from Mexican control even before the war concluded. One of those settlers was John Sutter who had failed in the Taos trade, tried and failed in Russian Alaska, and finally wound up with Mexican permission to trap on the Sacramento and American rivers in California. In 1840 he built a small fort where the city of Sacramento stands now, and soon expanded into trading and ranching in the fertile central valley.

By late 1847, with the war winding down, and dreaming of stretching his small empire, Sutter started construction on a sawmill to provide lumber for construction. He gave the job of locating and building the mill to James Marshall, who moved up the American some forty miles to the Coloma Valley. Marshall and his men worked quickly, and by January 1848 the mill was completed and ready for

THE BUFFALO HUNTER

Buffalo, roaming the plains in their millions, were the plains Indians' main resource, a seemingly limitless supply of meat and hides so essential to the lifestyle of the nomadic tribes. In harmony with nature they seldom killed for sport and viewed with disgust and deep concern the rapid decimation of the herds (between 1872 and 1874 1.5 million hides were carried by the Kansas railroad alone). Dressed in virtually plain buckskin jacket and trousers, with the heavy Sharps .45 M1874 sporting rifle, a hunter could kill scores of animals without moving from one spot. By 1884, the great herds were all but gone, the plains Indians' commissary destroyed forever.

THE BUFFALO HUNTER

The original buffalo hunter was the Indian who used all parts of the animal for food, shelter, clothing, fuel and weapons. In the early 1880s there were herds of 10,000 animals and more to supply his needs. Then, white explorers came West, followed by hunters and settlers. The building of railroads was the beginning of the end for the buffalo because railroad workers subsisted largely on their meat provided by hired hunters.

Young William F. Cody earned his nickname supplying the Kansas Pacific crews with meat in 1867. Tanning methods of hides greatly improved and slaughter for hides greatly increased after 1870. Some one and a quarter million hides were sent east in 1872-3 and railroads promoted excursion trips for 'sport hunters'. It is said that buffalo carcases lined the tracks of the Kansas Pacific for 200 miles. Professional hunters were interested in the hides only, leaving thousands of tons of meat to rot on the plains. Buffalo bones

were found to be useful as fertilizer and in 1874 alone some 3500 tons of bones were shipped east. To accomplish this slaughter, Sharps and Remington rifles in calibers .49-90, .44-90, .45-120, .50-90 and others were used. It is estimated that 80 per cent of all buffalo were killed with such weapons. The railroad and hunting split the herds around 1874; the southern herds were virtually exterminated by 1878. Hunting rapidly declined in the 1880s but by then the buffalo was all but gone from the plains.

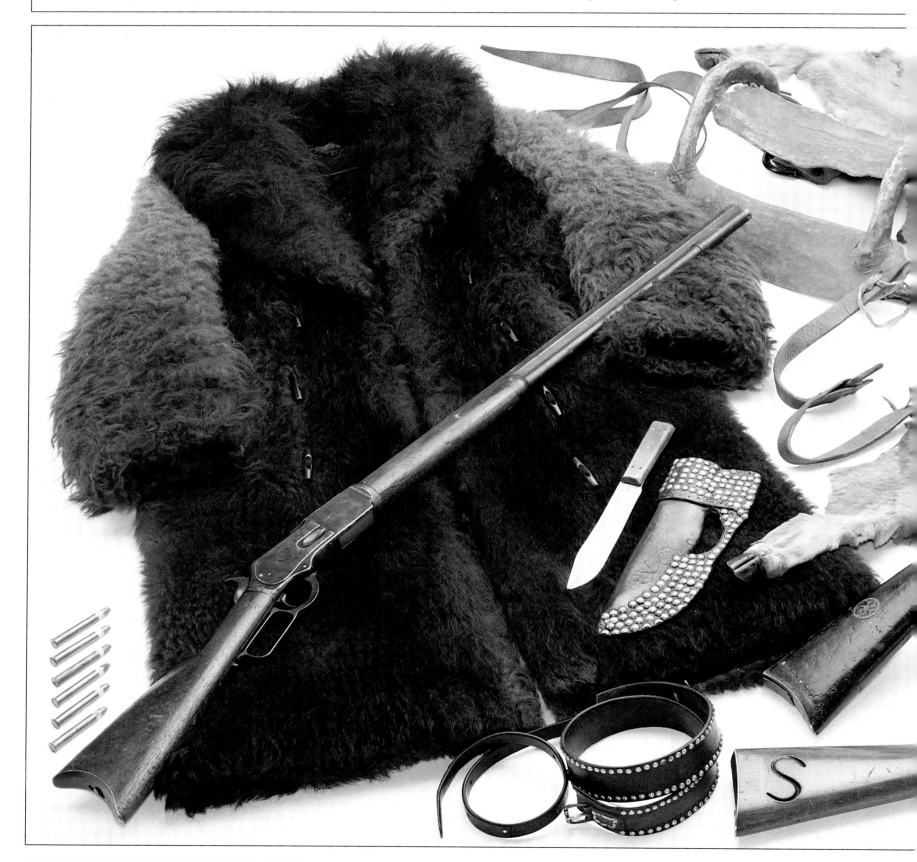

THE OPPORTUNISTS

1 Heavy lined buffalo hide coat with double frog closure.

2 .40-70 caliber cartridges.

3 Winchester Model 1873 lever action rifle, .45-60 caliber.

4 Wooden handled skinning knife.

5 Brass studded leather sheath of Indian origin for above.

6 Brass studded leather belt of Indian origin associated with above knife and sheath.

7 Rudimentary rawhide covered pack saddle of probable Indian origin, for transport of hides, equipment.

8 Rolled tanned buffalo hide.

9 Tanned hide of small buffalo calf, hoofs still attached.

10 Bleached buffalo skull.

11 Spencer rifle altered to a buffalo gun by adding heavy .50 caliber octagonal barrel and set trigger.

12 Rifle cartridge belt, leather with nickel buckle.

13 Sharps Model 1874 sporting rifle, .45 caliber.

14 Utility side knife with stag horn handle.

15 Leather sheath for above.

16 Colt single-action Army revolver, .45 caliber, with nickel finish.

17 Braided leather quirt.

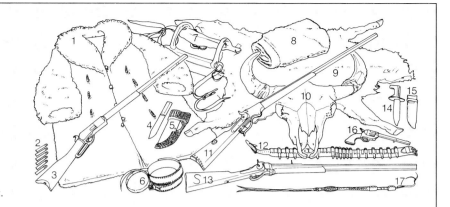

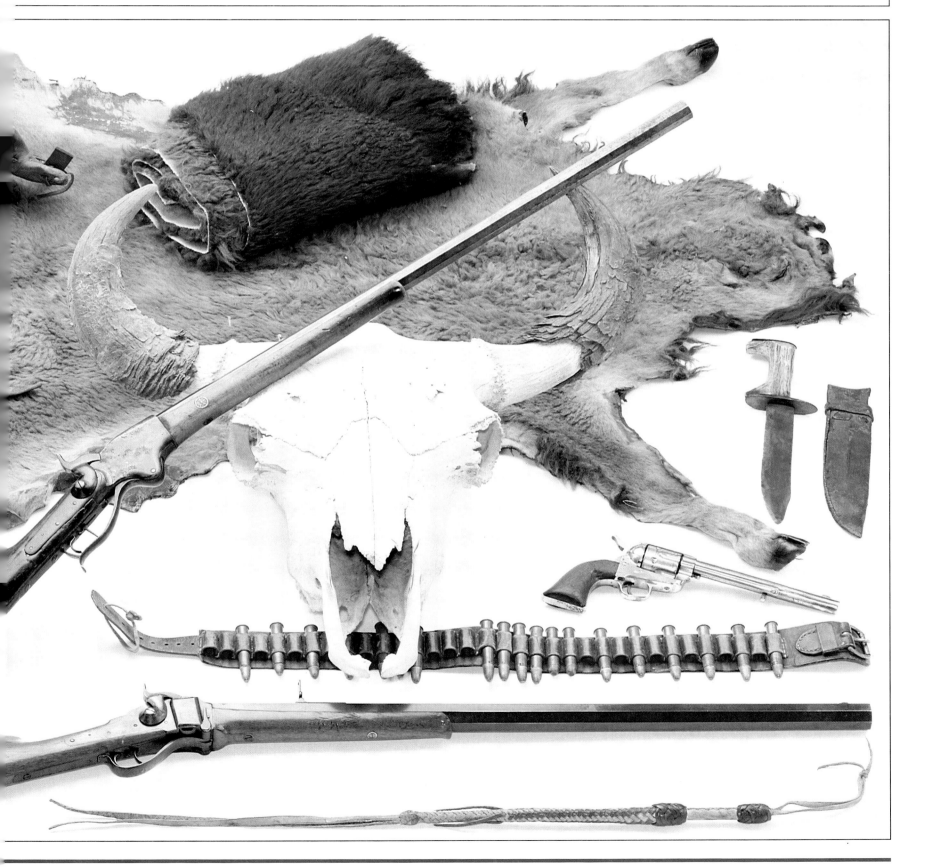

operation. There were fine points to set aright with the machinery and the mill race, and on 24 January Marshall inspected a newly dug channel through which the river's water was diverted to run the mill wheel. In the material washed out of the banks by the racing water he found several small, heavy bits of ore that he took back to show his crew. One of them wrote in his diary that night: 'This day some kind of mettle was found in the tail race that looks like goald.' 'Goald' it was![3]

Marshall later told his own story. 'My eye was caught by something shining in the bottom of the ditch,' he recalled. 'I reached my hand down and picked it up,' he said, 'then I saw another.' Excitedly he and his crew tried to determine for certain that it really was gold. They bit it and found it soft enough that their teeth left impressions. They hit it with a hammer, and instead of breaking it changed shape and flattened. Others went back to the mill race to look for more, and they found it, while Marshall reported back to John Sutter. They went back to the mill, and more looking revealed bits and nuggets of the stuff almost everywhere.

Above: *In 1847 John Sutter built a lumber mill on the American River at Coloma. What was found in the millrace was to provoke a gold race, but Sutter was not one of the many to become wealthy.*

At first Sutter tried to keep it a secret, not so much from fear of outsiders invading his domain, as from its interrupting the work on his mill. But he could not stop his men from talking of what they had found, nor did he keep quiet himself. In less than a month, workers from other parts of Sutter's extensive lands were coming to Coloma in their off hours to dig. Others tried other stretches of the American, and found gold there, too. Almost overnight all of Sutter's plans collapsed. Virtually all of his workers walked off their jobs, took picks and shovels, and started excavating the banks and stream beds north of Sacramento. The word spread slowly at first, even in California, and it was not until 12 May when a particularly fortunate prospector arrived in San Francisco fresh from the diggings, with a bottle filled with gold dust in his hand. 'Gold!' he cried, brandishing the flask aloft. 'Gold!

Below: *Hard on the heels of the first '49ers with their wash pans and shovels came others with more refined methods – water-fed sluices which could more quickly process gold dust from the earth.*

Gold from the American River!' Two weeks later the flood of would-be fortune hunters from San Francisco was such that the local press decried that 'the whole country from San Francisco to Los Angeles . . . resounds to the sordid cry of gold, gold! GOLD!' A month later, San Francisco was almost a ghost town, stores closed, ships abandoned in the harbor, streets empty, and three out of four men gone to the diggings.[4]

It did not take long for the news to spread, even given the slow communications of the times. By August the newspapers in the East were printing the first reports of the discovery, along with boasts that California's streams were awash with gold. Some were still sceptical. After all, there had been numerous gold findings in America previously, all of them turning out to be small deposits speedily exhausted. But then in December the govern-

Above: *John Bidwell, Sutter's trusted associate, made a massive gold strike on 4 July 1848. Thereafter he made a more permanent mark, setting himself up as a wealthy and influential landowner.*

ment published official findings from its agents in California, with President James K. Polk himself proclaiming this to be the find of the millennium. After that, there was no stopping the rush as men from every part of the United States responded to the call of adventure and easy money, as proclaimed in story and song:

Gold out there, and everywhere.
And everybody is a millionaire.
You'll get rich quick by takin' up a pick,
And diggin' up a chunk as big as a brick.

In the early days, in fact, it could be almost that easy. Possibly the largest gold deposit on earth had been placed here in the distant eons past, and uncountable years of erosion and geologic turmoil had placed much of it so close to the surface that it is amazing that the discovery was not made long before Marshall. Indeed, it probably was found by local Indian populations in times past. Having neither knowledge of the metal nor a use for it, it meant nothing to them, and would have been ignored. Now the first fortune seekers on the scene picked up nuggets of half a pound or

Below: *It was eventually called Placerville and before that Old Dry Diggings. But in 1849 this mining town was nicknamed Hangtown, for obvious reasons. It could match any post-bellum frontier town.*

MINERS

Discovery of gold in California at Sutter's Mill in early 1848 was the beginning of 'gold fever'. Gold seekers headed West by land and sea; responsible men left their families, soldiers and sailors deserted their posts, drawn by the all-consuming quest for easy riches. Towns sprang up overnight at sites of gold discovery, disappearing as quickly when it ran out. Civilization, if there was any, was self-imposed by vigilante miners' courts whose justice was swift, sure but arbitrary. Small-time entrepreneurs had a field day. Nearly half a million people went West in the search for riches. Discovery of gold in Colorado Territory in 1859 brought another 100,000 immigrants to the area. The huge Comstock Mine in Nevada brought big business into mining. Corporations replaced small prospectors and mining became an industry. Modern mechanical and chemical methods replaced man's efforts and the spirit of the adventure was gone by 1890.

1 Heavy iron-bound, wooden stave utility barrel for general camp use.
2 Metal and glass lantern, oil fueled, for camp and mine use.
3 Hand-forged metal pry bar, about 6 ft overall, from the Old Gold Reef mine.
4 Tin cash or valuables box.
5 Shallow pan, primary tool of gold seeker.
6 Small hammer and pick combination tool.
7 Standard pick with wooden haft.
8 Heavy sledge hammer with wooden haft.
9 Colt Model 1849 pocket revolver, .31 caliber, a type of firearm carried West on the gold rush.
10 Colt holster Model Paterson revolver, .36 caliber. Note folding trigger that extends when revolver is cocked.
11 English percussion double-barreled

shotgun, made by W. & O. Scott. 12 gauge.

12 Wooden brass-tipped ramrod for shotgun.

13 Blunt and Syms standard frame saw-handled under-hammer percussion Pepperbox pistol, .31 caliber, a popular type of weapon in rough mining camps.

14 Iron-bound, wooden stave whiskey barrel, a fixture in many isolated, primitive mining camps.

15 Weight scales, brass, iron and wood construction, a common instrument in the assayer's office.

16 Brass weights for the above scales.

17 Allen and Thurber dragoon size percussion Pepperbox, .36 caliber, another popular multi-shot weapon that was carried West in some quantity.

18 Wooden soles, leather uppers mucking boots

worn by miners standing in damp areas for prolonged periods.

19 All-purpose tin cup used as a drinking utensil or for holding lighting device down in the mine.

20 Fancy leather-trimmed vest of the type worn for some special occasion.

21 Silver dollars – the end result of many a miner's hard work and one of the standard mediums of exchange.

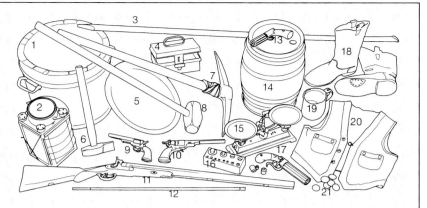

more with regularity, and almost everyone could wash at least a few ounces of the small grained 'dust' out of the stream beds in a day. The requisite tools were only a shovel, a frying pan or bowl for washing the 'paydirt', and perhaps a pick. Some men found small fortunes using nothing more than their knives. The technique itself was wonderfully simple. A prospector found what he took to be a likely spot and sampled a few pans full of stream gravel, first picking out the pebbles, then swirling the remainder around in his pan with water. The lighter dirt was washed over the lip while the gold dust, if any, being heavier, sank to the bottom of the pan. If the quantity looked sufficiently promising, he either continued panning, or else built a sluice box on rockers that performed the pan's function on a larger scale. While one miner rocked the box back and forth, another shovelled in a bushel or so of dirt and gravel and then poured water in at the higher end. The water washed the dirt out the lower end, while the gold dust settled and was caught in small ribs on the bottom of the box. Even years later when huge jets of water washed down virtual mountains, the principal remained the same. Only the scale changed.

By January 1849 the rush was on as the East, and later the world, digested the news of what had happened. Every week brought news of a new strike farther from Coloma and the American, until the established gold region

Above: *The idea was to wash the rich California dirt with water. First, pans were used, then a network of sluices as mining became more concentrated; a little later hydraulic jets would be employed.*

Below: *Mining for gold with a sluice near Sugar Loaf Hill, 1852. Only three years after the cry had gone up, the land was yielding less. Optimistic miners still worked over apparently exhausted claims.*

Above: *California attracted black and white prospectors. In addition to white Americans there were some 2,000 blacks, slaves as well as free men. Some mining camps barred 'foreigners' of any kind.*

Below: *Mining at the head of Auburn Ravine. These Chinese were some of the many thousands who had fled famine and hardship in their own land in the 1840s. Many still wore traditional clothing.*

covered several hundred miles around and north of Sacramento. Mining camps sprang up everywhere, and to them the prospectors flocked, staking out their 'diggings'. By January 1849 there were nearly 8,000 of them, with no law governing them, and no government either, for California was an independent territory with statehood fully a year away. Men made their own laws, and on the crowded riverbanks their population determined the 'claim' each man was allowed exclusively to himself, often no more than ten square feet – a spot just over 3 feet by 3 feet![5]

Hundreds of thousands dreamed of having their own 10 square feet to mine, and untold thousands of them answered the spirit in their feet that called them to California. It was neither an easy, speedy, nor inexpensive journey. There were only two ways, overland across the plains and mountains, or else by sea south to Cape Horn, then up the Pacific to San Francisco. The voyage could occupy four months or more, yet it was the preferred route by as many as eighty per cent of those living on the eastern seaboard who journeyed forth. About 6,500 others in 1849 tried a faster, though more dangerous, passage to the Isthmus of Panama, across it by mule, and then another voyage from the other side, but the jungle fevers claimed many.

The overwhelming majority went overland, the cheapest route, and thanks to the explorations of the mountain men, one with well

THE FORTY-NINERS

In 1849, the eastern states learnt that land recently acquired by the United States from Mexico was rich in gold. Within a few weeks a gold rush was on, with some 85,000 men swarming into California. Known as the '49ers, they participated in a boom which lasted for less than a decade. Some, with little more than a shovel, tin pan and 'cradle', made a fortune. Most, however, did not strike it rich, but adventures into the unknown gave an experience which lasted a lifetime. The man in the foreground is using a simple gold separator, a 'cradle', an extension of the washpan method which alleviated the tedium and hardship of squatting in icy water.

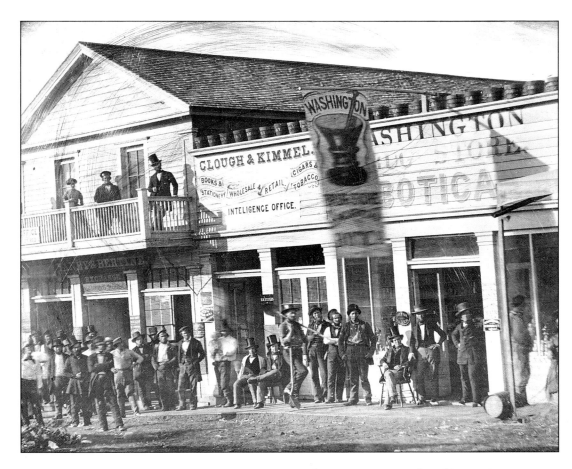

established trails. Men formed 'companies' for mutual benefit, pooling funds for supplies and guides, and mustering at jumping off places like St Louis to await the April weather that signalled the start of the trek. Chiefly they used the old Santa Fe Trail, or the Oregon Trail, and at least 30,000 of them set foot across the Kansas plains in 1849, the first of an even greater flood that by 1851 had swelled to over 100,000, with another 50,000 the following year. Men came from England some 30,000 strong, and even an estimated 25,000 Chinese crossed the greatest of oceans to seek fortune. By any measure, it was an incredible exodus such as the world had never seen before.[6]

Moreover, that exodus did not just lead to a quantum increase in the population of California. For every ten prospectors who set out from St Louis or Independence, there were another four or five who only intended to make part of the journey. Such a mass of travelers brought with them a mass of material and personal needs, and more conservative or thoughtful men who could resist the lure of the 'get rich quick' slogans, realized that there were good livings and profits to be made in Missouri, Kansas, and all along the trails, operating hotels and taverns, mechanics' shops to repair wagons, and stores to furnish the dreamers' needs. It was the same all the way to California, where a few wise men resisted the temptation to rush to the diggings, and instead let the miners bring the gold to them – in return for picks, shovels, clothes, liquor, provisions, and more. When the first rush commenced, every sort of consumer good was in

Above: *Sonora, southeast of Sacramento, was the center of the southern mining area, and a cut above the likes of Placerville. It could boast a miners' 'inteligence' (sic) office and a drugstore.*

Below: *Few women lived in mining towns such as Nevada City, on Deer Creek, in the 1850s. One man wrote: 'Got nearer to a female this evening than I have been for six months. Nearly fainted.'*

short supply, and men who could get them could make huge profits of as much as 500 percent. A store operator working for Sutter in the first months of the rush took in $36,000 during the spring of 1848, well before word of the strike had even reached the East.

Ironically, in fact, those who profited from the miners rather than the mines were almost the only ones who truly got rich. Even though 1852 saw some $81,000,000 worth of gold come out of the ground, the streams quickly played out as they became overpopulated with prospectors. It was only those with more capital and better business sense who outlasted the first brief explosion of strikes. With the surface nuggets and dust stripped away, it required machinery and large cash outlays to dam the streams or set up the high-pressure water jets that they needed to get at the riches buried deeper than the '49er' could reach with pick and shovel. By 1858 the gold production was cut in half but, more importantly, the gold producers had been reduced at least ten-fold. Tens of thousands of gold-hunters gave up after a year or two and returned to their homes in the East, rich only in the stories of adventure they would tell for generations. Of those who remained, most either turned to other pursuits or else took jobs working for the large mining companies.[7]

What had started as a great rush of hope and dreams ended largely in disillusion and disappointment. Some had foreseen this. 'The rush to California,' wrote Henry David Thoreau, 'reflects the greatest disgrace on mankind.' 'That so many are ready to live by luck and so get the means of commanding the labor of others less lucky, without contributing any value to society – and that's called enterprise!' Certainly there were dire effects from Marshall's chance discovery. A social upheaval reshaped the population of the eastern United States, and almost overnight turned a small Pacific coast outpost into a region rivalling in wealth and influence anything in the East. It

Above: *In 1853 a miner came up with the idea of directing powerful jets of water against gold-bearing hillsides. Gold buried hundreds of feet underground would be washed with the dirt into sluices.*

Below: *Such hydraulic mining, as here at French Corral, Nevada County, had labor-saving advantages. Where men originally used water as an auxiliary, now it was used as the laboring agent.*

led directly to statehood for California, and the debate over that had political ramifications far beyond its own borders in the days ahead. The settlement pattern of the Plains, the Rocky Mountain territories, Oregon and more, was permanently influenced, and that, in turn, would govern growth in those regions until the coming of the railroad and beyond. But most of all, the California Gold Rush infused new vigor into the age-old impetus that had always lain at the root of American settlement and expansion from the earliest days at Jamestown – dreams and opportunity.[8]

Indeed, the notion of getting rich quick did not die just because California's bonanza gradually faded into a big business in the hands of a few companies. Other gold and silver strikes occurred with regularity as the influx of settlers and prospectors generated by '49 steadily peeked and poked into more and more corners of the western country. Ten years after Sutter saw his land overrun by teeming masses, new deposits were found, first near Pike's Peak, and then in the Sierras

Below: *Places like Virginia City, Nevada, and Cripple Creek, Colorado, took pressure off California in the 1860s. A different terrain meant a new style of deep mining to get at huge veins of gold and silver.*

of western Nevada, then still a part of the Utah Territory. The Pike's Peak strike played out in barely a year, but not before the rush to it brought in enough settlers to get a movement started to break themselves off from the Kansas and Utah Territories to form the new territory of Colorado.[9]

Far more significant was the Comstock strike. The gold content of the ore proved to be disappointing initially, but then the miners found it rich in silver instead, and another rush was on. This time it lasted well over a decade, each year bringing more and more silver strikes in the canyons northeast of Lake Tahoe, creating the fabled Virginia City, and

leading ultimately to the Big Bonanza of 1873, when the so-called 'mother lode' was found. That year alone the ground yielded $21,000,000 in silver, with more in each succeeding year, until, by 1875, the total approached $150,000,000! The Big Bonanza was a series of deep galleries, the California Mine extending 600 feet along the massive vein of rich silver ore, the Consolidated Virginia Mine running another 710 feet along a vein that was at places hundreds of feet wide.[10]

Again, such strikes caused much dislocation and disappointment. But they also gave rise to cities like Denver and Carson City, and led inevitably toward the settlement of new territories that would become future states. Equally important to the settlement of the West as a whole, they also spread stories of other riches. Men who came, prospected, and went back east took with them tales of the broad prairies, the lush grasses, and rich earth that had never felt the cut of a plow. There was other wealth, other opportunity out there besides glittering metal. And there were other breeds of opportunists in the East looking for a chance, men – and women with them this time – who had the staying power to come, wrest a living from the land, change it to suit their needs, and then remain on it, content to make a new place for themselves.

Of course, land for tilling and raising families and livestock had always been at the heart

Above: *Virginia City, east of the Sierra Nevada, became the center of the silver-rich Comstock Lode. California's wealth would finance the Comstock development and ultimately that of the railroads.*

Below: *Cars coming out of the Comstock Mine, c. 1868. The deeply buried ore needed heavy mining equipment to get at it, and a new breed of men to labor hundreds of feet underground.*

of the spread westward from the Atlantic. But progress had been slow toward the Mississippi, impeded by mountain barriers, dense forests, relatively large populations of native Americans, and political and even military restrictions. But once across the Mississippi, all that changed, and in jumping that mighty stream the pace of settlement advanced as far in two generations as it had in the previous two centuries.

It began with a place that, like California, was as much an idea as a territory. Texas. The Spanish had held on to but settled it only sparsely with a few tiny hamlets at El Paso, Nacogdoches, San Antonio de Bexar, and elsewhere along its southern border, the Rio Grande. When Mexico achieved its independence in 1821, permission was granted by the authorities for Moses Austin to found a colony of Americans on the Brazos River. He died before he could get there, but his son Stephen carried on the father's dream. By early 1822 he had 150 colonists building a small settlement at San Felipe de Austin, in the center of a 150-square mile reservation on the Gulf of Mexico, roughly between the Colorado and the Trinity rivers, just east of San Antonio.

From the start, the colony's course was a troubled one, governed by the volcanic state of politics in the new Mexican state. Still the younger Austin was able to confirm land grants allowing each of his farmers 177 acres for planting, and a staggering 4,428 for grazing, reflecting the notion that this was destined to be cattle country. By 1829 the American colony had expanded, some 5,400 additional families immigrating as beneficiaries of a number of grants, some associated with Austin's settlement. The demands of hungry farmers from Missouri and Tennessee and Mississippi saw the colony grow rapidly. Austin's colony alone had over 900 families by 1828. Other colonies grew around Nacogdoches and elsewhere, the settlers including, ironically, some Cherokees who had been driven out of their homes east of the Mississippi, and were now joining in the white man's quest for a better future in the new West. As a result, what began as a trickle in 1821, turned into an *Americano* population of more than 20,000 by 1830, and such a growing pressure for more that the Mexican government closed Texas to further settlement rather than risk seeing it completely overrun by Anglos.[11]

There were no such checks to settlement north of Texas, however, and during that same decade and the ones to follow men who might once have come as passersby now stopped and settled. They came in an interesting pattern. Families from the colder northern reaches like New England moved to the northern reaches of the new lands, to what would become Minnesota, Michigan, and the other Great Lake states. People from the middle Atlantic states like New York and Pennsylvania, moved into the Iowa territory and on to what would become Nebraska. Southerners from Virginia and the Carolinas headed west for Arkansas, Missouri, and on into the Kansas Territory. In short, in moving west, they truly headed straight west, seeking climates much like those they left behind.

At first there had been a prejudice against open ground, oddly enough. After all, the only settlement experience that they and their ancestors had thus far was in taming the wooded lands of the trans-Appalachian wilderness. They long believed that such ground offered the most fertile soil, but by the 1840s, as more and more men tried the untimbered prairies of Missouri and Iowa, they discovered just how fertile it could be, and without the exhausting task of clearing timber first. After that, and with government owned land in the new territories going for a mere $1.25 per acre, the move was on.[12]

The settlers brought with them whatever they would need for the new life on new land – a bull and cows, hogs, chickens, plow and harness, seed, and their families to help work the

Below: *Denver for one grew from a dream of gold, and developed from the reality of silver. The city burgeoned after the discovery of high-grade silver ore in outlying places such as Oro City.*

THE <u>COVERED</u> WAGON

Adventurous pioneers began trekking west as early as 1835 in wheeled conveyances known as covered wagons, or 'prairie schooners', adaptations of the heavy Conestoga wagons of Pennsylvania that brought a generation of pioneers over the eastern mountains in earlier immigration. These vehicles were generally very sturdy but light transports designed for hauling heavy loads over distance rather than providing creature comforts for passengers or any semblance of speed. The wagons consisted of three basic components – bed, undercarriage with wheels, and fabric cover. Most were constructed of hard wood such as maple, oak and hickory. Iron was used for the tires, axles and hounds, the undercarriage connecting rods. Springs were unnecessary for freight hauling and these wagons carried loads of 2500 pounds and more. The only allowance for comfort was a cloth or canvas covering supported by ash or hickory bows which shielded occupants from snow, rain and dust. This covering could be rolled back in summer to let air circulate. Lack of springs encouraged those who were able to walk to do so. The jolting movement of the wagon would incapacitate a healthy person quickly and the severely limited space precluded many passengers anyway. These wagons were pulled by slow moving teams of oxen or mules, assisted frequently by muscle power of occupants, which could only travel fifteen to twenty miles on a good day. The bed or load area was about four

feet wide and ten to twelve feet long, large enough for household necessities and not much else. A jockey box on the front of the wagon contained rudimentary repair tools such as a wagon jack and spare metal fittings. A grease bucket slung beneath the carriage held some type of lubricant for the wheelhubs and axles. Contrary to Hollywood history, Indians rarely attacked wagon trains or circled wagons, but lone wagons and stragglers were altogether a different story. Danger was ever present. In reality, accident or illness was far more deadly than Indians. Cholera was a terrible killer. On one wagon train there reputedly was one grave every eighty yards. A discouraged pilgrim described his wagon in the wilderness as '250 miles from the nearest post office, 100 miles to wood, 20 miles to water and six inches from hell'. Guide books were published by some successful travelers and also by opportunists who never made the trip. Journeys consisted of eighteen hour days beginning at 4 am, followed by more endless days without any comforts.

Weather was a variable factor of great importance, when days or a week could mean the difference between being snowed in for the winter or safe passage through the mountains. Key traits of the indomitable pioneers who undertook this journey in spite of all odds were endurance, stoicism and iron determination. They were ordinary men, women and children with iron in their souls. The peak of this migration period occurred in 1850 when more than 55,000 individuals headed their wagons along the western trails.

farm. The quality of their livestock was a matter not yet scientifically considered by most. Breeding to improve strains, better milk yield, put more weight on a pig, was not yet practiced. Swine foraged wild on the claim, while cattle, if any, were small, tough, and a careless mixture of breeds. In 1844 and afterward, large numbers of sheep came into the middle and northern reaches west of the Mississippi, and later into Texas and the Southwest. To pull his plow and to the other back-breaking heavy work of clearing land and hauling, the first settlers brought oxen, but the ox teams rapidly dwindled as the desire for speedier production on ever larger holdings made the lumbering beasts impractical. Instead, the farmers on the plains and prairies turned to horses, nearly as strong, and able to move much more quickly.

Once their plows broke that virgin sod for the first time, the settlers began to sow much the same crops they had planted east of the Mississippi. Corn, cotton, flax, oats, and other grains, constituted the overwhelming contents

Above: *Settlers' covered wagons heading for Red Buttes, Colorado. Excluding the gold rush, early movement and settlement was relatively slow as new lands were formally organized into territories.*

Below: *The rigors of the trail could be exhausting, but most emigrants learned that if they outfitted properly, stuck to the trail and kept to a daily routine, they stood a chance of reaching their goal.*

of the settlers' storehouses at the end of harvest, matters of climate and soil determining what should be grown. And of course, every farm had its own subsistence vegetable garden, produce for the farmer's table alone.[13]

The movement of these settlers was not a steady progress, but one of fits and starts, with a brief rush here, then another there. Partly it was controlled by the government, for new lands, on being organized formally by Congress as territories, had to cede to the Federal authority large tracts of land. These public lands were then sold by acres or by whole sections, as the government chose and the economy would allow. Consequently, settlement was largely a matter of chance, and the blowing of winds in Washington City. Texas saw settlement first, after Missouri and Arkansas. By the 1830s Iowa was luring thousands, chiefly from Kentucky, Indiana, and Illinois. As Missourians reached Independence and nearby Westport Landing became an infant settlement (later to become Kansas City), the land across the border in what was then called the Nebraska Territory, comprising latter-day Kansas and Nebraska, assumed attractive proportions. It was created for the plow.

But the settlement of those lands had to await a waning of the surpassing fascination with Oregon in the 1840s, and then the Gold Rush of 1849-52. Legions passed through these lands on their way west, but few were interested in stopping. Native Americans also constituted a disincentive for a time. Those indigenous to the region were hardly amenable to seeing their hunting and living grounds overrun, while other tribes like the Delaware and Shawnee, who had been displaced from easterly lands by the whites, also offered a forbidding prospect. Only when the government provided increasing Army protection, a by-product of the overland immigrant trains, and when legislation was passed enabling men to buy cheap land now and pay later, did the prairies finally experience a 'rush' of their own.

A few enterprising people sought to get ahead of the rest, not so much to achieve fortune, as for an opportunity simply to get away from the rest of their kind and find peace. Utopians and outcasts had always shared a mutual need for the west, as far back as the time when the term 'west' meant Indiana or Kentucky. By the 1840s there was a growing group of people who combined elements of both, a community with a distinctly different social order than the rest of white America, and one that had made them anathema wherever they settled in the past. Latter-Day Saints, they called themselves, but almost everyone else called them Mormons.

The religious denomination had been founded in 1830, and thereafter was never far from controversy. Its odious doctrine of polygamy outraged frontier society, while the intensely close-knit nature of the Saints enabled them, through mutual assistance, to acquire covetted land and prosper where others had failed, earning understandable envy from neighbors. As a result, they had been pushed from state to state, usually by violence. By the mid-1840s they were settled in their own city,

Above: *The prairie lands of Nebraska Territory – which comprised latter-day Kansas and Nebraska – appeared ideal for farming. The 1841 Preemption Act offered land at almost negligible cost.*

Below: *Immigrants moving West passed through Indian lands. While many went unscathed, others did not, and the Army was increasingly called on to provide protection for overlanders.*

Nauvoo, Illinois. But their founder Joseph Smith was killed by an angry mob, and his successor Brigham Young saw the old cycle of resentment and violence starting all over again. He determined to take his people somewhere far enough away that no one would bother them again.

In 1845 Young was thinking about California, and emissaries made the long journey late in 1845 to look at the terrain. They reached California safe enough, but then learned of reports of good land east of the Sierra, near the Great Salt Lake in the territory of the Ute Indians. Word went back to Young, who now was being forced to leave Illinois. He told people that he wanted to take his flock to California, but said nothing more definite than that, and on 4 February 1846 the trek began. Young was a born organizer, and he conducted the march west like a military campaign. The Mormons moved in small parties, each with separate tasks, some moving ahead of the others to prepare the way, leave shelter behind, and even plant crops, for those who would follow. It was not for nothing that they looked to the bee for a model. On their march to the new Zion, the Saints worked like a well-schooled hive.

There were some 15,000 of them on the great march, singing their hymn 'Come, Come Ye Saints'. Their progress was slow, many being entirely on foot, and storms, blizzards, droughts, and seemingly every other natural hazard was arrayed against. So were the United States authorities until the war with Mexico erupted, and 500 of the Saints enlisted to form the so-called Mormon Battalion. Their pay went to the church to finance the march west, while their enlistment bought a little favor from the government. The rest wintered in 1846 in Iowa, then set out again the following April, Young going with the advance party of seventy-two wagons. By the time they got their first sight of the Salt Lake and its valley, most of them were ill and suffering from hunger. Young himself arrived on 24 July 1847, looked out over the barren landscape, saw the dry soil and, in the distance, the salt flats, and had a vision of what his people could make of it. 'This is the place', he supposedly said to them, for up to that time he had kept so carefully guarded his destination that most still thought they were going to California. But here, hundreds of miles from any white civilization, on land that no one would immediately begrudge them, he would build his temple and his new Nauvoo.

Within twenty-four hours, the Saints were at work planting their first crops. Young laid out their home, Salt Lake City, and soon the men were studying ways to divert the clear

Below: *The Latter-Day Saints, or Mormons, were led out of Illinois by Brigham Young (seated on chair, center) in 1846. Their ultimate destination and haven from opprobrium was not California but Utah.*

Above: *The Mormons founded their new Zion beside the Great Salt Lake. They did not buy the land but simply arrived and settled it, quickly establishing a halfway house between east and west.*

Right: *Overlanders heading West would pause at Salt Lake City to stock up and refresh themselves. The Deseret Store, on South Temple and Main Street, welcomed the opportunities for profitable trade.*

mountain streams behind them to irrigate the parched valley floor of the Great Basin. They began to dream of not just their home beside the Great Salt Lake, but of an inland Mormon empire, stretching far to the south, with even a corridor to the Pacific through southern California, and a domain more than 200 miles wide. Like so many of the opportunists who came to the west for their destiny, the Saints saw the hand of the Almighty in their settlement, especially the next year when first frost destroyed most of their vegetable crop, and then massive locusts threatened to devour their ripening wheat. With seeming providential timing, the seagulls that dwelled around the giant saltwater lake swarmed over the horde of insects and devoured them.

More than gulls, however, the Mormons owed their salvation to Brigham Young, who kept them together with a mixture of threats, cajolery, inspiration, and a host of other appeals to their spiritual and mental needs. He even prevented all but a few from answering the siren call of gold in 1849. His people formed their own government, with him as governor. They spread out and started other towns and villages in the plain, most of them models of neatness and style that made other frontier communities appear pitiful by contrast. In short, they forged a new alloy of religious faith with the American ideal of opportunity and the inevitable El Dorado awaiting those who went west with enough courage and imagination to find it. By the 1850s their new land was called Utah and was recognized officially as a territory by Congress. They still had a host of obstacles ahead of them, but they were surviving. And they set a new pattern. Unlike the other opportunistic exoduses to the West for furs or gold, the Saints came for a place to *live*. They were there to stay.[14]

Therein lay the beginnings of a pattern. The Mormons did not buy this land from anyone, they simply came and settled it. Tens of thousands of others were to follow, people too poor to buy large tracts, or even to pay the $1.25 per acre. The trappers had been followed by the miners, and after them came the ranchers. Inevitably, the simple farmer was destined to come in the wake of those who preceded him looking for a quick profit. Like the Mormons, the farmer would come to stay. He was the last of the opportunists to commence invading the West, excepting the railroad builders, yet the iron horse was itself only a further aid of the inrush of the plow.

The 1841 Preemption Act first opened the door to the tillers of the soil. It granted people title to a quarter section of land, if they improved and lived on it, with payment for the acreage deferred, and sometimes entirely forgiven. Under such an act were Kansas and Nebraska, Iowa, and more settled, eventually to become territories, and then states. In the 1850s even more liberal policies encouraged further agricultural exploitation. In 1854 the $1.25 was reduced on a scale according to the

quality of the land being purchased, allowing poorer farmers to buy land, even if not of the best. Then came the land bonus or 'bounty' for all veterans of any of America's wars. A bona fide veteran could apply for a claim of a full quarter section – 160 acres – often absolutely free.

Further inducements soon followed. Washington offered half sections in the Oregon Donation Law to families who would settle and farm for at least four years, and thereby more than 8,000 new settlers put over 3 million acres into cultivation. The Civil War interrupted such measures for a few years, but after 1865, with thousands of veterans looking to start new lives to the west, more legislation followed the heels of the 1862 Homestead Act that allowed any head of a family to stake a claim to a quarter section in a United States territory, farm it for five years, build a house, and thereafter obtain legal title to it at no cost. With a view toward the future, however, many would-be settlers chose to buy their land from the railroads, who had been granted vast tracts of land, usually a full section in width either side of their track right of way. This land was where the cities would naturally grow, and where the farmer would have the easiest access to the markets of the East for his grain and livestock.

They followed the river valleys at first, where the land was more level and the water immediately available. Then they settled

Below: *Families kept moving on, hoping to seize the many opportunities on offer. After the 1862 Homestead Act they continued to cross the Plains, then over the Rockies onto the fertile western lowlands.*

Top: *Bromley's Station, Echo Canyon, Utah Territory, 1863. A Pony Express station, then a stage stop, it stood in an important position between Salt Lake City and Fort Bridger in the Wasatch Range.*

Above: *By 1852 nearly every Mormon who wanted to had joined his sect in Utah. Such missionaries as these went east from Salt Lake City to other parts of America and to Europe to find fresh converts.*

along the rails, and gradually spread across the plains to the Rockies, into and through its more tillable lowlands, and then spilled out on to the other side, with even Young's Utah experiencing a non-Mormon homesteader influx. It amounted to a virtual invasion until, by 1890, the 'squatter' had penetrated to even the most remote parts of the West.[15]

Thus it would have seemed that the cycle was complete, from boom or bust adventurer at the beginning, to the steady, conservative, eternal hand of the farmer. But the West as a land of opportunity contained still more surprises. From time to time men forgot that the West was an idea, a state of mind, as much as a place. Definitions could change and a new 'West' could still be found. It came again in 1896 at a place about as far west as one could go on the continental American domain. The United States had purchased the Alaska territory from Russia in 1867, but thereafter hardly knew exactly what to do with it. Few were interested in settling in what most erroneously believed to be a barren, frozen waste. But then in 1896 men looked down in the waters of the Klondike and Yukon Rivers and saw what James Marshall had seen almost fifty years before. A Yukon rush commenced almost at once, and though the gold itself was chiefly in Canada rather than Alaska, still the quickest and least arduous routes to the diggings were through Seattle, Washington, by boat to Alaska, and then overland. The gold found in Canada was brought back to mining camps like Nome and Anchorage, there to go into the hands of traders around whose operations more entrepreneurs flocked. It was 1849 all over again, and it closed the book on what had been a century of unparalleled adventure and exploitation, from those first daring traders on their keelboats tremulously poling up the Missouri in the wake of Lewis and Clark, to the sourdough prospector who started the killing trek up the Chilkoot Pass toward the Yukon, with gold in his eyes.

Above: *Government surveyors eventually followed the Mormons into Utah. John Wesley Powell's photographer, E.O. Beaman, recorded these first generation settlers as Powell mapped the Utah plateau in 1872.*

Below: *Ute Indians in Salt Lake City, 1869. Brigham Young urged a policy of non-aggression toward them: 'I have not made war on Indians . . . My policy is to give them presents and be kind to them.'*

REFERENCES

1 Daniel Boorstin, *The Americans*, pp. 60-61; David Lavender, *Great West*, pp. 130-34.
2 David J. Weber, *The Taos Trappers* (Norman, Oklahoma, 1971), pp. 192-3, 210, 227-9.
3 Lavender, *The Great West*, p. 237; J.S. Holliday, *The World Rushed In* (New York, 1981), p. 25.
4 David Lavender, *California, Land of New Beginnings* (New York, 1972), p. 150; Rodman Paul, *The California Gold Discovery* (Georgetown, Calif., 1967), pp. 71-2.
5 Holliday, *The World Rushed In*, pp. 42-3.
6 *Ibid.*, pp. 452-3.
7 Lavender, *The Great West*, pp. 260-61.
8 Holliday, *The World Rushed In*, p. 458.
9 Boorstin, *The Americans*, p. 301.
10 William Wright, *The Big Bonanza* (New York, 1947), pp. 372-3.
11 Lavender, *The Great West*, pp. 121-23, 135-6.
12 Richard A. Bartlett, *The New Country* (New York, 1974), pp. 190-91.
13 *Ibid.*, pp. 192-7.
14 *Ibid.*, pp. 386-8.
15 Lavender, *The Great West*, p. 259; Bartlett, *New Country*, pp. 112-14.

III

FRONTIER POLITICS

Below: *Free-state battery, Topeka, Kansas, 1856. The issues of statehood and slavery led to open warfare on the plains.*

FROM THE MOMENT that Americans looked to the West, the land and its fate were inextricably intertwined with events decided in domestic and foreign capitals. Political and military affairs governed the opening of the West from the outset, dictating where the new immigrants settled, and those settlements in turn helped govern the unfolding history of the land.

White Americans' very first organized foray into the mist-shrouded world west of the Mississippi was as much politically motivated as it was simply a good real estate deal. The Louisiana Purchase was a strategic move designed to afford protection to the infant United States from the foreign powers surrounding it on almost every border. In 1803, with Britain in Canada on the north, with Spain in Mexico on the south, and with France owning the Louisiana Territory, President Jefferson felt rightly concerned that his nation could get caught in the middle. Napoleon had designs on re-establishing France's earlier New World prominence. When officials in New Orleans closed the mouth of the great river to any further American trading, the alarm spread all the way to Washington. Jefferson proclaimed that any foreign nation controlling the river's access to the ocean must be Americans' 'natural and habitual enemy.'[1]

Thus Jefferson commenced negotiations to buy the territory and remove the threat. It also effectively got France out of North America for good, ending the possibility that France and Britain, still mortal enemies, might do battle with each other on this continent and catch the United States between them. Jefferson had other things on his mind, too. Certainly the vast territory west of the Mississippi offered unlimited possibilities for new settlement. But also he did not envision it all necessarily becoming a part of the United States. Eventually, he felt, other new nations might grow up in the region, friendly to the United States and allied with it in common defense,

speaking of them as 'free and independent Americans, unconnected with us but by the ties of blood and interest'. Thus, from a host of viewpoints, the Louisiana Purchase was not just a land bonanza, but a political coup as well.[2]

Still, the schemes of foreign powers could not be kept out of the new lands without resort to arms. By 1811 it was widely believed that England was providing large numbers of weapons to the Indians of the Mississippi Valley, from the banks of the Illinois all the way down to Mississippi and Alabama. Widespread uprising led to harsh military action by United States forces, confirming suspicions that Britain was inciting the savages in what would be the prelude to another attempt to subdue the former crown colonies. In the ensuing War of 1812, Americans were chiefly preoccupied with an attempt to wrest Canada from England. Few Redcoats were ever seen west of the Mississippi, but their influence was felt. The Indians of Missouri and the upper Mississippi reaches, taking heart in the preoccupation of American armies with the British to the east, launched a series of successful raids against infant trading settlements along the Missouri River that put even St Louis in a panic. Meanwhile, far to the west where John Jacob Astor had established his Pacific Fur Company at Astoria, in the Oregon Territory, trade came under threat of a British blockade from Canada, and the Americans

were forced to abandon their small foothold on the Pacific. Some, like Jefferson, had foreseen that this might happen, but did not despair, hoping that the eventual peace would see Oregon recognized as neither American nor British, but 'the germ of a great, free and independent empire'.

However successful the War of 1812 was seen to be by Americans east of the Mississippi when it was done, to the west it had advantaged them little if at all. Oregon was securely in British hands, and the only benefit seemed to be that the Indians along the Mississippi had temporarily been subdued. Traders and settlers could once more start their slow spread westward.

But among those settlers lay the catalyst for the next crisis, this one purely domestic, and not long in coming. Missouri was settled rapidly, and by 1819 the men of the territory were talking of statehood. There lay the problem. Already a fragile balance of power in Washington between Northern 'free' interests and Southern slaveholding interests was tearing the nation apart. Now the new lands of the Louisiana Territory were being opened up, and if more states were to be formed west of

Below: *A view of Market Square, San Antonio, Texas, in the 1870s. The hordes of volunteers to defend the town never materialized: Travis' small force was annihilated on the 13th day of the siege.*

the Mississippi, would they be slave or free? The question was not so much one of humanitarian impulses as it was one of simple power. Make Missouri a slave state, and the balance shifted toward the Southern dominated Democrats. Make Missouri a free state, banning slavery in its borders, and only slaveless men, predominantly Northern Whigs, would settle it, thus ensuring that its representation in Congress would be Whig. The debate in Congress raged for months until, in 1820, a compromise was effected that was to govern all of the Louisiana Territory. Henceforward, no state formed from lands north of the line of 36° 30' could countenance slavery within its borders. States formed from below that line could if they so chose. Missouri itself was admitted as a slave state that same year.

This at least averted the crisis of the moment, but in reality only postponed it. Southerners were not happy with the decision but accepted it as the best they could get. The chief trouble was that *most* of the Purchase territory lay above that dividing line, thus almost ensuring that eventually it would provide more free states than could be matched in the lands below. Out of this dilemma came a renewed impetus for men of the South to look due west, to Texas.

The Louisiana Territory's southern boundary had always been indefinite. When the Adams-Onis Treaty of 1819 finally settled it, excluding Texas and recognizing Spain's claim

to it as unchallenged, Southerners were outraged. Seen in tandem with the Missouri Compromise of the next year, it seemed to present a clear case of Yankee conspiring to contain slavery to the states where it already existed, and thereby eventually reduce the South's voice in Washington to that of a pitiful minority. It is not coincidental, then, that Moses Austin and his son Stephen began their efforts to found a colony in Spanish Texas the very next year, nor that thousands followed them during that decade, bringing their slaves with them. If Southerners could not form new states to the north, they would try to wrest new territory from the Spanish.

The Texas experiment was always a troubled one, though at least it remained peaceful, helped by its isolation from Mexico City and by the turmoil within Mexican politics of the time. When Mexico closed the borders to further immigration in 1830, Texans supported a new revolutionary leader, General Antonio Lopez de Santa Anna, hoping that if successful he would be sympathetic to their interests. Unfortunately, even after Santa Anna took power, the colonists pressed for more and more autonomy, seeking to become almost independent, with their own legislature and answerable only to Santa Anna himself. At the same time, a growing movement for complete independence swept through the settlement, and one of their leaders, Sam Houston, started correspondence with President Andrew Jackson to sound his interest in acquiring Texas for the United States.

After that events moved swiftly. Austin was arrested and imprisoned for almost two years. On 30 June 1835 a young hot-head named William B. Travis led several other settlers in the armed eviction of a Mexican customs party from Anahuac near the mouth of the Trinity River. After that things escalated more rapidly. A small Mexican army of 1,100 marched north to San Antonio, only to find itself besieged by a scratch force of Texans some 600 strong and led by Austin. On 10 December 1835, their commander surrendered and a wave of euphoria swept the settlements.

Santa Anna, however, was not to be rebuffed so lightly. He commenced raising a much larger army to put down the insurrection, and was marching north toward San Antonio even while the Texans debated declaring absolute independence, and sent their own irregular columns out to expel other small Mexican garrisons. Houston was placed in command of all Texan forces, while young Travis took command of the small force left in San Antonio, headquartered in an old mission called the Alamo.

Each of the small columns sent out by the Texans met with disaster by 2 March 1836, the day that the convention meeting in Washington on the Brazos River formally declared independence. By then, however, all eyes in Texas, and even east of the Mississippi, were turned on San Antonio. Santa Anna himself had arrived with more than 1,000 soldiers, soon to be reinforced to 3,000 or more, and laid siege to Travis and his tiny garrison of no more than 150. At the first news of the uprisings in Texas, thousands of adventurers and would be settlers started west. A volunteer military company from New Orleans had arrived earlier, and parties led by men like David Crockett from Tennessee joined with earlier immigrants like the legendary James Bowie to bolster Travis' tiny ranks. As a result, daily expecting large reinforcements himself, Travis decided not to evacuate in the face of Santa Anna's overwhelming numbers. In the end, however, it all happened too fast for the ill-prepared and disorganized new authorities in Texas to deal with the situation. A mere thirty-five or so men actually slipped through to join Travis before the Mexican cordon around him drew tight. Travis, Crockett, Bowie, and about 180 others were trapped. On 6 March they died to the last man when Santa Anna's attack overwhelmed them in a fight lasting little more than an hour.

Below: *Alamo Plaza, San Antonio, 1870s, where Santa Anna's superior forces overcame the Texans in March 1836. Only six weeks later, the tables turned, Texas would declare independence from Mexico.*

Overnight 'Remember the Alamo' became a rallying cry for the rest of Texas. Houston, his small army still incomplete and ill-organized, withdrew before the Mexican advance. When other small Texan columns that were captured suffered the same fate as Travis and his defenders, hosts of families fled northward in a panic. All the while Houston kept his own counsel as he retreated back to the bank of the San Jacinto River, not far from Anahuac, all the while building his army. On 20 April an over-confident Santa Anna caught up with him, and the next afternoon, while the Mexican army slept in siesta, Houston and his 783 men attacked, taking the foe completely by surprise. Despite being outnumbered more than two to one, the Texans overwhelmed the panicked Mexicans and closed the battle in less than twenty minutes from firing the first volley. Santa Anna himself fell prisoner and all further efforts to subdue the revolutionaries ceased. While Mexico never formally recognized the independence of Texas, Texans took it for an accomplished fact, elected Houston their president, and started off on their career as an independent republic.

Right: *San Houston failed to reach the besieged Alamo in time. Forced to retreat before the pursuing Mexicans, his ragged army, remembering the Alamo, overwhelmed them at San Jacinto that April.*

Below: *Veterans of the Battle of San Jacinto in about 1870. Although their victory meant independence from Mexico, the American government was unwilling at once to annex Texas to the United States.*

For the next several years Texas endured a rocky existence, benefitting mainly from internal turmoils in Mexico that kept Santa Anna, following his release, from launching another invasion. Meanwhile, to the surprise of no one, repeated probes went out to Washington to raise the issue of admission to the union and statehood. Nothing came of them until 1843, when Houston cannily started playing a new friendship with Britain against United States' foot-dragging, and Washington finally took the statehood issue seriously. Once more the old debate on slavery erupted as the North saw a conspiracy in the Texas adventure to enhance slave interests. Nevertheless, by 1845 the debate ended with President John Tyler signing a Congressional resolution approving annexation of Texas if a ballot by its citizens so willed.

During the debate of the past two years, Mexico looked on in alarm. It had never recognized the independence of Texas, and seeing now that it could become a part of the United States, the new government under Mariano Paredes quite rightly read into the act a first step on a road to the acquisition of more of Mexico, perhaps even all of it. Mexico broke off diplomatic relations with the United States and started marshalling an army. Contrary to later evaluations, the two nations were not that unevenly matched militarily. President James K. Polk had a Regular Army of fewer than 8,000 in uniform, and spread all across the country. Mexico could count more than that, and easily raise more. Moreover, Paredes had hopes that a boundary dispute over Oregon might once more precipitate Washington to go to war with Britain. Thus circumstances seemed to indicate that Texas, certainly worth fighting for, could be contested at least with an even chance of victory.

General Zachary Taylor had been sent to command the small army of occupation at Corpus Christi, on the Gulf of Mexico, and in March 1846 set forth to march to the mouth of the Rio Grande, which Texas – and now the United States – claimed as the legitimate southern boundary of the Republic, which had the year before resoundingly voted for annexation by the United States. During much of that month and the one following, Taylor stared across the Rio Grande at the small 2,000-man Mexican army sent to re-assert Mexican authority in Texas. Finally, late in April, the Mexicans crossed the river above Matamoros, and on the twenty-fifth they attacked and captured or killed a small party of sixty-three dragoons. The next day, receiving word of the scrape, Taylor sent word to Washington that 'hostilities may now be considered as commenced'. The Mexican War had begun.[3]

During the next two years the major events of the war pursued their course south of the Rio Grande, with little impact on the western region above the river. Despite the seeming equality of the two sides at the commencement of hostilities, the United States very quickly assumed a dominance in the campaigning that it never lost, though a few of the battles were close-fought affairs. The Union did not go to war with Britain over Oregon, and thus one potential distraction was removed. Worse for the Mexicans, there was a patriotic wave of volunteer enlistments that more than doubled the size of the American army, and backed by economic, manufacturing, and transportation systems that far outstripped those supporting Santa Anna, who commanded Mexico's armies. At least 40,000 men from the Mississippi Valley's contiguous states went into uniform, along with another 20,000 from the South, both reflecting the obvious interest the war had for the aspirations of men from those regions. It was to be a war for westward expansion.

While most of the action took place in Mexico itself, the expanding American West saw its share of activity almost from the very first as the army, and even more so a host of civilian opportunists, lunged to seize Mexican territory in California and the territory centered around Santa Fe and one day to become Arizona and New Mexico. Colonel Stephen Watts Kearny was ordered to lead a column from Fort Leavenworth in the territory west of Missouri, and take it south to Santa Fe, subdue any Mexican resistance there, and then push on to southern California. If possible he was to seize the entire province. At the same time, Washington sent a naval squadron off around Cape Horn with orders to blockade the Mexican ports in California and cooperate with Kearny.

Meanwhile, even before Kearny was to arrive, Captain John C. Frémont, a topograph-

Below: *John Charles Frémont (1813–90), called by some the Great Pathfinder. As a captain, Frémont arrived in Sonoma in the summer of 1846 and was declared head of the 'Republic of California' by residents.*

ical engineer, was already in northern California, having come on a survey with a party of sixty men and obtained permission from local authorities to winter near Monterey. Even before word arrived of the outbreak of war, the Mexicans ordered him to leave in early March, and Frémont slowly made his way north into Oregon, only to turn around when he received news of the war. By late May he was at Sutter's Fort, and in June he was striking the first blows at Mexican authority when he seized the small Mexican garrison at Sonoma. Immediately afterward, in what was more a drunken revel than a serious civil-military move, Frémont's men proclaimed the California Republic, raised a new flag with a bear on it, and sent word off to American authorities that they hoped to see California joined with the United States as quickly as possible.

While the new Bear Flag Republic as it came to be called was a somewhat comical affair, inspired largely by captured Mexican brandy, more serious efforts were being made by the Regulars and volunteers under Kearny, and by the Navy off California's shores. Kearny's Army of the West numbered nearly 1,700 when it set out for Santa Fe in late June. By 15 August they had reached Las Vegas in the province of New Mexico, and there they formally declared that henceforward the territory belonged to the United States. Three days later the exhausted column marched into Santa Fe, having met no opposition from the Mexicans at any point in their journey. The first discharge of their guns came that afternoon in saluting the raising of the Stars and Stripes over the governor's palace. Kearny

U.S. MILITARY UNTIL 1871

The military presence on the frontier was small before the Civil War, but there were some 300,000 Indians in the West in about 1845. Military units were widely scattered in isolated outposts, charged with protecting civilians in their area of responsibility and immigrants traveling through these areas on trails west. The soldier was always greatly outnumbered; daily he confronted fear, fatigue, poor rations and little appreciation from those

he tried to protect. To assist these small garrisons, a number of volunteer militia units were raised but were basically ineffectual, often exacerbating already tense situations. Still, because of the small numbers involved, incidents were relatively few and actual fatalities small in number, although considerable livestock was lost. But, as white immigration increased and their influence expanded, Indian resistance stiffened and tribes began uniting to raid and pillage small settlements and outposts.

1 Cavalry enlisted man's shell jacket, yellow indicating the branch of service.
2 Colt Model 1860 Army revolver, .44 caliber.
3 Pack of six .44 caliber combustible paper cartridges for above.
4 Model 1842 Aston single-shot pistol, .54 caliber.
5 Colt Model 1860 Army revolver, .44 caliber, with detachable shoulder stock affixed for use as a carbine.
6 Model 1865 first model Allin alteration rifle, .58 caliber.
7 Model 1858 tin canteen with cotton sling.
8 Model 1861 contract rifle musket, .58 caliber.
9 Paper-wrapped copper percussion caps for above.
10 .58 caliber paper cartridges; left standard, right Williams Patent Cleaner round, for (8).
11 Model 1840 non-commissioned officer's sword.

12 Brass-mounted leather scabbard for above.

13 Sharps Model 1859 breechloading carbine, .54 caliber.

14 Saddle cinch for (15).

15 Model 1859 brass-bound officer's McClellan saddle, with padded seat.

16 Colt Model 1851 Navy revolver, .36 caliber.

17 Pack of six .36 caliber combustible paper cartridges for above.

18 Model 1850 staff and field officer's sword.

19 Brass-mounted metal scabbard for above.

20 Artillery enlisted man's shell jacket, red indicating the branch of service.

21 Model 1858 infantry forage cap or kepi, the brass horn indicating branch of service.

22 Colt third model dragoon revolver, .44 caliber, with detachable shoulder stock affixed for use as a carbine.

23 Colt Model 1851 Navy revolver, .36 caliber.

24 Remington new model Army revolver, .44 caliber.

25 Model 1855 triangular socket bayonet for (8).

26 Brass-mounted scabbard for (25).

27 Wooden tompion to keep moisture out of the barrels of items (6) and (8).

28 Model 1855 cartridge box with shoulder belt. The box holds forty rounds of .58 caliber ammunition, such as item (10).

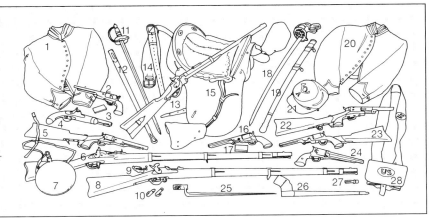

soon formed a civil government for the New Mexico Territory, sent part of his army south to join in the main operations in Mexico itself, and with the rest set out for California on 25 September. Along the way he encountered Christopher 'Kit' Carson, sent by Frémont to bring news of California's occupation to Washington.

Frémont would try to take credit for California, but in fact it was the Navy, under Commodore John D. Sloat, who achieved the coup. On 7 July he sent a party ashore at Monterey and raised the flag after the Mexican authorities left the town without a fight. Two days later another commodore formally occupied Yerba Buena, future San Francisco. That same day the Bear Flag came down in Sonoma after its brief reign, to be replaced by Old Glory. Officially, at least, all of northern California belonged to the Yankees. The few Mexican officers and men withdrew to Los Angeles, where about 800 of them fortified and prepared to make a stand under General Pio Pico.

When word of what had happened reached Kearny, he sent all but 100 of his Regulars and a few volunteers back to Santa Fe, and pressed on. By 22 November they were on the Colorado, with California on the other side, and there they learned that the peaceful acquisi-

Above: *Kit Carson guided Frémont on three topographical expeditions in the mid-1840s. Pressed into service as a scout during the Mexican War, he was thereafter denied a commission in the Union Army.*

tion of the province had suddenly turned hostile since Carson left Frémont. On 20 September the Mexicans in Los Angeles began an uprising that quickly escalated, with them declaring their independence from the newly American California, and soon forming their own government once more, covering much of the southern half of the future state. Only San Diego remained securely in American hands.

Kearny marched on hurriedly, and by the night of 5 December was approaching the small Indian village of San Pascual, barely thirty miles from San Diego. He received word that Mexican cavalry had been seen in the vicinity, and at dawn the next morning the Regulars attacked. Kearny conducted a poorly planned and executed fight, not surprising after an 1,800-mile trek with exhausted men and animals. Kearny himself was wounded, and several of his officers killed, while the Mexicans left the field in the end, but clearly having gotten the best of it. Now Kearny's

Below: *Although apparently celebrating the Bear Flag Republic, this 1877 photograph shows Pacific Coast Pioneers in Carson City, Nevada. The original flag, raised in 1846, was not long unfurled.*

command tried to limp on to San Diego, but got only as far as the San Bernardo ranch, where they fortified a small hill and survived for the next several days on horse and mule meat until a relief party from San Diego finally came to 'Mule Hill' and escorted them into San Diego on 12 December at last.[4]

On 29 December a combined command of Kearny's Regulars along with sailors and other volunteers, set out northward to put down the uprising. Two weeks later, after occasional skirmishing on the way, they marched into Los Angeles on 10 January 1847, with no opposition. Three days later Frémont, marching leisurely south to join Kearny, signed a treaty with the last remaining Mexican opposition near Mission San Fernando, just north of Los Angeles. It was the virtual end of the Mexican War in the American West. Conflict did continue, but only as the ambitious victors fell out among themselves, vying for credit and power.

The Mexican War itself dragged on for another year, before a treaty of peace was finally executed on 2 February 1848, at Guadalupe Hidalgo. It was a conflict that had startling impact on the West. Virtually all of the territory below the Louisiana Purchase line, in what is now the United States, came into American hands. A subsequent, more peaceful acquisition came in 1853 when the Gadsden Purchased added more territory between the Colorado and the Rio Grande, comprising southern portions of latter day Arizona and New Mexico. Meanwhile, the United States had managed to stay out of war with Britain over the contested Oregon Territory. Instead, in June 1846 the two nations negotiated their differences and agreed upon a boundary along the 49th parallel, the modern border between Washington and Canada. Thus, excluding only minor adjustments in the years ahead, the contiguous continental United States was complete.

Equally to the point, for the first time the government had revealed the same bent of opportunism until then demonstrated by so many of its private citizens. The West *was* a place where fortunes and futures could be made, and under President Polk the nation had doubled its uncontested western holdings. Now there could be almost unlimited new

Below: President Polk's urging of war against Mexico in 1846 was seen by some as warmongering. But under his presidency America increased its western holdings, annexing Oregon Country in 1846.

territories and states, not separate nations as Jefferson had dreamed, but all part of a huge, powerful, and wealthy United States of America.

Predictably, the domestic turmoil that always lay beneath the surface of American politics emerged with renewed vitriol when the guns fell silent. Indeed, there had been an immense opposition to the war all during its course. In the North, Whigs and 'Free-Soil' men opposed to slavery, saw in the conflict nothing but a massive land grab, almost all of it below the Missouri Compromise line, calculated by pro-slavery Democrats to provide land for slave states to counter the free states that were coming from the Louisiana Territory. Certainly it was the South that had responded most enthusiastically to the war, both in Congress and at home.

All it took was the first debates over the admission of a new state to bring it all out in the open again. California, spurred by the impetus of the Gold Rush, applied for statehood in 1850. So did the Mormons in Utah, claiming a vast province that included several future states, while a rump session of men in New Mexico made the same request. Texas laid claim to a large portion of New Mexico. Everybody wanted a slice of the pie; everyone it appeared, was out to capitalize with unseemly haste on the bonanza the war produced, and the whole mess, as usual, fell into Congress's lap.

Months of heated debate finally led to a series of measures identified under the heading 'Omnibus Bill'. No one was entirely happy with it, but each side gave a little, and gained something in return, and the backing of Zachary Taylor, now President, helped most Senators to swallow it. Stephen A. Douglas of Illinois authored many of the separate bills, while the old compromiser Henry Clay of Kentucky helped steer them through to passage. California would be admitted as a free state, while the Mormons had to settle for territorial status for their desert colony, redubbed Utah. Its land claims were also drastically scaled back. New Mexico, too, would be a territory, to include future Arizona. Texas lost its claim to the New Mexico land but received a large monetary compensation instead.

The so-called Compromise of 1850 also addressed the slavery issue in yet another attempt to put an end to the seemingly constant agitation. In future, all territories could decide the matter for themselves at the time they applied for statehood. Meanwhile, a Fugitive Slave Law was passed compelling citizens and authorities in free states to assist slave catchers who came looking for runaways from the South.

No one got all that they wanted out of the Compromise, but it gave each side something, and well-intentioned men hoped that it would settle once and for all the agitation of how to handle the new territories to the west. Unfortunately, like most of the compromises over sectional issues, it treated only a symptom, and not the basic malady of slavery and balance of power. Instead, it set the stage for a rush of settlement intended to determine the political future of the territories and, with them, of the nation.

GATLING & HOTCHKISS GUNS

Patented by Richard Jordan Gatling of Maney's Neck, North Carolina, this Model 1875 gun was manufactured by the Colt Patent Firearms Manufacturing Company. The Model 1875 was chambered for the .45-70 government cartridge, the same ammunition used in the standard Army shoulder arm of the period. Ammunition was gravity fed from the box magazine mounted on top of the bronze breech housing. The gun had an effective range of about 1000 yards. Nearly all garrisons in Indian country had such ordnance on post and these guns on field carriages normally accompanied any sizeable expeditions in the field. It may be noted that Brevet Major-General George A. Custer left behind three Gatling guns in June 1876 because he felt they would slow down his rate of march. The results of his engagement with the Indians at the Little Bighorn may have been somewhat different had these early rapid fire guns been present.

The Hotchkiss two-pounder mountain gun (right) was a French design adopted by U.S. military forces about 1885. Actual caliber was 1.65 in. and the gun could be transported by a team of horses assembled, or carried by a team of four mules. In this mode of transportation it was mobile over the most difficult terrain. Normally a crew of six manned the gun of which two were assigned to animals and ammunition. Two types of projectiles were issued, common shell with a percussion fuse and cannister. Maximum range was about 4000

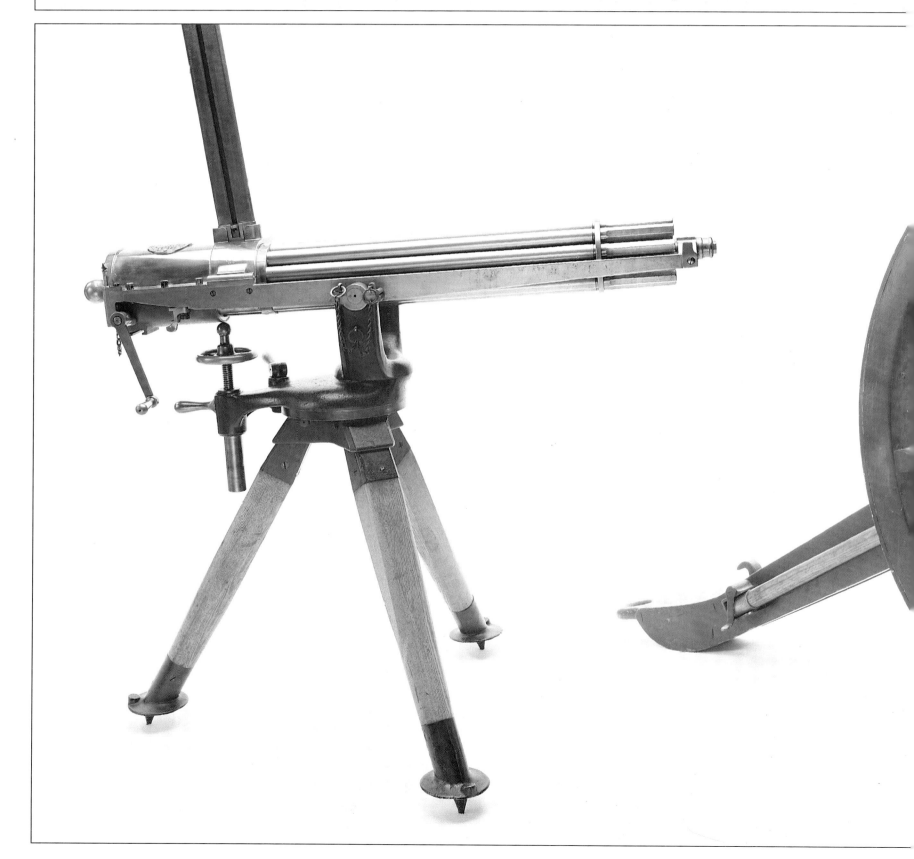

yards at elevation 14° 15'. The slow moving projectile had only a velocity of 591 ft per second at maximum range but an initial velocity of 1298 ft per second. When disassembled for mule transport, the barrel weighed only 121 pounds, the wheels each 66 pounds and the carriage 220 pounds, plus the standard load of 56 rounds of ammunition. Because of its light weight, mobility and efficiency, this gun was used extensively by the Army in the West during the later Indian conflicts. The Indians had no defense against it.

1 (Left) Gatling gun, Model 1875, on wooden tripod with crude elevating mechanism, ammunition magazine in place, operated by the hand crank seen extended below breech.
2 (Right) Hotchkiss two-pounder breech loading mountain gun. Light artillery piece.
3 1.65 in. cannister round for above.
4 1.65 in. common explosive shell for above.

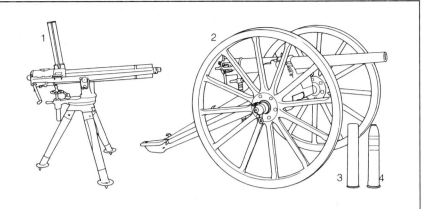

The immediate focus was the land west of Missouri. Slavery advocates could look across the line to the wide, rolling prairies of what was then called the Nebraska Territory, and envision its suitability for the plow, and slave labor. But since the 1820 compromise line prohibited slavery above the line of Missouri's southern border, all of Nebraska was destined to be free country. This alone rankled the conservative elements in Missouri. Since the West had been either won or purchased with national blood and treasure, what justification could there be for Congress prohibiting any citizen from going to the new land and taking all of his property with him, including property in slaves?

Worse, by 1853 most of the Indian tribes in the territory had been pacified or moved out, and the land was begging for settlement. Then when talk of a trans-continental railroad going through began to circulate, a group setting themselves up as a rump convention elected a governor and nominated a delegate to be elected to Congress, though any such actions were extra-legal since Congress had not yet formally organized the territory. The convention did not address the issue of slavery, tacitly accepting the dictate of the Missouri Compromise line, which slave interests in Missouri felt ought to be challenged, especially in the light of the Compromise of 1850, whose provisions for slavery being decided at the time of a territory's admission as a state seemed to abrogate the 1820 restriction. Another pro-slavery 'convention' was hurriedly assembled, and it nominated its own Congressional candidate. Then in the fall election, hundreds of Missourians crossed the border at night to cast illegal votes electing the pro-slave men.

Of course none of it was legal, and Washington refused to recognize any of the candidates, but the growing controversy did punctuate the need to settle such issues. It fell to Stephen Douglas to attempt a permanent resolution that, in the end, only made matters worse. First he adopted the idea of separating the territory in two, Nebraska and Kansas, and pushing a bill for their territorial organization simultaneously. Then Archibald Dixon of Kentucky addressed the underlying issue of slavery. He and others persuaded Douglas to adopt his idea of adding a repeal of the Missouri Compromise into the new Kansas-Nebraska Bill. This way, pro-slave people might settle in one and see it eventually become a slave state, while abolitionists might settle the other. Furthermore, Douglas proposed that the issue not be settled by Congress as each territory applied for admission to statehood, but that the matter be settled internally within each territory prior to statehood. This doctrine of 'popular sovereignty', combined with the repeal, put the nation on the road to chaos.

At first the bulk of the settlers flowing into Kansas were non-slaveholders, if not entirely anti-slavery in their sentiments. But then wildly exaggerated stories began to circulate about the several emigrant aid societies formed in New England to encourage and finance the settlement of the territories with free-staters in anticipation of having a majority when the populations reached the mandated minimum for territorial organization

and the framing of constitutions. This put the pro-slave people in a fury, and spurred an immediate reaction from the Missourians when elections were held for Kansas' first legitimate territorial Congressional delegate. Hundreds of bogus votes were cast by men who rode across the line from Missouri. Later they repeated the fraud to elect a pro-slave legislature. In response, the abolition elements tried to form a free state on their own, though entirely outside the law. Missouri slave proponents threatened to attack and pillage the free-state headquarters at Lawrence.

As the troubles that soon had the territory called 'Bleeding Kansas' escalated, extremists on both sides sent men, money, and guns, into the area. Shots were fired early in 1856, at last, and on 21 May Lawrence was attacked and its abolition newspapers and headquarters buildings destroyed. There was open warfare on the plains. Into this arena stepped a man who presaged much of what in another century would be called terrorism, John Brown. A man of limited emotional stability, who had failed in most of his several callings previously, he had adopted abolition with a fanatical frenzy that ignored all boundaries of law and humanity. Assembling a small cadre of followers, he

began to spread terror through the pro-slavery settlements, achieving national infamy for his 24 May attack in the night on Potawatomie Creek. Armed with broadswords, Brown and his men, including several of his sons, appeared out of the darkness and knocked on the doors of five known pro-slave cabins. When the man of the house answered, he was taken outside and slashed to death.

What followed became known as the August War, as marauders from both camps roamed the moonlit plains by night, appearing from nowhere to kill and burn. More than 200 people died that summer before a new territorial governor arrived to bring order out of the chaos, with Brown himself nearly suffering death in the only substantial 'battle' of the war at Ossawatomie, when a few hundred met in a desultory skirmish.[5]

While Kansas cooled for a time, it would not be for long. The free-soil elements in Kansas decided to boycott any participation in the government of the territory. Worse, when balloting was held to select delegates for a constitutional convention to meet at Lecompton in 1857, anti-slave men boycotted that as well. This, plus the importation of thousands of bogus voters from Missouri, virtually ensured

Left: *John Brown was to be hanged at Harpers Ferry, Virginia, in 1859 but not before he had fomented trouble in Kansas in 1856 as a leading light in the violence against pro-slavery factions.*

Above: *The epithet 'Bleeding Kansas' came about largely through the actions of men like James Lane, the 'Grim Chieftain'. A fervent Free-stater like Brown, he was to die by his own hand in 1866.*

Below: *Dr John Doy (seated) was kidnapped and imprisoned in Missouri by Proslaveryites in 1859. Swiftly freed by fellow Kansans, he would help win the day: Kansas was admitted as a free state in 1861.*

U.S. MILITARY 1872-1900

After the Civil War, the U.S. Army was drastically reduced in numbers. Volunteers were discharged to return home or go West and the resulting small army was tasked with occupation of the defeated southern states and guarding the rapidly expanding western frontier. Even with additional regular army units that were sent west in the post-war years, the overall garrison forces never exceeded 5000 men of all ranks. All were volunteers on three to five year enlistments. A lowly private received only $13.00 per month. Needless to say, there was a great social gulf between officers and enlisted men. By 1874 the whole U.S. Army was limited to a total of 27,000 men. Those units sent west became 'Policemen of the Plains' and were understaffed and understrength. All manner of equipment was obsolescent and in short supply. With all these disadvantages plus a strong lobby in the east demanding the further expansion of the frontier, the Army was additionally forced to contend with an increasingly aggressive Indian population that had been pushed beyond its limits. What ensued was a deadly war of attrition with the Army engaging the Indian at every opportunity, destroying his villages, crops and herds, and on occasion his women and children. By the 1890s the Indian could no longer put up any resistance. Casualties, lack of food and disease combined with relentless pursuit by the Army defeated the finest light cavalry in the world.

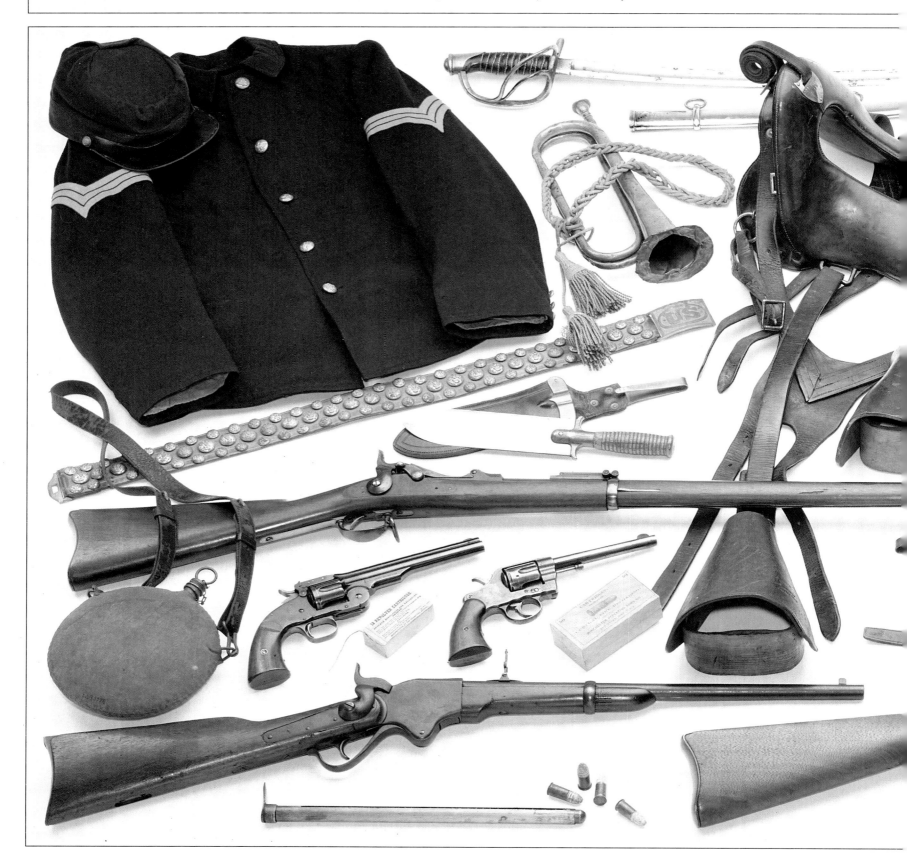

1 Forage cap, about 1889.
2 Model 1883 five-button sack coat.
3 Model 1874 U.S. belt.
4 Model 1880 Springfield armory hunting knife and scabbard.
5 Springfield Model 1884 breech-loading rifle.
6 Model 1881 canteen.
7 Smith and Wesson first model Schofield revolver.
8 Box of .45 caliber ammunition for (7).
9 Colt Model 1894 double-action revolver.
10 Box of .38 caliber ammunition for (9).
11 Spencer Model 1865 repeating carbine.
12 Magazine tube inserted in butt of (11).
13 Ammunition for (11), (12).
14 Model 1860 cavalry saber.
15 Metal scabbard for (14).
16 Brass bugle.
17 McClellan saddle.
18 Colt single-action Army revolver, .45 caliber.
19 Two boxes of .45 caliber ammunition for (18).
20 Riding gauntlets.
21 Scabbard for (22).
22 Entrenching bayonet.
23 Scabbard for Model 1873 triangular socket bayonet.
24 Model 1885 carbine boot.
25 Springfield Model 1884 carbine, .45-70 caliber.
26 Box of .45-70 caliber ammunition.
27 Brass spurs, about 1872.
28 Monocular or telescope.
29 Cavalry dress helmet.
30 Cavalry officer's campaign hat.
31 Cavalry officer's forage cap, 10th Cavalry, 1874.
32 Leather monocular case.
33 Cavalry breeches, c.1890.

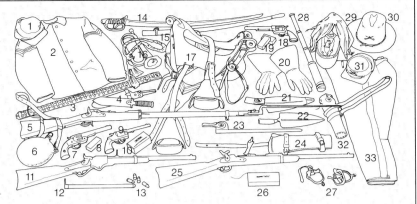

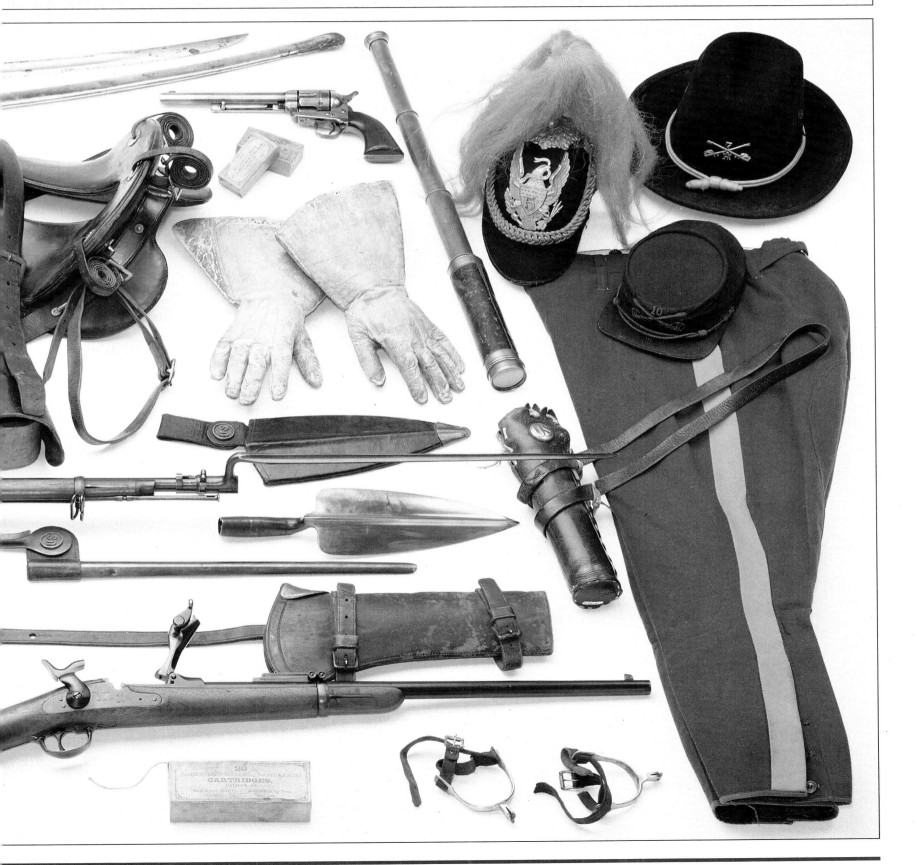

that the subsequent convention would have a pro-slave majority. Soon afterwards, in the election for a new territorial legislature, the pro-slave men tried the same tactics, but this time the governor threw out most of the fraudulent votes, and meanwhile the free-staters had turned out in numbers for a change. The result was a free-state majority in the new legislature. The constitutional convention, an independent body, now redoubled its efforts and soon produced a constitution recognizing slavery. President James Buchanan endorsed the constitution, in spite of a national outcry, and on 21 December it went before Kansans in a referendum. In the face of another free-soil boycott, the constitution was approved resoundingly. But once the free-state dominated legislature came into power, it called for another referendum. This time the slave men boycotted, and the constitution was rejected. The morass only got deeper and deeper before, in the end, the slavery provisions of the constitution lost out. When Kansas was admitted as a state in 1861, it was a free state.[6]

And when Kansas was admitted, the Union was at war with itself. The agitation over slavery had finally driven the two sections so far apart that compromise was impossible. In December 1860 South Carolina seceded, to be followed by seven other states of the border and South, and Texas, Arkansas, and Louisiana from the West. Firing erupted at Fort Sumter on 12 April 1861, and the war was on. Ironically, for both sides early in the war, its conduct lay largely in the hands of men who had made their names or gained their first experience out beyond the Mississippi, men like John C. Frémont, now a major-general, Jefferson Davis, who served in Arkansas as a dragoon in the 1830s, and thirty years later found himself president of the new Confederate States of America. General Robert E. Lee had been a cavalryman in Texas, and General Albert Sidney Johnston had seen service all across the West, including a stint as secretary of war of the Republic of Texas. Others like U.S. Grant and William T. Sherman had seen obscure service in California and the Oregon Territory, and were now equally obscure colonels destined to rise to great heights.

While the West thus contributed some of the leading lights to the war that ensued east of the Mississippi, it proved an ironic twist that the men sent to fight the Civil War on the opposite side were almost virtually unknown and, to an alarming extent, untalented. Moreover, the West was so vast that neither side ever fully came to grips with how to hold on to or administer it. When Davis organized the military defenses of the Confederacy, he designated the Department of Texas and the Indian Territory, roughly to encompass Texas, future Oklahoma, and as much more of the southwest as could be taken. A year later, however, he changed his mind, and simply designated everything west of the great river as the Trans-Mississippi Department. Throughout the war he placed it under one inept commander after another, from the womanizing inebriate General Earl Van Dorn, to Theophilus Holmes, who some said suffered from 'softening of the brain'. Finally he assigned it to General Edmund Kirby Smith, who ruled it so autocratically that some came to refer to the region as 'Kirby Smith-dom'. Across the lines, the Union went into the war with most of its vast territories administered as the Department of the West, with smaller commands for California, Texas, New Mexico, and other organized territories. Exigencies of the ensuing war led to a redivision, with a Department of the Pacific, and a massive Department of the Missouri encompassing most of the old Louisiana Purchase.

Once the firing began, immediate attention focused on the southern half of the West, the New Mexico Territory, the Indian Territory, and lands running west to the Pacific. The Confederates, hoping eventually for a transcontinental railroad of their own, needed a dominion that stretched to the Pacific. The gold and other riches of California also loomed invitingly and, ever-acquisitive, they could use a foothold in New Mexico as a base for further expansion into Mexico itself. Much of the settlement of the region had been by Southerners or men of Southern leanings, even if they left their slaves behind, and when war broke out they hoped to ally themselves to the new Confederacy. In faraway Taos, New Mexico, someone took down the Stars and Stripes and raised instead the new Con-

Below: *Frémont, who had made his name west of the Mississippi, appeared in the theater of war, but his star was on the wane. Briefly a major-general, he was removed by Lincoln for military mistakes.*

federate banner. Kit Carson quickly appeared to yank it from its staff and order Old Glory raised once more. He was soon a lieutenant colonel in the newly raised 1st New Mexico Infantry. The war for the southwest was on.[7]

Texans inaugurated the battle for the region when they forced the surrender of General David Twiggs' command at San Antonio in February 1861, though it was not much of a coup, for Twiggs himself was a secessionist who soon donned Confederate gray. Confederates immediately started occupying old Federal frontier posts along the Rio Grande to the south, and the Indian lands to the north. Davis soon sent envoys to try to woo the Cherokee and other tribes into taking side with the South, and Lincoln did the same. The Indians, throughout the conflict, mustered little enthusiasm for either cause, probably suspecting that in the end, regardless of who won the white man's war, the red man would lose.

Van Dorn, on taking command in Texas, immediately looked to the far western border with New Mexico, and the remaining Yankee garrisons in that territory. Fearing a threat, he strengthened his outposts along the border, and then looked beyond to consider the possibilities of launching an invasion of his own. One of the officers in his command was 45-year-old Henry W. Sibley, newly commissioned a brigadier general in the Southern forces. His eyes were on New Mexico, too. He knew the country well, and watched with interest as communities and frontier posts all across the territory were unsettled by widespread Confederate sympathy. He watched, too, as a small command of Texas cavalry met with little successes and much sympathy and assistance on a march into New Mexico. By late summer 1861 all of southern New Mexico Territory was more or less securely in Rebel hands, providing a pathway to California. On 1 August they announced the Confederate Territory of Arizona with its capital at Mesilla.

Sibley now secured authorization from Davis to attempt a campaign that would conquer the rest of the old New Mexico Territory. Sibley later claimed that his plan went even farther, to including the taking of Colorado, Utah, and California. Perhaps so, but Davis seems only to have authorized him to go after New Mexico. Enthusiastically Sibley went back to Texas and started recruiting a 3,500-strong brigade, finally setting out on 22 October for El Paso. Once there, they continued on into New Mexico.

Facing Sibley in the region were less than 4,000 Yankees commanded by General E.R.S. Canby, who had been best man at Sibley's wedding some years before. During the next few weeks the two sides feinted and shadowed each other, occasionally skirmishing, with Canby generally getting the worst of it until they reached Valverde, a ford on the Rio Grande. Here they met in the first real battle in the far West, and Sibley emerged the victor. Soon the Confederates set off once more on their march of conquest, taking Albuquerque, and on 10 March 1862 marched into Santa Fe unopposed. But then it started to turn against them. Rapidly converging Yankee reinforcements from Colorado and elsewhere met a column of about 400 of Sibley's men in Apache Canyon on 26 March and routed them. Two days later, at Glorieta Pass, the Confederates were the victors, but while the battle raged, a party of Yankees had surprised and destroyed the enemy's supply trains. The Rebels had no choice but to retreat to Santa Fe. As Federal columns finally began to converge on him, Sibley soon thereafter found that he had no alternative but to withdraw, bringing to an end his invasion and with it hopes of a Confederate southwest. Along the way, the battered, hungry, and demoralized Confederates fell out among themselves, and desertions escalated. By July, Sibley was rushing back through west Texas to San Antonio. More than a third of his small army was no longer with him when he arrived, and the Confederacy never again attempted to spread itself to the Pacific.[8]

The war for the southwest was virtually ended before much of the rest of the West came into play. Blue and Gray battled far more for Arkansas and Missouri, with the war's greatest battles west of the Mississippi taking place here, and inaugurated by the Battle of Wilson's Creek, Missouri, on 10 August 1861. The Union defeat there, followed by other reverses, saw the Confederates in control of much of central and western

Right: *While civil war raged in the east a forgotten war was going on in the West for vital territories such as New Mexico. Colonel E.R.S. Canby's force thwarted Confederate claims to the area in 1862.*

Missouri through the balance of the year. Later the scene shifted south to Arkansas, and there, at Elkhorn Tavern, on 6-8 March 1862, the Confederates suffered a serious reverse that forced them to yield all of Missouri then held and much of northern Arkansas. Thereafter the Rebels never again made a serious threat to Missouri until the fall of 1864, when General Sterling Price led a massive invasion army, chiefly cavalry, northward to the Missouri River itself. He was met at Westport Landing, near present-day Kansas City, on 21-23 October and decisively defeated. It was the Confederacy's last invasion of Union territory, though a rump convention of secessionists had voted in 1861 to take Missouri out of the Union, with no effect.

The conflict in Missouri and Arkansas in most ways bore more of a relation to the war east of the Mississippi than to the West. The same was true of the Red River Campaign of spring 1864, when a small Union army attempted to move up the Red, through western Louisiana, accompanied by a naval flotilla. It ended ignominiously with a few small battles and the near loss of the fleet when the level of the river dropped, almost stranding the Yankee vessels, and the whole operation,

Below: *New Mexico Territory also included modern Arizona and was held tenuously by a string of frontier forts such as Fort Marcy at Santa Fe, headquarters of the Federal department.*

BLACK TROOPERS

Those black troopers who, after the Civil War, wished to remain in the U.S. Army were organized into the 9th and 10th Cavalry regiments, commanded by white officers, where integration was unheard of. The soldiers operated under intense disadvantages, with limited mention in despatches. Plains tribes, however, respected these blacks as worthy antagonists, referring to them as 'buffalo soldiers', a name derived from the similarity they saw between the buffalo's coat and the soldiers' hair. Perhaps the name was a form of honor, the buffalo being sacred to plains tribes. The association stuck: a buffalo was the insignia of the 92nd Division, Negro division, in World War I.

again, was an extension of grand strategy for the war in the east, not the West.

However, a very distinctive kind of war was waged elsewhere, from the plains of Kansas to the Indian Territory, and far to the north, in the land of the Sioux. For the pro- and anti-slave forces who made Kansas bleed, the war had already been going on for years when 1861 came. Thousands of them simply continued on a course that had become, for them, almost a way of life. Regular uniformed regiments were raised in Kansas, Colorado, and elsewhere, manned by local people, and then assigned the task of patrolling and holding their own territory. It made good sense, but it also ensured that old feuds and animosities were carried into uniform with the men who wore them. On the Southern side, enlistments were more sporadic, and hundreds simply joined irregular bands like those led by guerrillas William C. Quantrill, George Todd, and William 'Bloody Bill' Anderson.

In such an atmosphere, with governments more than a thousand miles to the east, and few authorities to check or control the activities of outfits west of Missouri, excesses and outrages very quickly came to characterize the frontier war. Quantrill, especially, made his name a terror, ambushing, marauding, and simply murdering and plundering, often with only a flimsy pretext of acting in the name of the Confederacy, whose commission he never officially held. In August 1863 he settled an old pre-war grudge by leading his men against Lawrence, Kansas, and almost destroyed the undefended town, leaving more than 100 dead in his wake. Anderson would murder and mutilate his victims indiscriminately, and on one occasion executed a train load of unarmed Federal soldiers on their way home from furlough. The actions of the Confederate guerillas became so outrageous that they embarrassed even Confederate authorities, who increasingly tried to disavow Quantrill and his associates. Few of them survived the war.

Interestingly enough, the very last land engagement of the Civil War was fought in the West, at Palmito Ranch, outside Brownsville, Texas, on 13 May 1865. It was, ironically, a Confederate victory. But everywhere else the Rebel armies were surrendering, Kirby

Below: *With men like Quantrill, 'Bloody Bill' Anderson (seen here in death) led bands of Missouri guerrillas in savage raids across the Kansas border. For some, the Civil War to the east was merely an extension of Bleeding Kansas.*

Smith's being the last to yield. With the notable exception of the Union Army's campaigns against the several Indian tribes of the southwest, the plains, the Pacific, and the northwest, the Civil War was largely something that Westerners read about but did not experience unless they lived in Missouri, Kansas, or New Mexico. To a considerably greater degree, in fact, the events following the surrender of the Confederate armies were felt more deeply west of the Mississippi.

Reconstruction, that much-misunderstood period when North and South struggled with how to live together once more, with the nature of the Federal Union, and with the role of the newly freed Negro, played a large role west of the Mississippi. States like Missouri and California, though predominantly loyal to the Union, still held large Democratic factions sympathetic to the Southern point of view. Kansas, made a state in 1861, on the other hand, had purged most of its conservative factions and stood firmly with the new Republican majority. Even more challenges faced the government, with peonage – virtually a form of slavery – still being practiced by Mexican-Americans in New Mexico in spite of the Thirteenth Amendment to the Constitution. On the other hand, in some areas attitudes towards the newly freed blacks were more hospitable than in New England.[9]

Throughout the ensuing years of Reconstruction, the West took an active role in national politics, really the first time its people's voices exerted genuine influence. In the great battle between President Andrew Johnson and the Radical Republicans bent on a more stringent imposition on the South, for instance, Western statesmen spoke up strongly, and generally in favor of the President. When Johnson was impeached and tried before the Senate, he escaped conviction by a single vote – that of Edmund Ross of Kansas. When the issue of the vote for blacks occupied national attention, the western territories were among the first places where Negroes could go to the polls, and many westerners called for universal suffrage, which came before long. And when a resurgent Democratic party acquired dominance in some of the western states and territories, the people still refused to allow the party's conservative faction to reimpose the state rights dogma that had led the South to secede. From the first, Westerners were looking not backward, but ahead. It was a part of their creed.

Except when it came to the Indians.

REFERENCES

1 David Lavender, *The Great West*, p. 61.
2 Daniel Boorstin, *The Americans*, p. 270.
3 Robert S. Henry, *The Story of the Mexican War* (Indianapolis, Ind., 1950), pp. 48-9.
4 *Ibid.*, pp. 212-14
5 James C. Malin, *John Brown and the Legend of Fifty-Six* (Philadelphia, 1942), pp. 614ff.
6 William C. Davis, *Breckinridge: Statesman, Soldier, Symbol* (Baton Rouge, La., 1974), pp. 181-3.
7 M. Morgan Estergreen, *Kit Carson* (Norman, Okla., 1962), p. 230.
8 Martin H. Hall, *Sibley's New Mexico Campaign* (Austin, Texas, 1964), *passim*.
9 Eugene H. Berwanger, *The West and Reconstruction* (Urbana, Ill., 1981), pp. 13-14.

IV

THE CLASH OF RED & WHITE

Below: *Disinherited and soon to be erased from memory: Kiowa, Comanche, Cheyenne and Arapaho prisoners, St Augustine, Florida, 1875.*

GENERATIONS BEFORE THE westward spread generated by the aftermath of the Civil War overwhelmed the native Americans, the infant United States first addressed the problem inevitably to be posed by the conflict of red and white men vying for the same ground. As far back as 1787, the leaders of the new nation already knew enough to believe that such matters could not be left solely to local or state authorities. As much as foreign policy with other nations required speaking with a single voice and unified purpose, so did dealings with the western tribes. Moreover, local interests could not be trusted to pay any heed to the fair treatment of the Indian. Ironically, in light of future events, the new United States was actually interested in fair play for the indigenous peoples of the continent, and in that spirit the Constitution provided that all authority over Indian matters rest with the central government.

The first enactments actually protected Indian rights to the lands they lived on, exercising no eminent domain to claim those lands, but rather adopting the policy that Indian owned territory could only be taken by treaty and purchase. Furthermore, Congress required that all who would enter Indian nations for trade obtain licenses, refrain from importing liquor, and not attempt to purchase land or horses, or try to settle on Indian property. Such traders were required to pay sureties for their good conduct, to be forfeited on failure to comply with the law, and make themselves liable to arrest and prosecution as well. Washington also promoted the establishment of government trading posts that would sell decent goods at fair prices, thus driving unscrupulous private traders out of the business, and in the end benefitting the native Americans. Unfortunately, it all worked only in theory. Land-hungry settlers on the early western borders were far more interested in exploiting the new wilderness before them,

than in observing legal niceties. Their government should be looking out for *their* interests, they reasoned, not those of the savages. As a result, when lawbreakers were apprehended and brought to trial, rude country juries refused to convict them. When other well-wishers tried to educate the Indians, with the dream of eventually amalgamating them into frontier society and community – and thereby, incidentally, turning nomadic peoples into stationary farmers, thus reducing their need for large domains and encouraging them to sell – uninterested whites subverted the scheme. Worse, when the Indian occasionally reacted violently in keeping with the mores of his own culture, the whites' conviction that these were barbaric savages was only reinforced. Despite the best of intentions on both sides, it should early have been obvious to all but the most visionary that the future of white and red in the expanding West was not destined to be a happy one, and one, moreover, with only one unavoidable conclusion.[1]

Indians were on Jefferson's mind when he bought the Louisiana Territory and sent Lewis and Clark off to survey the wilderness. The President foresaw the conversion of the red men into an agrarian society, and part of the mandate of the explorers was the identification of tribes far to the west, and the opening of friendly relations with them. Foreseeing that unscrupulous traders and Canadian adventurers might try to 'excite in the Indian mind suspicions, fears, & irritations toward us', he enjoined Lewis and Clark to be diplomats as well as explorers, and so they were. A host of myths and misconceptions about the Indians flourished among white easterners; that they were descended from pre-Columbian Europeans, even that they could trace their lineage back to one of the 'lost tribes' of Israel. Thus they were seen as having Irish, Welsh, even Nordic blood. Only thorough acquaintance would settle the issue.[2]

Unfortunately, Lewis and Clark's would be not only the first, but practically the last peaceful contact that the two peoples would enjoy. During the next two decades, as white adventurers and trappers gradually penetrated deeper and deeper into the wilderness, clashes became more and more frequent. Some were entirely inadvertent. The Anglos brought with them their diseases of civilization, to which Indians had never been exposed, and against which they had no immunities. Measles and mumps and whooping cough spread rapidly through native villages once contact with whites brought about initial contamination. In time more virulent viruses took even greater tolls, the worst being smallpox, which almost annihilated some peoples like the Mandan of the Missouri. There would later be charges that the whites intentionally introduced the diseases into Indian communities to exterminate competitors for covetted land, but the fact was that the average frontiersman knew as little about his own diseases as did the unsuspecting natives.

Far less innocent confrontations rapidly developed. White trappers and explorers dabbled with Indian women, cheated the natives in horse trades, gave them alcohol that led inevitably to fights, and built cabins on Indian land they had not purchased. Indian reactions were many and varied, reflecting wide differences in temperament, and no concerted or consistent plan for dealing with the Anglo invasion. In the first decade after Lewis and Clark, isolated attacks, usually on lone individuals, started to take white lives. In 1807 Arikaras attacked a larger party of traders on the upper reaches of the Missouri, killing three and arousing simmering hostility among other tribes growing increasingly resentful of American intrusions. Trappers gave the area a miss for a time to let things settle, turning to dealing with the more amenable Crows and Blackfeet, only to get caught in the middle of old tribal rivalries between the Blackfeet and the Flatheads. Indeed, some whites soon learned to turn the sporadic tribal warfare of the plains and mountains to their advantage, playing one Indian against another.

But more and more it was white against red. When the second war with Great Britain erupted in 1812, the British quickly sought to ally themselves with Indians to provide an enemy in the American rear, and it worked effectively for them east of the Mississippi. In the new West, however, the Indians acted largely on their own, seeing the advantage that Yankee preoccupation with England gave

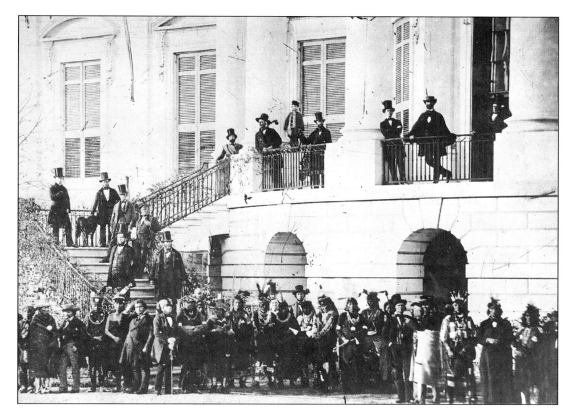

them. The Minnetarees in the future Dakota Territory rose up and drove out American traders, while natives lower down in Missouri started to attack isolated settlements. Frontier regulars at Fort Madison, in latter-day Iowa, abandoned their post and retreated, and resistance to the Indians was weak and ill-organized all along the line. Far to the west, in the Oregon Territory, fur traders found themselves increasingly faced by resentful natives whose threats forced them to withdraw their operations closer to their bases at Astoria and elsewhere.

With the war concluded, the relentless westward move redoubled, this time supported by an expanded military and the new demand for furs. Now more of the tribes turned unfriendly as they saw larger and better equipped parties of Americans coming upriver in their keelboats or overland with their wagons. Attacks on trappers' parties became frequent, with the whites usually outnumbered. Violent death became a constant threat to those brave enough to venture into the mountains. Henry Ashley saw fifteen of his men killed by Arikaras in a single engagement in 1822, resulting in Army reinforcements from Fort Leavenworth coming to his aid with cannon. Following a brief bombardment, the Indians abandoned their villages and withdrew into the interior, becoming among the first native Americans voluntarily to give up their land and remove themselves from contact with the whites. More would follow. Behind them,

Above: *Pawnee, Ponca, Potawatomi and Chippewa: a delegation group at the White House, 1857-8. As early as it could, the U.S. Government encouraged diplomatic tours to the East.*

Below: *Delegations continued into the 1870s. The Dakota, led by Red Cloud and Spotted Tail, attended one in Washington in 1877. The aim was to impress Indians with the white man's power and culture.*

whites burned their villages so that they might never return.[3]

Throughout the rest of the heyday of the mountain men, the Indians seized advantages when opportunity offered. The Blackfeet closed the upper Missouri. Further south the Mohaves rose up against Jedediah Smith, and did so again in 1828 in faraway Oregon when the Umpquas hit Smith yet again. None of this was lost on authorities back in Washington, for whom the growing pressure to spread west made the Indian question all the more important. Those Indians with whom the government had negotiated before the war had pressed for their own separate nation, recognized by Washington. The Americans could not stomach that at the time, but after the war they did almost the same thing on their own initiative, in an attempt to cut down on the clashes between white and red. In the vast land west of Missouri and north of Texas, Congress created the Indian Territory, and during the 1810s and 1820s several eastern Indian tribes were relocated to what is now Kansas and Oklahoma. Contrary to popular misconception, some went voluntarily in order to get away from white pressure in the east. In time, others would be forcibly removed, especially the so-called Five Civilised Tribes, the Cherokee, Choctaw, Chickasaw, Creek, and Seminole, whose removals during the 1830s were accompanied by such hardships that their route west to the Indian Territory became known as the Trail of Tears.

Still, Washington did attempt a measure of fair dealing, giving them presumably irrevocable title to new land in return for their old ancestral property. And to keep the new Indian Territory inviolate, more legislation outlawed white settlement and unauthorized trading. Three new frontier forts were erected: Fort Leavenworth in what would be Kansas, Fort Gibson in future Oklahoma, and Fort Towson near the Texas line. Their mandate was not to contain the Indians, but to protect their borders and keep whites out, as well as maintaining peace between the indigenous plains Indians and the new arrivals.

In all the 1830s was a dreadful decade for the Indian, and a triumphant one for the new wave of whites. The Sauk and Fox Indians rose up briefly on the upper Mississippi, but were handily put down. Out in the new Indian Territory, even the imposition of passport requirements for white travel did not keep out the more adventurous, or less scrupulous. Soon Indian was fighting Indian as they clashed over hunting grounds, and the Army was forced to march into the territory to try to keep the peace, only to see its commander, General Henry Leavenworth, die of sickness, and hosts of others fall by the wayside. Even attempts to do right by the Indian seemed doomed to end in death.

With the Indian Territory closing off – or so it seemed – the central route to the far west, traders and settlers moved by northern and southern routes instead, but could not avoid coming in conflict with increasingly militant native inhabitants. During the Texan Revolution the ever-warrior-like Comanche and Kiowa took advantage of Texans' preoccupation with Mexico, and rose up in a series of raids on the western settlements. But the conclusion of the Revolution allowed angry Texans to turn their attentions elsewhere. They formed the nucleus of the later famed Texas Rangers chiefly as an Indian policing force, and ruthlessly set about forcing the native Americans back, commencing one of the most virulent sagas of white subjugation of red in Western history. When the Mexican War came, the Indians attempted once more to rise, this time in New Mexico, where they attacked Taos and raided the spindly Army supply lines. Whites responded savagely. At Taos a relief column trapped the Pueblo Indians inside a fortified mission, breached a hole in the adobe with their picks, and then just kept tossing exploding shells inside until more than 150

Below: *Although shown here in a later photograph (1882), the Texas Rangers ruthlessly policed the southern plains Indians, notably Comanche and Kiowa, throughout the 1860s and 1870s.*

INDIAN TRADER

The brothers William and Charles Bent began to trade with the Plains Indians in the early 1820s. By 1829 they had built the first Bent's Fort on the north side of the Arkansas. William married the Cheyenne Owl Woman, and their son George is pictured here at Bent's New Fort, established in 1849. Behind him is his wife Magpie (Mo-he-by-vah) wearing typical S.Cheyenne costume for the period, c. 1880. The leggings are embellished with German silver buttons; the buckskin dress beaded across the shoulder is stained with yellow earth paint. She also wears a dentalium shell necklace. George assisted and interpreted for such writers on the Cheyenne as Dr George Bird Grinnell.

NORTHERN CHEYENNE

The Cheyenne were at one time a single tribe, but with the treaty of 1851 the Northern Cheyenne left the south and moved up into the Great Plains. In their move up the plains they met the white man in battle in 1852. They befriended the Sioux and along with their allies continued to travel north. Through the years a great many battles were won and lost fighting in the hierarchy of the plains tribes. They grouped together with the Sioux on the Little Bighorn in 1876, which culminated in the Battle of the Little Bighorn. After this battle they were sent to Indian Territory and placed on a reservation with their southern sister tribe. In September 1878, led by Dull Knife and Little Wolf, they headed north again. Numbering some 353, they were mercilessly harried by the Army. Many died but those who survived saw a reservation established for them in 1884 on the Tongue River. Their journey north was depicted in the movie 'Cheyenne Autumn'.

1 Headdress of bald eagle feathers, no trailer.
2 Peyote fan.
3 Eagle-claw necklace with hand-carved bone beads chipped and worked to round.
4 Breechcloth, red trade wool, decorated with butterfly motif. Fringed with sequins and bugle beads.
5 Hoof bag.
6 Black and white beaded pouch.
7 Paint pouch.
8 Strike-a-light bag.
9 Ammunition pouch.
10 Small utility knife with sheath.
11 Scout's peace medal.
12 Nickel-plated tomahawk.
13 Roach of porcupine hair and deer hair.
14 Stone-headed club, head of crystallized rock.
15 Steel-tipped arrows, eagle feather flights.
16 Bull snake-skin covered bow, sinew bowstring.

17 Knife with sheath
18 Eagle-feather bustle, feathers tipped with yellow down (trailer below attaches).
19 Bustle trailer, with eight eagle feathers.
20 Brass wrist bracelets.
21 Crazy Dog Society dance rattle, buffalo hair handle and made of raw dog skin.
22 Curved knife with beaded sheath.
23 Pipe bag, adorned with seed beads and porcupine quills.

24 Sandstone-headed club, beaded handle, with hand-tanned buckskin attachment.
25 Steel-tipped arrows.
26 Crazy Dog Society ceremonial whip, dog fur strips, showing face of dog, with rawhide strap.
27 Old-style beaded breastplate: white seed beads, eagle plume, peyote stitched onto buckskin straps.
28 Peace medal, silver plated nickel.

29 Buffalo-headed tomahawk.
30 Tomahawk.
31 Bird's nest pouch, including cottonwood down and animal hair.
32 Necklace of seed beads, blue and white tile beads (glass), brown and white wooden beads.
33 Rawhide concho belt, nickel plated
34 Mocassins.
35 Softwood deer flute, possibly birchwood.
36 Hand-drum and stick.

were dead and the rest surrendered. It was the way in which whites would deal with hostiles here in the southwest for the next generation.

Meanwhile relations on the northern route to the Pacific were no better. During the late 1830s and more into the 1840s, settlers had begun to trickle into Oregon, settling first in the fertile Willamette Valley, until there were soon some 10,000 of them, with no military protection from Washington, and with increasingly unfriendly Nez Perce and Cayuse Indians providing an unsettling threat. Incidents over land and animals escalated, and then in November 1847 Cayuses attacked a mission and killed the missionary, Marcus Whitman, his wife, and a dozen others, taking nearly fifty more as hostages for ransom. Whites responded quickly for their defense, but not until the territory was formally organized was the threat substantially subdued, and that came largely as a by-product of the massive stampede to California. With such large numbers of people moving overland, the Army came increasingly to find itself employed on convoy duty protecting immigrant and prospector trains.

Indeed, it was now that the United States Army finally began to come into its own as the chief arbiter of peace on the western frontier, and the leading instrument of white policy from Washington. The reason was simple. Everywhere the pressures of white expansion were forcing red and white into more and more contact, with ever-increasing incidence of violence as the Indian tried to resist the advance. The impact affected more than just the land they lived on. Game, once blessedly abundant, began to disappear as more and more fell to white rifles. The spread of disease continued to decimate populations, while the Americans' liquor, which the Indian was constitutionally unable to assimilate as well as the European, made many more dependent on white charity, and objects of scorn to peoples white and red. Defense, manhood, and survival, demanded some action. Some tribes simply gave in. Others tried to adjust to the inevitable. Most decided at some point to resist.[4]

That resistance was almost certainly doomed from the start if for no other reason than the radically differing nature of the Indian's concept of warfare from that of the whites. A cult of bravery flourished in almost every native American tribe, one that exalted individual acts of daring and heroism, memorializing them in warriors' names, and in campfire songs and stories told for years afterward. Wars might seemingly have no beginning and no end, but merely drag on in a series of raids, chiefly conducted to capture booty, especially horses, and to furnish opportunities for individual acts of daring. As among most aboriginal peoples of the world, deaths in battle were relatively few. Symbolic 'death' was more important, such as 'counting coup' by touching a foe on the head with a coup stick, or merely touching any part of his person with the hand and escaping unscathed, while others witnessed the act. Death did occur, to be sure, and was often ritualized in the form of elaborate torture of captives, designed not as an inhumane expression of bloodlust, but to give the victim an opportunity to display his bravery and earn honor in

Above: *Powder Face, an Arapaho chief, 1870. Signatories of the Medicine Lodge Treaty in 1867, the Arapaho later faced reservation enclosure and exile. By 1875 they no longer threatened white expansion.*

Right: *The Comanche were a constant threat to central Texas during and after the Civil War. Despite their mobility and fine leadership they, like their allies the Kiowa, could not resist forever.*

the manner of his death. It was a concept that the whites did not, and never could, understand. To them it was simple barbarism.

Also difficult to fathom, at first, was the Indian way of making war, a way in which individualism overrode unity of action. A warrior rode into battle for himself, not as part of a unit, and Indian leaders exerted just as little control over their braves in a fight as they did in peaceful councils, where a chief's agreement to a treaty might only be binding on himself and his family. The native American of the plains was a masterful horseman who practised for years the use of his several weapons while mounted, often training his animal to turn, stop, and start again, by pressures from the rider's knees, thus leaving hands free for bow and arrow, club and lance. However, he would not act in concert with other braves once the fighting began, with rare exceptions. Moreover, warriors went off to fight in the most haphazard of ways. No chief commanded them to do so. Rather, individual warriors sang and orated to fire the spirit of as many as would follow, and off they went usually in groups no larger than thirty. On the way, the rest paid no more heed to the 'leader' than suited them. Once they spotted their objective, if the foe looked too numerous, they turned back.[5]

Against such a mode of warfare, the Army now called on to preserve peace on the frontier had many advantages, chief among them being its superior weapons, and its infinitely superior tactics. Individual bravery could almost never be a match for organization, and so long as the bluecoated soldiers held their ranks, they had the advantage. It was only when they separated themselves from their main body, or straggled in ones and twos, that the lightning swift red men swooped down upon them with deadly result.

Nevertheless, when the Army set out to subdue the Indians, it did so with no real policy or plan. The end of the Mexican War left

Above: *Little Wolf, Cheyenne. Cheyenne and other central and southern plains tribes fought the Army constantly as their land was invaded by gold miners, white immigrants and buffalo hunters.*

Above: *Quanah Parker, Comanche. Quanah led resistance to the whites on the southern plains until, in the mid-1870s, he sensed the inevitable and sought to negotiate for peace with the whites.*

Above: *Kicking Bird, Kiowa. A spokesman for peace, he broke away from Fort Cobb in 1868 after the Medicine Lodge Treaty. He was poisoned, probably by Kiowa, after he had listed militants for exile in 1875.*

enough men in uniform to make a feeble attempt at doing the job, but with more than 100,000 Indians among various tribes facing them, the 16,000 Regulars remaining in uniform could hardly contain them all. Worse, the government in Washington inaugurated a policy of constructing a host of frontier forts and outposts all across the west, and then garrisoning them with fragments of regiments too small to provide an effective deterrent to a determined band of the foe.

During the dozen years leading up to the outbreak of the Civil War, a long string of posts was constructed, from Fort Brown at the southernmost tip of Texas, northwest along the Rio Grande to El Paso, and northward through the Texan interior to the Indian Territory. More were located in what would be western Kansas, at Fort Kearny in the future Nebraska, and on into the Dakota Territory at Fort Pierre east of the Black Hills. Thus came into being a host of names redolent of frontier lore – Fort Laramie, Fort Union, Fort Worth – many of them destined to grow into great cities. This chain of installations faced a twofold challenge. Those in Kansas, Nebraska, and the general region of the central plains had to protect overland travelers on the Oregon and California trails from the Sioux, Cheyenne, Arapaho, Kiowa, and Comanche,

the most dreaded of the plains Indian raiders. Farther south, the frontier garrisons faced the duty of keeping Kiowa and Comanches from infiltrating Texas on plundering raids. None of these forts fit the latter-day concept of a pallisaded square with corner blockhouses. That sort of fort was strictly a thing of the past in the Allegheny 'West' of several generations before. Many of these forts did not have walls of any kind, and were, in fact, small communities of houses and barracks, chiefly safe from attack because their garrisons, small though they might be, were still larger than most Indian parties would dare attack.

Symbolic of their mission to procure peace, the forts often acted as host to hostile tribal delegations in the almost constant attempt to negotiate treaties. At Fort Laramie in September 1851 authorities made a treaty with some of the northern plains tribes, and two years later at Fort Atkinson in western Kansas did the same with some of the southern groups. The immediate goal of these treaties was to secure Indian promises not to molest the Oregon and Santa Fe trails, a promise the chief present gave and generally kept for a time. Well into the 1850s emigrants passed over both routes without molestation, and meanwhile on appointed dates the Indians them-

selves came to some frontier post to receive the gifts of cloth and food and other trinkets promised them in return for their peaceful ways.

It was too good to last, of course. Every wagon train brought more whites west, and more opportunities for unexpected confrontations. Back in Washington politicians began to discuss the concept of reservations, large tracts of land set aside legally for the sole occupancy and use of the native Americans. It was a well-intentioned scheme, but it ignored the fact that for centuries these people had been nomadic hunters, wandering the plains freely and at will. They could not suddenly plant themselves on one piece of ground and turn into farmers. Culturally, socially, and emotionally, it was an idea unacceptable to all but a few. Still, reservations were created in western Texas in 1854 for its Indian population, and some few bands of Indians agreed to settle within them.

The string of forts continued to spread throughout the 1850s, heading westward along the border with Mexico to Fort Yume, on the California border, and northward from El Paso toward the Rockies and old Bent's Fort. On the southern line the bluecoats were trying to live up to treaty agreements with Mexico, promising to protect Mexicans from Apache raids across the border, while the line

running northward guarded the overland trails through New Mexico.

In all of these frontier military departments, the troop allocation was almost amusing. In the massive Pacific Division, containing California and the Oregon Territory, a line extending from the border with Mexico to Canada, no more than 1,000 Regulars served at any time, and occasionally as few as 600. It was much the same in the other divisions and departments, and with a two-fold result. The 7,800 soldiers manning the fifty-two frontier forts erected by 1854 were too few adequately to protect the citizens from the Indians should an uprising come. At the same time, they were almost powerless to prevent the settlers from taking matters in their own hands and willfully setting about to exterminate the native Americans, as they attempted to do in California and Oregon in particular. Caught in the middle, the bluecoats earned the enmity of both sides.

Then came the first great uprising. On 18 August 1854 an aggrieved settler came into Fort Laramie with a complaint that some Sioux had butchered one of his cattle. The next day an officer and thirty men set out to take the offender, and foolishly marched right into an Indian camp, made demands for the man's surrender, and then opened fire indis-

criminately when refused. A chief fell, and then the Brulés themselves attacked, killing all but one, who died of his wounds later after telling the tale at Fort Laramie. Thereafter attacks on the overland routes resumed, and the Army responded by sending more men charged with putting down the uprising. Retaliations came swiftly, and severely. A Brulé Sioux village was attacked and destroyed. A lengthy expedition into the Black Hills scattered many more, and a bitter peace was finally accepted by the Sioux.

But then the Cheyenne rose up in the summer of 1856, this time over ownership of a horse and the resultant killing of three braves by an Army captain. The following spring the Army sent a powerful expedition through Kansas and along the Platte, intimidating the Cheyenne until 29 July, when the two forces met in a genuine battle in eastern Colorado. The Army Cavalrymen advanced first at a trot, then swung into a gallop in line, their sabers drawn and pointed forward. The Indians stood their ground at first, then raced forward toward the attackers, only to recoil when they met those polished steel swords. The fight quickly turned into a pursuit as the soldiers raced after fleeing Cheyenne, most of whom eluded capture or injury. They soon struck back in a series of raids on civilian out-

Left: *The Indian Wars were not confined to the plains. Fort Bowie, Arizona, was built in 1862 to control Apache Pass. The Army patrolled the vital route through the Chiricahua Mountains to Tucson.*

Above: *From 1865-7 Red Cloud, Oglala Sioux, battled the Army to a standstill. In 1868, it closed the Bozeman Trail and abandoned three forts. Red Cloud's voice was later to be heard urging peace.*

Below: *Arapaho, Caddo, Cheyenne, Kiowa and Comanche 'militants' at Fort Marion, St Augustine, Florida, 1875-8. Prisoners far from home, they no longer threatened white settlement of the southern plains.*

SIOUX

The great Sioux nation consisted of three major divisions distinguished by three language dialects. Among this famous and notorious tribe were leaders who were highly honored, notably Sitting Bull, Crazy Horse, Red Cloud and Rain-in-the-Face, to name a few. These chiefs led military war parties against their many enemies to establish their territory among all tribes of the early Plains era. Being a proud, noble people, the Sioux rarely complied with the cavalry's orders to stabilize their whereabouts. Numbering in the thousands, young warriors were ready to go into battle to protect what was theirs, often in an individual way. Warfare allowed for counting coup to become an important asset. A young warrior, if he wished to be highly regarded within the tribe and his warrior society as well, had to count coup. Those going into battle had their spirit helper at their sides, which was part of their protection and their teachings. A warrior carried medicine given him by his spirit helper for power. The shield that he held high in front of him was covered with painted pictures that may have depicted his visions. In his mind's eye he was ready body and soul to do battle for himself and his people. After they had won a battle, warriors would participate in dances and celebrations which went on for days. During this time, warriors would recall their deeds in battle, especially if they had successfully counted coups.

(Continued on p.116)

1 Eagle-claw necklace.
2 Man's buckskin shirt, with beaded panels and fringed with human hair at neck and on arms.
3 Pair of man's deerskin leggings, beaded, with buckskin fringes.
4 Pair of man's moccasins entirely decorated with seed beads, including on soles. Note that these are not so-called 'death' moccasins.
5 Pipe: catlinite bowl with wood stem, decorated with beads and horsehair.
6 Pipe bag: deerhide with beads and porcupine quills, with tin cones holding fringe of feathers.
7 Stone-headed club with horsehair attachment.
8 Brass-head tomahawk, with wooden handle with brass tacks.
9 Quirt with antler horn handle.
10 Horsehair hair ornament, of porcupine quills and feathers attached to rawhide.
11 Bronze-bladed knife with beaded sheath.
12 Roach, decorated with porcupine hair, deerhair and horsehair.
13 War shield: made of rawhide stretched over frame, centrally adorned with small bird of prey carcass, hawk feathers and horsetail.
14 Full headdress and trailer, made from red trade-cloth with plain and dyed eagle feathers.

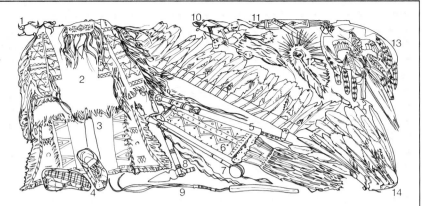

posts, but by 1858 their fury had spent itself as the intimidating show of force by the bluecoat horse soldiers had them once more pacified temporarily.

To the south of Texas, however, the Kiowa and Comanche were not to be so easily subdued. There, too, increasing misunderstandings led to outbursts of violence, and a large scale military response. But when the Comanche suffered a considerable defeat in one of the few battles involving more than a dozen native Americans – some 300 of them were routed on the Canadian River at Antelope Hills – they responded not by retreating, but became even more bellicose. Even larger battles ensued, and the campaign lasted through 1858 and into the next year, with more engagements including one in which forty-nine Comanche men – every warrior present – lost their lives. Even in 1860, with sectional problems in the East occupying most of national attention, campaigns continued in Texas to subdue marauding hostiles, but without complete success.

In April 1861, when the Civil War erupted, the Army and civil authorities could look westward to see only mixed results from their efforts to deal with the indigenous peoples of the continent. True, there were several chains of forts protecting most of the frontiers, the major trails, and the line of white settlement. But there were also a number of Indian nations, spread in a long line from Canada south to Mexico, who harbored smoldering resentments against the whites – the soldiers, the corrupt government traders, the miners, farmers, and everyone else. The military may

Above: *Although this trio survived the Minnesota massacre of 1862, many innocent whites, including the father and two other sons of the family, did not escape the wrath of Little Crow's agency Sioux.*

Below: *Refugees from the massacre, these settlers were warned by friendly Sioux of the onslaught to come. Some 400 others were less lucky, victims of years of Indian anger and justifiable resentment.*

have gotten the best of it in their few battles, but it was hard actually to beat a foe who more often than not simply refused to fight on disadvantageous terms, but melted into the shadows, to reappear later without warning. It was like chasing ghosts.[6]

As for the Indians, though the several tribes could never act wholly in concert to unite against the Anglos, any more than they could unite within themselves on any particular course of action, still they saw in the sudden preoccupation of North and South with each other a chance to reclaim the West for themselves, and to drive the invader out of their homeland and back to his own. They did not wait long to launch their counterstroke.

When Yankees and Rebels started shooting at one another, Washington pulled most of its professional Regular Army troops out of the West as quickly as possible, to serve as a nucleus for the growing armies in the East. In their place it assigned newly raised volunteer regiments, chiefly ones enlisted in the region itself. This boded ill for the Indians, for these men went into uniform with generation-old prejudices and attitudes toward the tribes, founded on years of close conflict. They would be far less inclined to use discretion than the Regulars, as quickly became evident, nor were they at all reluctant to be themselves the aggressors in renewing hostilities when opportunity afforded.

The crisis commenced on the northern frontier, with the several tribes generally falling under the overall designation of Lakotan, or Sioux. In 1862 confrontations began to alarm settlers in Minnesota. Then in August it

broke out in earnest when a few Indian youths killed five settlers, largely on a dare. Inflamed warriors started the war talk that night and with the acquiescence of their leader, Little Crow, decided to launch a war to drive the whites out. They went on the offensive the next day, starting a rampage of butchery and wanton killing that paled even the worst atrocities usually laid at the feet of the Indian. By nightfall some 400 whites had been massacred in farms and small settlements, many of them hacked to pieces in bloodlust and the vented outrage of a generation of resentment. When a small company of soldiers from Fort Ridgely went out to the scene, the braves cut it off and killed half its complement, leaving the rest scattering for safety. The next day the Sioux marched on Fort Ridgely itself, and in two days of fighting some 800 braves repeatedly attacked the 180 defenders. Only the soldiers' cannon stopped their assaults.

A wave of panic and outrage swept the region simultaneously, for by the end of the first week of the uprising, some 800 civilians lay dead, with hundreds more taken captive. Volunteers poured out to form militia regiments as settlers raced into the larger towns for safety, yelling that behind them the Indians were 'murdering everything'. Some speculated that the Confederates had somehow bribed the Sioux to rise up, but in fact the Rebels had nothing at all to do with it. Minnesota soon had 1,500 men called out and armed, but in the first engagement with the Indians, the soldiers were almost wiped out in a surprise attack. Then on 23 September some 700 of them almost brought off another surprise

Above: *Medicine Bottle was one of the leaders of the Sioux uprising. His escape to Canada was short-lived. Kidnapped back to the United States, he speedily went to the gallows at Fort Snelling.*

Below: *In December 1862, only months after the massacre, both Medicine Bottle and Skakopee were hanged side by side. Little Crow, who had evaded capture, was killed by a farmer the following summer.*

ambush at Wood Lake, but it went against them and the soldiers instead put them to flight. The defeat took the heart out of the uprising, which was always plagued by internal dissent from the first, and hundreds of the Indians gave themselves up and turned over their hostages. Known or suspected killers were soon arrested, and 300 sentenced to death, though President Lincoln later pared the number down to forty.[7]

The most seriously hostile warriors did not surrender, but withdrew in small bands into the Dakota wilderness. Rumors circulated for months that Little Crow was raising another small army to renew the outrages, whereas he was, in fact, attracting little support. Then Little Crow himself was killed while on a horse-stealing raid. In the late spring of 1863 a new, stronger, column of Yankee soldiers started to move up the Missouri to pacify remaining hostiles, but in July found their 1,900 bluecoats engaged in a kind of running skirmish with perhaps 1,600 members of several Sioux tribes. The result, though hardly decisive, was that the native Americans were pushed back beyond the Missouri, leaving Minnesota safe. But then on 3 September a different column of soldiers, led by Alfred Sully, stumbled on as many as 4,000 Sioux, 1,000 of them angry warriors who quickly surrounded the 400 bluecoats. Only the Sioux concept of ritualized warfare saved the Americans, for instead of swarming over them at once, the Indians delayed to paint themselves for battle. It gave time enough for a relief column to arrive, scattering the surprised warriors, and in the end killing over 300 of them, a casualty

rate equal to that of some much larger engagements in the Civil War raging to the east.

The next summer Sully led a small army up the Missouri once more, intending to put a complete end to the uprising and exact either treaties or death from the foe. On 28 July he caught up with about 2,000 of them at Killdeer Mountain in the Black Hills, numerically an even match for the 2,200 that he led. But when the battle was joined, the soldiers had it all their own way, and by next morning the surviving Sioux had fled. What was worse, they had been forced to leave all of their stores of food behind them. 'I would rather destroy their supplies than kill fifty of their warriors,' Sully later remarked, and it was, indeed, a devastating blow. Throughout the Indian wars the hunger that the white man's forces could inflict by capturing stores inflicted far greater hardship, and exerted more influence on Indian movements than anything else.[8]

By the time Sully dispersed most of the Sioux, the rest of the frontier was ablaze as the plains Indians followed the lead of their northern neighbors. In part it was caused by overreaction among fearful whites, who heard the stories coming out of Minnesota and consequently took any Indian action as a veiled threat. Sporadic raids had continued, as always, on the immigrant trails during 1861-3, but nothing on a truly threatening scale. But people in Colorado especially were convinced that the Arapaho and Cheyenne were only biding their time. When large numbers of livestock began to disappear in the spring of 1864, this seemed to signal the beginning, and white leaders responded quickly. While several military commanders were involved in the subsequent 'campaign', it was chiefly the work of a former Methodist minister, Colonel John Chivington, described by one as 'a crazy preacher who thinks he is Napoleon Bonaparte'. He was also a pathological liar, intensely ambitious for political advancement, and virtually immune to any humanitarian feeling for the Indian, as he soon demonstrated.

Below: *A casualty of General Crook's ill-starred 1876 campaign against the Sioux, here at Slim Buttes in the Dakota Badlands. Crook's pursuit of hostiles had quickly turned into a nightmare.*

Right: *Colonel John Chivington won his reputation in the Civil War. A former Methodist minister, his action at Sand Creek in 1864 prompted Congressional investigation into unmitigated brutality.*

Chivington sent out parties with orders to do nothing but kill and burn, and when some Cheyenne retaliated, it raised the ardour of other more peaceful peoples. Soon small bands of Kiowas and Comanche joined the Cheyenne and Arapaho in avenging and raiding, and military authorities from Kansas and Colorado both were singularly ineffective in containing them. With winter coming, however, the Indians calmed themselves, and soon chiefs like Black Kettle of the Cheyenne were suing for new peace treaties. But by this time the people of Denver especially were only just coming into their full war fever, with Chivington organizing a new regiment of volunteers filled with angry miners, the 3rd Colorado Cavalry. Just at the time that the Indians wanted peace, the whites bristled for war. 'I want no peace till the Indians suffer more,' General Samuel Curtis told Chivington, and that was all the colonel needed.

Black Kettle brought several hundred Cheyenne to a camp on Sand Creek, where they had been told to wait for authorities to allow them to surrender properly. Despite this, Chivington was able to rationalize that, not having officially surrendered, they were still foes. As a result, on the morning of 29 November he and about 700 troopers made a surprise attack on Black Kettle's camp, about 500 Cheyenne and Arapaho of whom the considerable majority were old men, women and children. The result was a bloodbath of which only a psychopath like Chivington could be proud. Only a handfull of warriors managed to mount a defense. The rest tried to run away, but there was no escaping the carbines and sabers. The bluecoats, especially the men of the 3rd Colorado, slaughtered indiscriminately, gleefully practising their marksmanship on toddlers wandering amid the carnage, slashing women open with their blades, and scalping the living and the dead. When it was over, more than 200 had been killed, and Chivington would proudly report that his command 'did nobly'. Later others would not agree. So great was the outrage at his act that the Government was forced into action and a Congressional investigation was launched. It concluded that the colonel 'deliberately planned and executed a foul and dastardly massacre which would have disgraced the veriest savage among those who were the victims of his cruelty'. At least the verdict demonstrated that there was a large body of whites who could see beyond racial prejudice to maintain that the Indian was entitled to fair and decent treatment, even as a foe.[9]

It was in 1865 that the rest of the plains peoples found themselves more fully at war with the bluecoats, and even with some Confederates who, taken prisoner, were granted release if they volunteered to fight Indians in the West as what were called 'galvanized Yankees'. Native American outrage over Sand Creek saw the Sioux join forces with their cousins the Cheyenne briefly to pose a new and genuine threat to Denver. Operating in bands as large as 1,000 braves, they struck government storehouses, overland stage coach stations, telegraph lines, and every avenue of commerce and communication in the territory, completely isolating Denver in January and early February. But then the nomadic peoples left to follow the wandering bison herds that were their livelihood, and the Colorado threat disappeared almost as suddenly as it had started.

By now Major-General John Pope had been sent to take command of all of this territory, embraced in the massive military Department

Below: *Black soldiers of the 10th Cavalry escort to General Wesley Merritt. The 10th Cavalry was posted to Montana and North Dakota to fight hostiles after twenty years in the southwest.*

SIOUX

The greatest honor went to the warrior who was in the most danger yet returned unscathed. Such honors as taking an enemy's weapon would be greatly praised by his peers and his warrior society. In the early 1800s the Sioux were faced by the oncoming hoardes of settlers who were protected by soldiers. Their only recourse was to fight: they could not move west since that meant encroachment on enemy lands. As years passed the fighting began to wane. Most of the battles involved the resisting and fleeing of Indians off the reservations. Their forced return by the military agitated the young warriors and skirmishes continued. In 1876 Sitting Bull's and Crazy Horse's bands, with the Cheyenne and Arapaho, were camped on both sides of the Little Bighorn River. The Federal policy at that time was to gather 'hostile Indians' who were not on reservations and move them onto reservations. That summer, Custer set out to enforce Federal law. Appraised of the situation but ignoring orders to await reinforcements, Custer attacked the encampment. When the Indians' counter-attack led by Crazy Horse was launched, the battle began. Custer was quickly overwhelmed and the rest is history. The star of the victorious tribes remained in the ascendancy only briefly. The Battle of the Little Bighorn represents the last for the Sioux and Cheyenne; the Nez Perce would follow soon. The date 1876 began a new period in Indian history. Battles of the future would be fought in the courts.

THE CLASH OF RED & WHITE

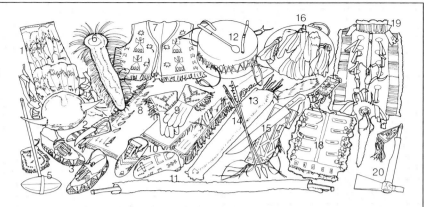

1 Buffalo horned headdress with short trailer with golden eagle feathers and bear fur.
2 Small single-edged knife with sheath.
3 Beaded mocassins, strong diamond patterns typical Sioux beadwork.
4 Cedar pouch.
5 Stone-headed club.
6 Roach of porcupine hair and deerhair.
7 Man's beaded vest.
8 Man's deerhide leggings.
9 Deerskin gauntlets, decorated with porcupine quills, with canvas-lined wrist guards.
10 Moccasins (also beaded on sole).
11 Wooden bow and cover, made from skin of mountain lion.
12 Drum and drumsticks, one with padded head.
13 Bow quiver, probably skin of mountain lion.
14 Steel-tipped arrows.
15 Large knife, c.18 in. long, with painted rawhide sheath. This was influenced by soldiers' swords.
16 Medicine shield, with gathered feathers, including those of bald eagle.
17 Strike-a-light bag.
18 Quilled breastplate, feathers held in tin cones.
19 Quilled and mirror-embellished breastplate, includes skin of river otter, ribbons, yarn.
20 Tomahawk.

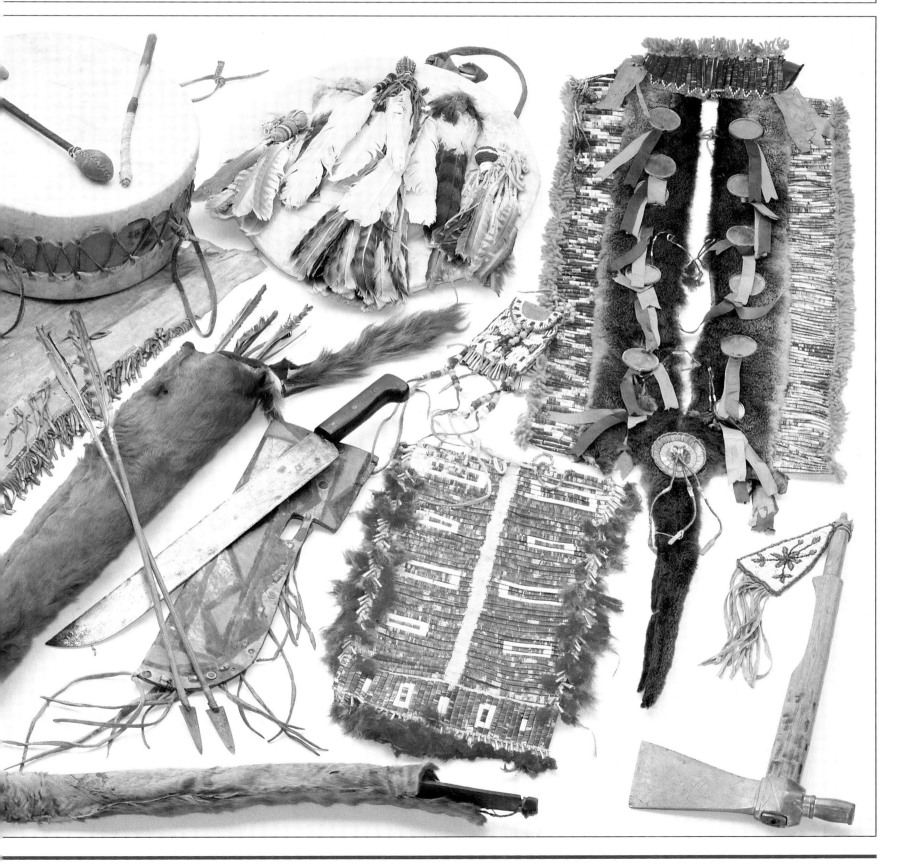

of the Missouri, and he planned a brace of campaigns to end the frontier threat once and for all. He wanted to send a column against the Kiowa, Comanche, and some northern Apache in the area south of the Arkansas River, and another to subdue the Sioux, Cheyenne, and Arapaho above the line of the Platte. Pope intended sending 1,200 men on the southern expedition, and two columns totaling 3,200 against the northern hostiles. But then the Civil War came to an end, Congress started looking into the Sand Creek disgrace, and a renewed wave of agitation for more peaceful, humanitarian, means of dealing with the Indian ensued. The southern campaign virtually disintegrated under these pressures, and peace treaties once more began replacing carbines and sabers.

To the north, however, a different story ensued. A number of Sioux gave themselves up to the military and volunteered to be relocated to places where they could be watched and contained. Others, however, in some numbers, took a more warlike stance. A number of hit and run attacks saw the Indians chiefly the victors, though Army casualties were more in horses than men's lives. But then that summer the several war chiefs managed to agree upon one great concerted attack on a station guarding the Oregon Trail crossing of the Platte. Up to 3,000 braves struck on 26 July, ambushing a small wagon escort. They then surrounded and killed the escort of a small wagon train and burned it before withdrawing into the hills, their offensive spent. The Army responded with an expedition up the Powder River, but on 5 September met with a surprise attack from the victors of the raid on the Platte that was only turned back by the soldiers' repeating carbines. Still the campaign ended in

failure as the distance conquered the whites' horses, and hunger their bellies.

Indeed, at the end of the summer all onlookers had to concede that the campaigns had all been failures, espending a great deal of money – $20 million by some estimates – in order to kill perhaps 100 Indians. Thus the authorities did an abrupt about face and once more pressed hard for peace treaties instead, and most of the tribes willingly obliged, especially when tempted by renewed annual bonanzas of trade gifts.

But if Washington thought that the end of 1865 meant universal peace between whites and with the red men, it was to be disap-

pointed very quickly. With the Civil War concluded, there was to be an immediate pressure of new settlers on the West, and on a scale dwarfing anything seen before. Hundreds of thousands of veterans got land bounties if they moved to the new territories. Pressure for new Homestead laws mounted. Southerners, finding their homes ravaged by the war, or unwilling to live under a Reconstruction government, looked westward to start anew. Thousands of deserters, prevented by shame from returning home, chose to go west instead, while hundreds of others, accustomed by four years of war to a level of lawlessness, soon drifted beyond the Mississippi where the

Above: *Nelson Miles (center, rear) hounded Kiowa and Comanche from the southern plains in the mid-1870s. After Little Bighorn in 1876 he harried the remaining Sioux into submission.*

Below: *Geronimo of the Chiricahua Apache with his band of renegades in 1886. His continual breakouts from the San Carlos Reservation and sporadic raiding kept the southwest on a knife edge.*

constraints of society and statute were less severe.

Thus was presented a new dilemma. With the war done, the Army demobilized drastically as war-weary citizens welcomed the reduction in military expense. But with a reduced military, the only hope of preserving peace with the native Americans lay in treaties and, even more so, in relocating them to places where they did not pose a threat to white settlements, or an impediment to future expansion. Such impulses were in part humanitarian, and part practical. Contact between red and white would be greater than ever before after the Civil War. More and more

areas of the West were being opened and settled by whites, and a very real question arose of whether or not there could be found places large enough to provide reservations for the native peoples where they could subsist, especially the nomadic peoples accustomed to roaming vast territories. General William T. Sherman, though no humanitarian where the Indian was concerned, sympathized with their plight. The red man was so surrounded by white expansion, he said, that 'the poor devil naturally wriggles against his doom'.[10]

It should hardly have surprised anyone. Old Chief Bear Rib of the Hunkpapa Sioux ex-

pressed the problem aptly during treaty negotiations in 1866. 'To whom does this land belong?' he asked. 'I believe it belongs to me. If you ask me for a piece of land I will not give it. I cannot spare it, and I like it very much. All this country on each side of this river belongs to me, . . . and if you, my brother, should ask me for it, I would not give it to you, for I like it and I hope you will listen to me.'[11]

No one could be certain, but there were somewhere in the neighborhood of 200,000 Indians in the vast West, and perhaps 50,000 of them in total maintained some degree of overtly hostile attitude. Meanwhile, arrayed against them in the post-war demobilization were a mere 20,000 troops scattered over some 110 forts. Their numbers would fluctuate during the next twenty-five years, as would their fortunes in dealing with the native American. By 1890 they would fight twenty-four officially designated campaigns or 'wars', and participate in fully 1,000 engagements, most of which they won thanks to superior weapons and organization. It would take fifteen years finally to bring peace to the northern plains and contain the Sioux, Cheyenne, and Arapaho. Fully a decade would be required to end the depredations of Kiowa and Comanche on the Texas border, while Apache tribes would fight on until 1881. West of Texas the Apache held out even longer, and even in faraway California and Oregon the Modoc and others did not finally give up their way of life without some last resistance.

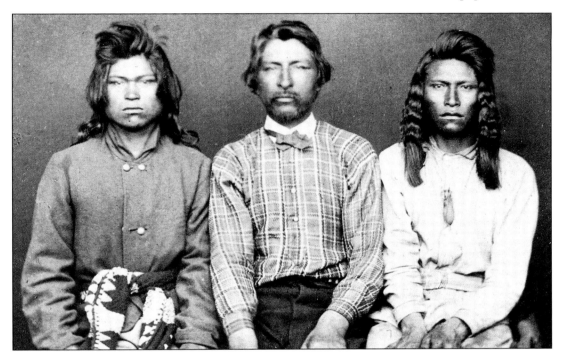

Left: *Farther west, the Modocs had been slow to bow to the whites. Donald McKay (center) and scouts of the Warm Springs tribe helped to capture Captain Jack for his part in the Modoc War, 1872-3.*

Along the way, the Indians scored their triumphs, few though they were, but shocking in scale. On 21 December, 1866 Sioux under the leadership of Crazy Horse decoyed eighty-one soldiers out of Fort Phil Kearny and attacked them in a ravine, killing them to the last man. Nearly ten years later the most dramatic Indian victory of the century came far to the north in the Sioux War of 1876. A column under General Alfred Terry set out from Fort Abraham Lincoln on the upper Missouri in present-day North Dakota, moving westward to the Yellowstone to find a confederation of Sioux and Cheyenne under the leadership of Crazy Horse, Sitting Bull, and other promi-

nent war chiefs. At the mouth of the Rosebud, one column of the 7th Cavalry swung off to the south, commanded by Lieutenant Colonel George A. Custer. One cavalry column had already been bested on the Rosebud on 17 June, as the Sioux and Cheyenne fought with unaccustomed unity in large numbers. Custer should have been more cautious. On 25 June he approached a large village in the vicinity of

Below: *George Armstrong Custer traveled the plains with an entourage of pets. An enigmatic figure to say the least, he badly misread the signs and led his troopers to annihilation in 1876.*

the Little Bighorn, but certainly had no idea of its true size. Leading just over 600 men, he was approaching a horde of at least 2,000 warriors, and perhaps many more.

Even had he known the actual size of the village, separated from him that morning by only an intervening ridge, he would not have been deterred. One of the lessons of the past generation of Indian fighting was that the plains tribes would not act in unity, that there was no coordination in battle, and that a force of well armed and trained soldiers could usually meet and best ten times its own numbers. Custer, therefore, was perhaps not as rash as later critics charged. Also, he probably did not

Above: *Sitting Bull of the Hunkpapa Sioux led the confederation of plains tribes that defeated Custer's force at Little Bighorn in 1876, a victory which was ultimately to seal the fate of his people.*

Below: *Officers and wives of the 7th Cavalry at Fort Abe Lincoln in 1876. Custer stands third from the left, his wife Elizabeth to his left. The figure at top right is his brother Tom.*

Above: *Little Big Man of the Oglala Sioux spoke as Crazy Horse's envoy against the selling of any Sioux lands, especially in the Black Hills. He fought at Little Bighorn and at Slim Buttes some months later.*

know that many of these hostiles carried rifles, not just bow and lance, and some even had repeating weapons. Custer split his command into three sections, intending to surround the village. Instead, the two others were pinned down by overwhelming enemy fire as soon as the action started. Custer, meanwhile, moved to seal off the lower end of the village. Too late did he discover that several parties, each much larger than his own, had moved out to surround him. He and his 215 men dismounted and took cover on both sides of a ridge and began to sell their lives. The only survivor was an officer's horse.[12]

It was the zenith of the plains Indians' resistance to the white man. Never again would they achieve such a victory, or such cooperation among themselves. But it came at a high price. For the next five years the United States Army conducted a campaign against the Sioux and Cheyenne that, in the end, saw them conquered. Sitting Bull himself was the last one to hand over his rifle and submit to relocation to a reservation.

Four years before another once-powerful tribe, the Nez Perce, were run to ground. They had inhabited the Wallowa Valley in Oregon for unknown generations, but by the late 1870s the pressures of expanding white settlement led to calls for their removal to a new reservation in Idaho. Not responding to negotiations, the Nez Perce finally started to move only in response to military threats. But then, once on the way to Idaho, they changed their

minds and decided to march to the east, across the Rockies. The Army started after them, but lost one skirmish after another as the Indians made a heroic trek across the mountains toward Montana. Only after months of pursuit did the Army finally corner the Nez Perce, and then they lasted through a five-day siege before their leader finally decided to yield. 'Hear me, my chiefs,' said Chief Joseph. 'I am tired. My heart is sick and sad. From where the sun now stands I will fight no more forever.'[13]

There were other uprisings among other tribes in the late 1870s, chiefly the Bannock, Paiute, Sheepeater, and Utes, but by 1879 they, too, had been contained. This left mainly

just the Apache. Under their leaders, chiefly the aggressive Geronimo, they chafed at remaining on the reservations to which their own treaties confined them. Finally Geronimo just left the reservation, rallied others to his name, and soon became a terror to the southwest. Some attacked and nearly captured Fort Apache, starting a five-year campaign to track down and subdue Geronimo. When finally forced to surrender, the wily chieftain and his people were removed the greatest distance ever imposed on an Indian people – to Florida, then Alabama, then Fort Sill, Oklahoma, and almost twenty years later, back to New Mexico.

The fall of Geronimo signalled the virtual end of substantial Indian fighting in the West. Almost all Indian tribes were contained on their reservations, often in squalid conditions, but leaving the overland routes, the railroad and telegraph lines, the settlements and cities, secure at last. Thereafter reservation policy sought to keep the red men away from whites, while at the same time educating them to function in a white man's civilization. After almost a century of conflict, the conquest of the Indian was complete, or so it seemed. Many had truly become docile. Many were never hostile to begin with. The bravest had died. Those who remained, tired, hungry, humiliated, had virtually all been banished from the lands they had loved for eons, to more barren reaches set aside for them largely because the whites did not want it. Even then, when settle-

Below: *Gathering the bones of the dead from the Little Bighorn battlefield. Thereafter called Custer Battlefield, only in 1991, well over 100 years after the event, did it revert to its original name.*

Left: *Joseph led the last resistance of the Nez Perce in the late 1870s. Pursued by the Army and captured miles short of the Canadian border, Joseph finally gave up: 'I will fight no more forever.'*

PLAINS INDIANS FIREARMS

Indian firearms are readily identifiable by their particular use of brass tack decoration, their generally hard used condition and typical Indian use of rawhide for all manner of repairs. Acquisition of arms was normally by trade, purchase or capture from an enemy since manufacturing expertise was beyond the Indian's capability. The Federal government and white traders, as a rule, only provided Indians with obsolete flint and percussion muzzleloading arms. Weapons taken from enemies, the Army and white settlers, were sometimes the most advanced modern metallic cartridge repeating rifles and revolvers but the Indian's lack of technology rendered these modern arms useless after ammunition was expended. The Indian also lacked maintenance skills to service his arms. Some specimens extant exhibit crude field expedient repairs, an effort to prolong the usefulness of a particular weapon. Indians are known to have used breech-loading arms as muzzleloaders with loose powder and ball when ammunition was unavailable. The Indian kept his arms functional long after a white owner would have discarded an arm as useless. The Indian was a master of adaptation and ingenuity in this regard. Indian firearms, because of hard use, are very scarce and few survive today. All specimens are considered rare and desirable. The relevance of the chief's staff (1) in this plate is that chiefs, rather than warriors, were the first to receive guns from the whites.

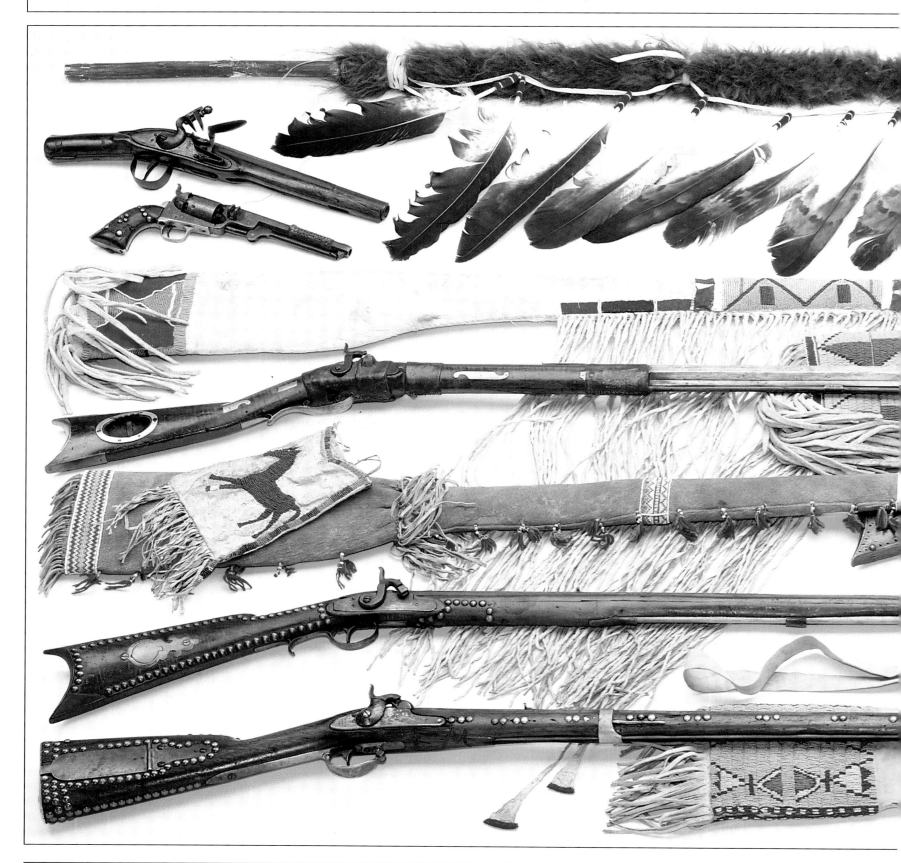

1 Crow chief's staff, representing a flag.
2 Flintlock pistol, made from cutdown trade musket. .50 caliber.
3 Colt Model 1851 Navy revolver with brass tack repair. .36 caliber.
4 Crow rifle scabbard, hand-tanned buffalo hide.
5 Unmarked percussion single shot rifle. Note rawhide repairs around lock area and rear of barrel. .45 caliber.
6 Sioux ammunition pouch, with beaded blue horse.
7 Santee Sioux rifle scabbard, hand-tanned smoked deerskin.
8 Percussion single shot trade rifle. Brass tacks decorate stock about .40 caliber.
9 U.S. Model 1841 percussion rifle.
10 N. plains ammunition pouch, buckskin or elk hide.
11 Flintlock trade musket.
12 Crow ammunition pouch.
13 Cheyenne or Santee Sioux ammunition pouch, may be elk hide.
14 Sioux Ghost Dance pouch.
15 Crow rifle scabbard.
16 Ballard breech-loading sporting rifle, dual ignition system, with altered forestock and brass tack decoration.
17 Winchester Model 1866 carbine, with added brass tack design.
18 Oglala Sioux rifle scabbard, hand-tanned elk hide.

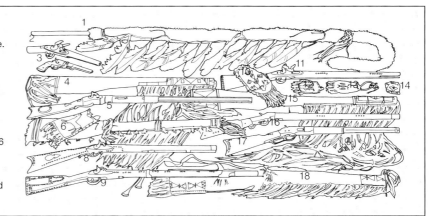

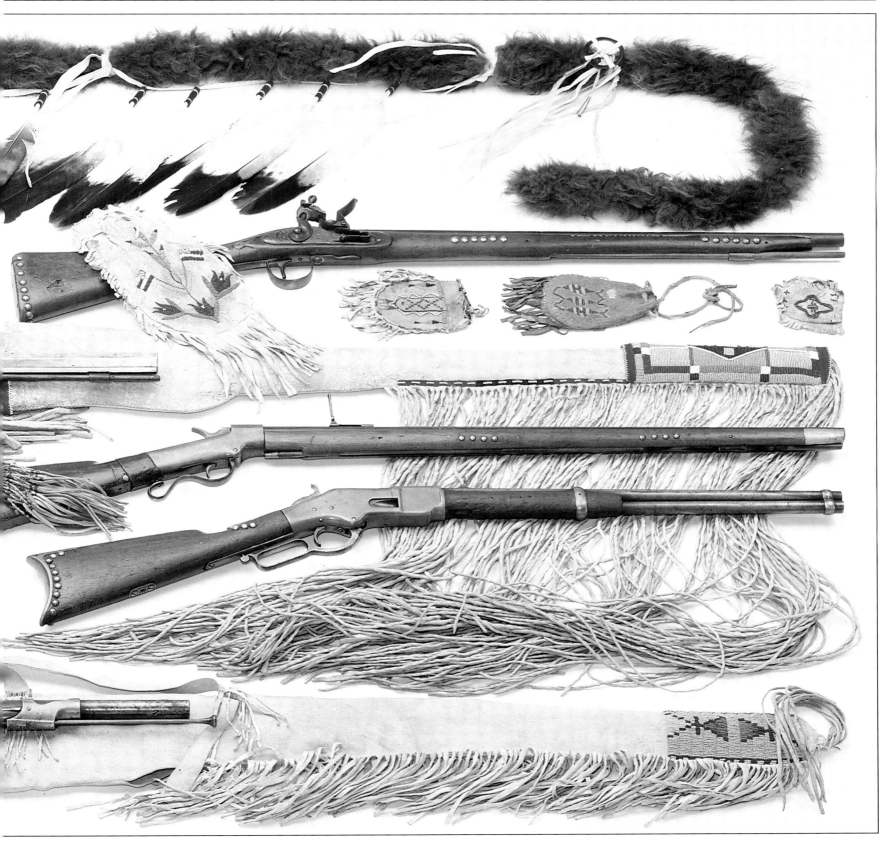

INDIAN U.S. ARMY SCOUT

The use of enlisted scouts not only introduced working capital among the Apaches but was an effective means of tracking down Indian offenders. It also provided an exhilarating break from routine reservation life and the chance to use U.S. power to elevate warrior status – the Apache war complex governing the behavior of army scouts. These scouts were an impressive sight, possessing great stamina, toughness and sharp intelligence. As illustrated, the Western Apache scouts usually wore scarlet headbands distinguishing them from Chiricahua hostiles. High bootlike moccasins with thick rawhide soles turning up at the toe were essential in the harsh desert environment.

ment began to crowd a reservation, Indians who owned land were persuaded to sell it, and if they did not, then their title was challenged, the presumption being that the only proof of Indian ownership was a willingness to part with his property!

It was an attitude of hypocrisy that capped the sorriest chapter in the history of the West. The clash of red and white had been inevitable, and just as inevitable was its outcome, considering resources and goals. Many whites, most usually in the Army's professional high command and in the Indian Bureau in Washington, approached the problem with some measure of humanity and even empathy for the native Americans. Unfortunately, that had not been enough, for the resistance that the Indian leaders' ethic of manhood required of them could only be met by equal or greater force, and by 1890 the force of a once-proud people who ruled half a continent had been spent. Almost.

REFERENCES

1 David Lavender, *The Great West*, pp. 59-60.
2 John Logan Allen, *Passage Through the Garden*, pp. 50-51.
3 Lavender, *The Great West*, pp. 125-6.
4 Robert Utley, *Frontiersmen in Blue* (New York, 1967), p. 5.
5 *Ibid.*, pp. 7-9.
6 *Ibid.*, p. 107ff.
7 Kenneth Carley, *The Sioux Uprising of 1862* (St Paul, 1961), pp. 34ff.
8 Utley, *Frontiersmen in Blue*, p. 278.
9 Stan Hoig, *The Sand Creek Massacre* (Norman, Okla., 1963), pp. 158ff.
10 Utley, *Frontiersmen in Blue*, pp. 341-2.
11 Daniel Boorstin, *The Americans*, p. 263.
12 Robert Utley, *Frontier Regulars* (New York, 1973), pp. 259-61.
13 *Ibid.*, pp. 302ff.

Top: *Soldiers and Apache scouts during a campaign in the 1880s. Apache hunting Apache was a result of intertribal rivalry and reservation boredom and led to a speedier conclusion of hostilities.*

Above: *The council between Geronimo and General Crook in the Sierra Madre in March 1886. Agreeing to surrender, the Apache fled the same night. This led to the replacement of Crook by Nelson Miles.*

Below: *Geronimo's (central figure) was the last effective resistance of the Indians in the southwest. Surrendering in 1886 and exiled to Florida, he died far from home at Fort Sill, Oklahoma, in 1909.*

V

FRONTIER COMMUNITY

Below: *Still-life with watermelons. A frontier sod-house, one of many photographed by Solomon Butcher, built into a bluff.*

ALMOST IN THE shadow of the relentless push and containment of the Indian, and largely removed from the opportunism of the gold and fur seekers, a teeming new white civilization sprouted almost as soon as trees fell to axes and soil felt the slice of the plow. With a rapidity that paled every previous exodus in human history, people flocked to the West, from the east, and from around the world.

In some places the new settlers presented a babel of tongues and myriad social and cultural peculiarities brought with them from their former homes. Initially it was peoples of English-speaking background who came west,

Englishmen, Scots, a few Welsh, along with a few Swiss and Huguenots, some Germans in Missouri and Texas, and a smattering of other peoples. But rapidly as the West opened up, more and more immigrants from across the Atlantic arrived to stake their claim. More than fifteen per cent of Californians by 1870 were Irish and German, with almost the same proportion in Nevada next door. In Virginia City alone half the population was not native to America, and foreigners also gave color and exotic overtones to the frontier Army, in which nearly a third were immigrants, chiefly Irish.[1] They would find their fighting qualities well suited to the new country.

In fact, the massive flood of expatriates from Europe prompted by its political upheavals of the 1840s and 1850s, saw huge numbers of them go west to make new lives. Literally millions of Germans came in the last half of the century, and another two million Scandinavians arrived after the Civil War. Almost all were poor, arriving with nothing but their clothing, and almost all of them craved one thing – land – and that meant the West. The Irish gravitated toward the towns and cities – San Francisco had 25,000 by 1870, more than a sixth of its population – while the Germans and Scandinavians came to find farms. The Germans embarked from St Louis and started

to spread westward along the Missouri. Typically they built their tidy little clusters of homes and farm buildings just as would have been expected from the German sense of orderliness. This, in turn, created a comfortable atmosphere for other new arrivals from the old country, resulting in a tendency – quite natural – for Germans to settle where other Germans had settled before them, creating substantial communities that lent a distinctive flavor to places like Fredericksburg, Texas. Moreover, they formed German-American friendship societies, and 'Leiderkrantz' clubs and literary societies devoted to their native writers. They promoted physical fitness and political debate in their 'Turnverein' clubs, which also served as a nucleus for recruiting when Civil War erupted and the German settlers responded in greater numbers than any other non-English speaking people. They started their own newspapers, began brewing old world beer, introduced their distinctive dishes and songs, and contributed overall what one of their own called 'a cultural leaven for the American frontier'.[2]

The Germans were not alone in adding to the well-spiced dough of the rising West. The Irish brought with them a host of their own distinctive features. Where the Germans were predominantly Lutheran, the Irish were Catholic almost to a man, and used this bond to retain a unity among themselves despite the homogenizing influences of frontier life. Moreover, they came chiefly to labor, not to farm, and their communities were to be found strung out all along the transcontinental railroads they helped build, and in the precincts of the cities whose buildings they constructed. Even more politically charged than the Ger-

mans, they lent volume, fervor, and occasional violence to frontier debate, especially whenever the subject of England should arise.

Iowa, Missouri, and the northern tier of territories from Minnesota through the Dakotas to Montana, hummed more to the musical speech of the Swedes, the Norwegians, and the Danes. Some Scandinavians also came as railroad laborers, but most came to buy cheap land, and those who hired themselves out saved their pay to buy their farms and raise their sheep and dairy herds. Lutherans like the Germans, they brought perhaps the strictest behavioral ethics of all European immigrants

to the northern plains. Even in the wilderness they prized education, hard work, and fair play, along with a liberal view of the world and government that often put them at odds with their neighbors.

The great wave of European movement to the West had largely abated by the 1880s, just in time for a new, smaller, influx of other peoples, chiefly Chinese, Italians, and Jews. The first came in primarily as laborers for the gold mines, and later the railroad. Many more came as indentured servants to wealthier Chinese masters. During the 1850s and 1860s they chiefly populated San Francisco and

Above: *A construction train in Granite Canyon, near Laramie, Wyoming, 1868. Fast-growing railroad companies like the Union Pacific had the same idea as their laborers – to go West as fast as possible.*

Below: *A section gang in Wyoming in the 1870s. Suggesting it could be a family affair, the foreman's daughter sits among the men, most of whom were Europeans come to the new country to labor.*

northern California, but in time they found their way to almost every frontier community, becoming universally associated with laundries and restaurants, as well as for their seeming incredible capacity for uncomplaining hard work and thrift. Moreover, when one family established itself, it soon sponsored the coming of another one to build a little community. More so than any other immigrant peoples, they worked, played, and lived so closely together that they kept their separate cultural identity more completely than any others. Every major city of the West and most of the smaller ones, had and still has its 'Chinatown'. It was no wonder that they, and the lesser numbers of Japanese who followed them, aroused considerable antipathy and resentment. Their hard work and thrift often led to their owning choice land that more profligate whites had overlooked. Their oriental features, strange language, and seemingly bizarre customs, further singled them out, and in the course of Western history they would come in for more persecution and harassment than any other people except the Indians.

Even Jews, so despised in the old world, fared better than the Chinese, though not so many of them came west. About one out of twenty immigrants to America was a Jew by the 1860s, though most chose to remain in the East. Still San Francisco had its first congregation by 1849, and more sprouted up in Sacramento, Oregon, and even in Nevada. Having suffered intolerance more intimately than any other immigrant people, they showed one of the most liberal attitudes toward the plight of the Indian and the rights of other immigrants. They, too, were more city dwellers. Few took up the plow, but instead they opted for the

Above: *In the gold camps of California, the Chinese were hated for many reasons: their color, their unfamiliar ways, their incomprehensible language. Some people even found fault in their diligence.*

Below: *The Chinese work ethic embraced more than mining and the railways. The now ubiquitous Chinese laundry had early origins on the west coast. Their tight-knit communities would later spread east.*

CHINESE COOLIES

Among the first Chinese in the West were two men and women who disembarked at San Francisco in 1848. They were the forerunners of thousands who flooded into California, to rework the gold mines abandoned by the '49ers. In 1870 the Chinese population there reached more than 70,000. To the large corporations developing the railroads, the Chinese were a boon, working harder and for less than any white man. Consequently, their lives were often made intolerable by resentful whites. Recruitment was initially from the Chinatowns of San Francisco and Sacramento but was later extended to the Cantons as the demand for labor, to tackle virtually impossible tasks, increased.

trades and professions they had plied in Europe, becoming merchants, jewelers and watchmakers, and educators. Inevitably they, too, suffered from considerable intolerance and anti-semitism. Ironically, the presence of more visible objects for xenophobic hatreds like the Indian and the Chinese gave the Jews a measure of safety they might not otherwise have enjoyed.[3]

One thing they all had in common was hope (excluding, perhaps, the indentured Chinese, who were virtual slaves, yet even they hoped for freedom, and many got it in the end). Another shared attribute was a willingness to take on hard work. The lazy and shiftless did not come up with the money for the long passage across an ocean, or brave the hardships of a harsh frontier, in order to be layabouts. They sought more freedom than they had known in their old homes, land that the crowded, aristocracy-ridden Europe did not have to spare, and came with a general conviction that out here they could make of themselves almost whatever they set their sights on. They brought a belief in equality, born in the inequities they had suffered in the past, far beyond what many of the native-born whites embraced, and in their hard-working quest for that equality they challenged those of Anglo-Saxon stock who had opened the frontier as far as the Mississippi.

The first of the flood were the overland immigrants, not interested in stopping at the near edge of civilization, but bound for the far West. Overwhelmingly they came to farm, more than sixty per cent of them bringing their plows and harrows and ox teams with them. Also, since their migration started in the

Top: *A rock train in Monterey, California. Chinese coolies who labored for the Central Pacific railroad did the perilous jobs no Europeans would touch; hundreds paid the price with their lives.*

Above: *The pull west was literally that. Wagons carried the settlers' past and future, a burden borne by mules or oxen, as here. Oxen were sturdier, hardier and more economical ultimately.*

Below: *Covered wagons camped near Boulder, Colorado. For greater safety most trains formed corrals at night. Nicknamed prairie schooners, wagons had to be versatile where water was concerned.*

1840s, most were native born Americans, with Europe's contribution yet to be felt. Those who would not farm came instead to provide services to the farmers. Trades like blacksmithing, tanning and harness making, carpentry and cooperage, predominated, along with a smattering of doctors, teachers, and the inevitable lawyer. Most came with 'a vision of a rich soil producing an abundant surplus'.[4]

To a surprising extent, these first emigrants were people who had moved before, almost as if it were in their blood. Some had moved several times before crossing the Mississippi on the greatest move of their lives. Moreover, they moved in a pattern keyed to the nature of frontier society. Their first move came in their early twenties, when young men left their parents and young women were taken to wife. A decade later, as the arrival of children put pressure on small holdings, they moved again. And ten or twenty years later, men and women in their forties and fifties looked to move once more, to find a place for their grown children sufficiently abundant that the family might stay close in the elders' later years.

A few, to be sure, were of another stripe, people in whose feet the itch was so strong that they could never settle anywhere for long. They were not favorably looked upon by the earnest settlers, and many acquired the derogatory nickname 'Pikers'. It stemmed originally from Pike County, Missouri, but came in time to apply to any of the poor whites from Missouri and Arkansas who, illiterate and uncouth, wandered westward without aim. They were immortalized even in songs like 'Sweet Betsy from Pike', their character being revealed in the company Betsy brought with her – two yoke of oxen, a spotted dog, a cross-eyed rooster, a hog, and 'her lover Ike'. One family of 'Pikers', the Newty's, actually left Pike County for Oregon, then moved to the Sierras in California, and then started talking of moving to Montana, pushing their herd of hogs before them. Father, mother, and all the children slept in the same filthy bed, out of doors, and presented such an appalling picture of 'weak-minded restlessness', thought one visitor, that they startled him with a 'horrible lesson of social disintegration, of human retrograde'. They were a 'race of perpetual emigrants who roam as dreary waifs over the west'. Anxious to make a little more room in

Below: *Trying to reproduce the comforts of home, such as it had been. These Kansas immigrants moved West in a simple box wagon fitted with bows and covered with canvas, generally not the Conestoga type.*

his crowded bed, father Newty offered a young man half the herd of pigs if he would marry his oldest daughter.[5]

There was a species of loner who came west who fit an entirely different mold. Tens of thousands of single young men struck out to make a place for themselves, and in the hope of finding a wife on the frontier. After the Civil War especially, a whole generation of men came home from the armies having seen a bit of the world, and no longer content to wait to inherit the parents' farm. These were no idle wanderers. They wanted property of their own to settle on, but having sampled a bit of adventure, they wanted a mix of the excitement of frontier life with their home building. Many came entirely on their own. Many more hired themselves out to families moving west, amounting to perhaps twenty per cent of the unmarried men who made the move. They gave their labor in return for room and board, and took wages where they could get them.[6]

At the other end of the scale were whole colonies who settled en masse to form instant communities. In Kansas, during the 1870s, Ellis County alone saw no fewer than twenty-four such colonies arrive, from places as diverse as Massachusetts, New York, Ohio, Pennsylvania, Ireland, Russia, France, Bohemia, Austria and Denmark, and including

Above: *The Moses Speese family, Custer County, Nebraska, 1888. After the Civil War, harrassed blacks moved West en masse. Many moved to Nebraska after some Kansas cities stopped them from settling.*

Below: *Some sod-houses grew almost organically from the barren plains. But three sons, two mules and a cow grazing the roof – plus wood-framed windows – were perhaps reward for a hard life.*

blacks from Kentucky. The impetus to settle this way was hardly mysterious. 'It is not at all surprising that the immigrant should wish to make settlement in a new country by the side of his old friends and neighbors,' commented an onlooker. Fearful of the 'strange and perhaps peculiar people' awaiting them on the frontier, the colonists brought the comfort of old associates along with them.

Their group immigration revealed something else that lay at the very heart of the new communities they came to create. These people were not rejecting society by coming to the wilderness. Rather, they were turning their backs on a society at home that for whatever reason had failed them – economically, culturally, socially. They came to build a new society in its place.[7]

First they had to build their own piece of that society, and that meant a house. The variety of structures that went up on the plains and prairies was as great as the imagination of the builders, divided by the building materials available. At its most rudimentary, the first home was the inside of the wagon that brought their possessions west with them. Quickly that gave way to something more, however. Tents sprouted on the grasslands in the summer and fall months, but they, too, had to be temporary. When timber was not available, they used the topsoil of the ground they hoped to plow. When in a hurry, they carved 'dugouts' into the hillsides facing away from prevailing northerly winds. They dug as deep as they wanted to go, then walled up the open side with sod and used what wood was available to roof it over, often placing a sod covering on top of it. The result was crude, leaky, dank, and prone to infestation, but it was better than sleeping in the open.

When more time afforded, and better sod was available, they built free-standing houses, sometimes of considerable size and durability. They cut the sod in the spring, slicing it into

Below: *Sod was cut from previously unplowed prairie to build the first, rudimentary dwellings. Backbreaking work though it was, there was no option, and even less choice of materials, available.*

FARMERS & HOMESTEADERS

In the twenty years after the Civil War, 1865-85, more land became cultivated than in the previous 250 years, 1615-1865. This incredible feat was accomplished by farmers who traveled hundreds of miles to inhospitable flat seas of grass, which also lacked trees, sometimes without water or shelter of any kind. Here they built sod-houses and struggled constantly against bitter cold, intense heat, floods and drought and huge swarms of locusts, sometimes six inches deep on the ground, that ate everything in their path. Add to these hardships the animosity of the cattlemen who detested the sod-busting plow, the farmer who drove it and the loss of the open range thus converted to farm land, and it is truly amazing that farmers survived, let alone prospered. Beside the sod-busting plow, the invention of barbed wire in 1874 by Illinois farmer Joseph F. Glidden was the other major factor that greatly hastened the closing of the open range. By 1873, wheat and alfalfa crops began to evidence greater profitability than ranching and these ranchers were astute enough to see that growing fruit and vegetables for the east, now that the railroads made these markets more accessible, was even more lucrative. By 1899, California was the largest producer of grapes in the country. The turn of the century saw steam-powered farm machinery and irrigation turn barren plains into the nation's granary. The farmer had become essential to the survival of the whole country.

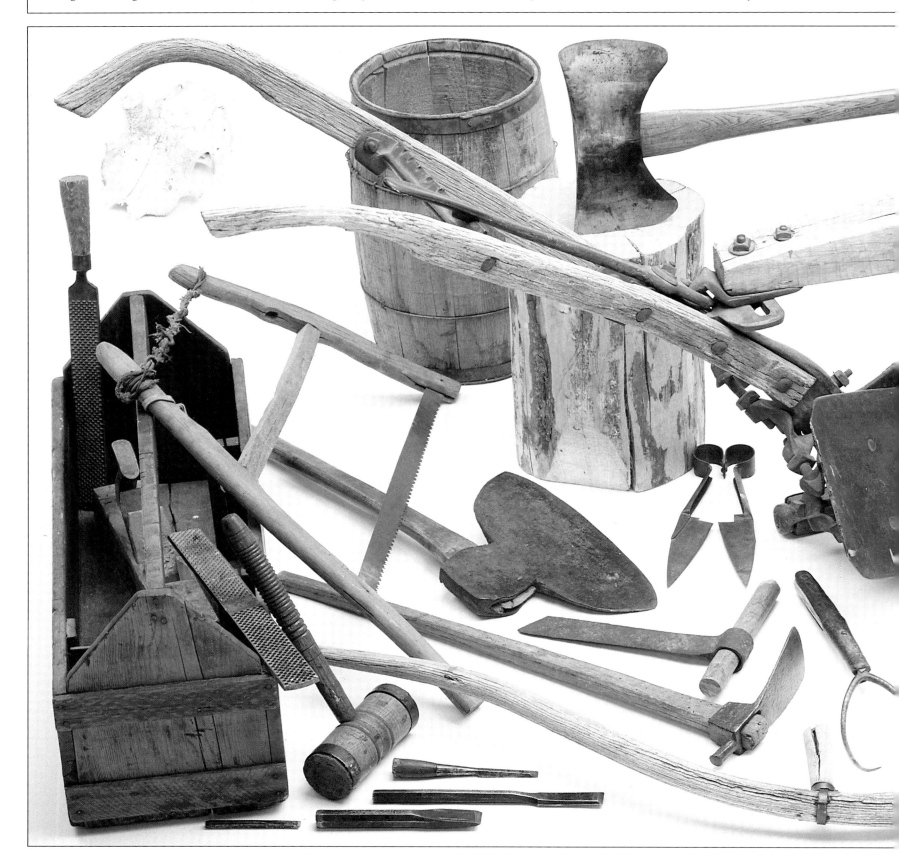

134

1 Top part of elk skull.
2 File with wooden handle.
3 Wooden plane, blade marked 'Ohio Tool Company'
4 Large file.
5 Wooden tool box.
6 Turned wooden mallet with iron-bound head.
7 Small chisel marked 'Winchester'.
8 Heavy wood chisel.
9 Long wood chisel.
10 Wood chisel with wooden handle.
11 Wooden keg.

12 Large double-bladed axe, head marked 'S. Francis Renfrew'.
13 Bow-saw, tightened by twisting rawhide (top).
14 Wide single-bladed axe.
15 Sheep shears.
16 Shingle splitter, iron, used in roofing.
17 Wooden handled mattock.
18 Pitchfork head.
19 Scythe.
20 Iron bladed sod-busting plow, pulled by mule or horse.
21 Brass cowbell with

leather strap.
22 Wooden plate with wooden three-tine fork and scoop.
23 Burl poplar wood bowl.
24 Wooden five-tine fork probably used for separating liquids.
25 Wooden pestle.
26 Iron cooking pot.
27 Stoneware whiskey jug.
28 Mule headstall.
29 Mule collars.
30 Dropped deer antlers, often to be seen adorning roofs or above doors of sod-houses.

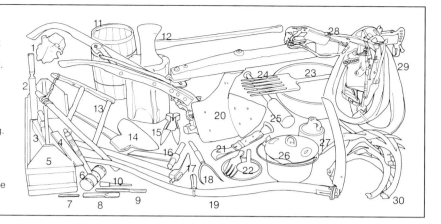

large 'bricks' a foot wide and eighteen inches long, and perhaps three inches thick. They looked for sod that had a thick mat of grass growing on it, ensuring an even thicker tangle of roots beneath that shortly acted as a 'mortar' in holding the bricks together. As the walls dried, the roots kept the earth from breaking apart. Thus, the older it got, the stronger a 'soddy' became. The most expensive part of a sod house would be its windows, which had to be purchased commercially in most cases, and could cost $1.25 – the price of an acre of public land. Then there was the lumber for the roof, which had to be strong to support the weight of the sod roof laid over the top. Here was the

only weak spot in the soddy, for after some years the wood would rot or the weight of the sod would bow it down dangerously. The walls could last almost forever.

It was truly a 'living' home, for more than the builders lived in it. Insects of all kinds bored into the sod. Mice and larger vermin nested in any cavity left unfilled. Rattlesnakes slithered under the door in summer to the cool interior, often settling under a farmer's bed, or even in it. There was no keeping anything truly clean, for the dried earth of the walls and roof constantly shed bits and pieces of dust and dirt on to everything. Still, it was cool in the high plains heat, and virtually immune to

fire. Moreover, it was adaptable. If the settler proved prosperous, it was easy to expand the house by simply building on new wings and cutting doors through the walls. A more conventional timber and shingle roof could be added, and even standard wood frame rooms tacked on. To 'beautify' the interior, they plastered the walls with mud, smoothed it down, and then painted it with lime whitewash. Many became so attached to their soddies that long after they could afford to build a proper house, they chose to live out their days in their earthen homes.[8]

For those who found timber available, more likely from a local sawmill than free standing on the largely treeless plains, they quickly built rude frame dwellings little more than shacks by the standards of the communities they had left behind. They erected the thinnest framework possible – to conserve wood – then covered it with planking, and sheathed that in tarred paper to keep out the drafts. In the southwest, learning the local technique of making adobe bricks from the Mexican Americans and Indians allowed settlers to construct arguably the best homes of all. The mud was mixed with grass or straw, formed into bricks, and sun dried. Erected using more adobe as a mortar, the houses built from such bricks withstood every fire and calamity nature could send, even proving resistant to tornadoes. They took longer to build because of the time spent making and baking the bricks, but they built houses of which the owners were proud – by frontier terms, that is.

Furnishing the interiors showed far more in the way of individuality, but one thing every

Above: *A 'soddy' may or may not have been an affectionate term for such a house . . . Jacob Smith and his large family and home at least had the support of a sturdy timber upright and rough beams for theirs.*

Below: *Relative prosperity is evinced by the baby carriage owned by Mrs Georgia McGaughey at her home in New Helena, Nebraska. The strongly Celtic surname suggests the immigrant family's origins.*

soddy or shack had to have was a stove, for cooking year round, and heat in the winter. Some were specially built in the east for western transportation and use, but in time almost any iron box could be used. Most typical was the eastern style 'ten-plate' stove, most of them cast in the iron furnaces of Pennsylvania. Two to three feet tall, eighteen inches wide, and perhaps three feet deep, such 'chunk' stoves as they were also called, had a firebox on the bottom, stoked through a door in the front. Above sat a large open chamber with wide doors opening from either side. Through convection, the smoke and heat from the fire passed up through flues at front and behind the chamber, then across another interior passage to the stove pipe, which then ran up through the chimney to the outside. A warming platform extended from in front of the door to the firebox, and food itself was cooked on the top surface, or baked in the central chamber, whose temperature could be regulated roughly by opening and closing the side doors. The same doors helped to govern heat for warming the house.

It required some ingenuity to find something to burn in those stoves when the settler found just how scarce wood could be. There was no coal here, and precious few trees, with some like the ironwood too hard to cut and too resistant to take flame. Sometimes the thick dried sod would burn after a fashion, rather like the peat that the Irish knew so well. Better still were tightly packed twists of prairie grass or, after the first year's crop was in, corn stalks and cobs. Most plentiful of all, however, was dried animal dung. The Indians had demon-

Above: *Some settlers, such as Al Wise, grew prosperous, hence the timbered house and shingled roof. Around 1892, he was both cattle rancher and county coroner. The elk skull and antlers are ornamental.*

Below: *The Schuch's ranch, a German settlement in Colorado. Germans and Scandinavians especially came West to farm, building strong community feelings and solid foundations for future generations.*

strated the properties of the buffalo 'chip', and farmers soon learned that cattle droppings would serve the same purpose. There was nothing refined about the fuel. It brought insects into the house, was dirty and smelly, and tended to ruin the stoves after a time, for it burned too hot. It left a terrible mess to clean all to frequently. But it provided heat, and at no cost.

The prairie and plains settler turned his attention to other vital matters as soon as his first rude shelter went up, and sometimes even before. He had to get the soil working for him right away. Since most immigrants went west in the spring or summer, this meant that when they reached their new homes, a good portion of the planting and growing season was already past. They had to race to get their parcel cleared of rocks, debris, even the few trees, and get their seed into the ground. Farmer, plow, and ox teams worked from just before dawn until last twilight to break the sod, tear up the tangle of roots, and expose the untapped earth beneath. Almost to a man, they brought the seed for the crops they had known in the past, chiefly corn and wheat, with a scattering of several other grains depending on the soil and the farmer's needs. They followed plows that first brought west names like John Deere and McCormick, dropped their precious seed in the furrows, and waited for sun and rain, and luck, to bring them a crop.

Water was the other essential, of course, and the farmer could not depend on the heavens to serve his needs in the right quantity or at the right time. Even before the house was

Above: *Life on the plains was crushingly hard for women, in an era when to be house-proud was to be eternally optimistic. This woman gathers buffalo chips – dung – to burn for fuel in the stove.*

Below: *Because they had to, sod-busters had faith in the limitless bounty of the land that gave them opportunity. Where some lost the battle, others took up the plowshares literally and metaphorically.*

THE SOD-BUSTER

Shortly after the Civil War, pioneers in their thousands swarmed into the region from the Missouri to the Rockies. While many came from the eastern states, significant numbers were recruited from Europe, as far as the steppes of Russia. On offer under the terms of the 1862 Homestead Act was potential ownership of 160 acres which had to be managed and occupied by the claimant for five years. Often called sod-busters (the name speaks for itself), these emigrants turned barren soil into a richly productive land. On the treeless plains, the only building material was sod which was used to construct one-story houses such as is shown here.

built, he started looking about for a likely spot to sink his well. It was a job for pick, shovel, and ladder, as he laboriously dug deeper and deeper. The lucky ones found good water at thirty feet; the rest had to go farther down. Then, when they found their water, they had to get it out, at first with a simple bucket on a rope, and later with hand pumps and, eventually, windmills. The steady breezes of the prairies made windmills ideal, and as the decades went on, more and more refinements were made in commercially manufactured machines so that tens of thousands of them could be sent west, sold through mail order catalogs, for sums as little as $25. With nothing

more important than water, it was money well spent. Moreover, the farmer learned to send the water where he needed it, either into troughs for the animals, or through irrigation ditches to the periphery and interior of his crop lands, even to the wife's vegetable garden. Few if any bothered with catering to convenience for human needs. Indoor water would not come until well into the next century for much of the West outside the cities.

The toil of being a prairie and plains farmer was little different from that known back in the East, with chiefly the added danger of sporadic Indian raids, and the drawback of iso-

lation and a less friendly environment. When it rained, some had to wear oilskin coats indoors to stay dry, wrapping infants in more oil cloths and holding umbrellas over them. 'Yellow mud' from the roof and walls could form a small torrent passing through the house. The earth floor, therefore, became a miry mush despite all efforts to harden it with salt and other preparations. 'You'll be perfectly delighted at the paradise you've found,' went one poem, 'as you build your castles in the air and dugouts in the ground.' In such times, few would have agreed. Yet a few wags could see humor even in such circumstances, giving vent to their wit in poetry and song:

Above: *Some of those who settled and stayed gave their names to towns. The biblically named Ephraim and Sarah Finch, Nebraska ranchers in the mid-1870s, saw Finchville named after them in 1880.*

Below: *Both Solomon Butcher and Laton Huffman recorded the settling of the plains. Butcher's pictures seem to take pride in the achievement of others; Huffman bewailed the loss of the last wilderness.*

Right: *Certain sod-houses put others to shame. The Belgian Isadore Haumont arrived from Europe in spring 1883, and built his magnificent two-story house in 1884-5. Nineteen feet to the eaves, walls three feet thick and tied through with timber, boasting a fine, shingled roof, and a brick chimney stack, the house cost $500 to build. Haumont lived in the house on the French Table, north of Broken Bow, Nebraska, until his death in 1920.*

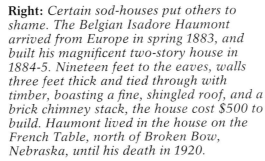

How happy I feel when I crawl into bed,
And a rattlesnake rattles a tune
at my head.
And the gay little centipede void
of all fear,
Crawls over my neck and down
into my ear.
And the gay little bedbugs so
cheerful and bright,
They keep me a-laughing two-thirds
of the night.
And the gay little flea with sharp
tacks on his toes,
Plays, 'Why don't you catch me'
all over my nose.

Others did not find it at all amusing. 'Rattlesnakes, bedbugs, fleas, and the "prairie itch" were what kept us awake nights and made life miserable,' remembered one.[9]

Men and women performed reasonably well-defined roles on the frontier, though definitions were often blurred by the simple necessity to get things done regardless of whether or not it was 'man's' or 'woman's' work. The men and older boys worked the fields and tended to the heavier livestock. Women and children looked after the family garden, the chickens and pigs, and all of the domestic chores. For women especially, it was killing labor that wore down the frail or timid

all too quickly. If it was not the constant carrying and fetching, it was the tedium of lonely prairie nights. 'Everything is so monotonous,' wrote one sad farm wife in 1873, 'almost unbearable.' Homesickness for the friends and family left behind almost inevitably afflicted the women especially, who spent so much of their day by themselves or with only the small children for company. 'I saw a vast expanse of prairie country in sunset,' wrote a Kansas woman, 'but it looked so very lonesome, and so I cried, in a moment of longing for my family so far away.' A letter from east of the Mississippi or a newspaper could bring back all of the memories, and with them a flood of

tears, for men and women alike, though more often than not the men relished the new life. 'Mother never became quite satisfied with Kansas,' one pioneer child recalled, 'but father loved it.'

In such an environment, the company of others, frontier society however rude and unrefined, was relished by the new westerners from the plains of Nebraska to the California coast, and they used considerable ingenuity in taking advantage of the chance for gathering. As soon as churches formed – often meeting initially in some pioneer's soddy – dozens of settlers in the locality became attendees, regardless of their denominations in former days. Catholics seemed to hold out until they could form their own congregations, but many of the young Jewish men who came west on their own quickly assimilated into gentile congregations and even took gentile wives. When pastors could not be hired, they held simple prayer meetings with the men taking turns at the readings, then afterward the day was given over to communal meals to which everyone contributed, perhaps some liquor for the men, and a ceaseless exchange of gossip and news stored up during the previous week or weeks since last they met.

Even more savored were the days set aside for pure frolic. The 4th of July, the 'harvest home' party that signalled the end of the harvest season, the passing through of traveling medicine shows, dramatic troupes, even lecture and debating societies, all produced an inevitable picnic and an afternoon of respite from the gruelling routine of work and sleep. It is no wonder that religious revivals and temperance meetings had such a profound effect on the frontier community. Those who attended came far more for the excuse of an entertainment – any entertainment – than

from deep sympathy with the cause at hand, but repeated attendance eventually swayed their convictions, giving fundamental ideals their deepest rooting in the sparsely settled regions of the Midwest.

Frontier people needed these entertainments to keep them sane in the face of cyclones, tornadoes, drought, crop blights, livestock epidemics, the almost inevitable death of at least one child from diptheria or undiagnosed fevers, the dust storms, prairie fires in summer and blizzards in winter. All the calamities the Almighty could send hit the new westerners repeatedly as the battle between man and the land see-sawed in the contest for victory. Death and tragedy were constant companions. Indeed, even funerals rated highly among the social gatherings, so precious was the need to be with others for a few brief moments of solace from the solitude. Alas, watching friends and neighbors being laid to rest, especially the children, became so commonplace that it confused the living children brought to watch. In 1885, in Kansas, one 6-year-old came back from a child's funeral so fascinated by the scene, and so unaware of what it all was about, that he took a stick and beat his little brother to death, then performed a solemn burial of his own. It had seemed so much a game, an almost happy occasion, that he wanted to repeat it at home, and went proudly to his mother afterward to tell her what he had done.[10]

It could hardly be a surprise that many could not face this kind of life when they came west,

Below: *'I will dwell in the house of the Lord . . .', even if it happened to be just another soddy, purpose-built for religion. Settlers of the Caldwell-Bluff City area had no qualms about the style of their church in 1880.*

Death on the frontier was sometimes swift and violent but occurred from natural causes in most cases, just as in other areas. Some unfortunates died alone, in remote areas, unattended and unmourned. There was no burial and no grave site or remaining trace of them after nature had done its work. Others received a short, perfunctory interment. The deceased was wrapped in a blanket, thrown over the back of a horse and taken to a hole in

the ground. Others went to their graves in farm wagons or on the back of a buckboard. In some cases graves were dug but in others rocks were just piled on the corpse to keep animals from it. Frontier justice was also swift and sure when executed by vigilantes. Results were usually the subject of a funeral of sorts. While no official figures are extant, it is estimated that considerably more than 700 wretches met their maker as a result of such impromptu justice before 1900. The deaths of notorious outlaws and

gunmen at times became more of a spectacle. It was not unusual for the local undertaker to have the deceased laid out in a store front or on boards on the sidewalk, mortal wounds exposed, for public viewing, and a form of advertising. Many of the well-known desperadoes of the time had their final photograph taken on this occasion. There were those who left this life in a more fitting manner. For formal funerals, the hearse was used for conveying the dead. The magnificent vehicle shown here, which is housed and

may be seen at Old Trail Town, Cody, Wyoming, was made in St Louis and sent to Miles City, Montana Territory, about 1880 to carry deceased gold miners. The body of the vehicle is beautifully carved rosewood that was painted in the early twentieth century. There is no visible manufacturer's plate. The hearse was used during Prohibition in the 1930s to transport bootleg whiskey in a concealed trap beneath the space where the occupant lay in state, an interesting alternative adaptation.

or else tried it but gave up in favor of a less solitary existence. Towns were few at first, generally growing up only as small clusters of shacks around the major trading posts, army posts, and overland trail river crossings. But after the railroad came through and started spreading its tentacles out in an ever-expanding pattern, hundreds of new towns sprouted along the iron road. Most started as collections of shanties, or even tents, or rude frame walls with canvas spread overhead for a roof. There was, of course, no concept of town planning. People simply built where it suited them, which usually meant in a straight line along a single street at first, and that one most often fronting the railroad or trail. It is no accident that almost every frontier town of the plains and prairies had at its center a 'Front Street'.

They grew in spurts and cycles, some governed by the changes in the westward movement itself, others dictated by good years and bad in the Eastern economy, fluctuations of drought, and most frequently of all the success or failure of speculators who made and lost fortunes in persuading immigrants to choose one spot over another. Speculators acquired title to large tracts beside the railroad, or where the track was expected to go through, and then set about a practised routine of city building. Setting aside what they believed to be the choicest lots, they sold at low rates, or even gave away, smaller lots on the periphery in order to encourage tradesmen and mechanics to settle, thus providing the underlying service structure needed to attract more substantial settlers and their

Below: *Starting, like Liberal, with the main street, a new town like Mullinville, Kansas, founded in the 1880s, was as open as the land around it. Some saw only bleakness; the optimists saw prosperity.*

Above: *Where there were people there were bound, sooner or later, to be towns. Only ten days after its founding in 1886, Liberal, Kansas, was already growing, as building along its main street indicates.*

Below: *Nicodemus was established by black homesteaders from Kentucky and Tennessee in 1877, in Graham County, Kansas. The cry was 'Ho for Kansas!' and it led many beleaguered blacks into a promising land.*

Above: *Many Kansas towns, such as Horton, owed their establishment to the railroad. Prospective settlers mill around an excursion special laid on by the railroad to promote sale of town lots in the 1880s.*

Below: *Saloons seemed to exist everywhere and baldly stated their presence. This one, in Nebraska Territory, its owners standing at the door, was described as stopping place, bar and restaurant.*

money. When the growth boom started, then the prime lots could command considerable sums that the bankers and business people were happy to pay in order to bring their operations into a town already established and ready to prosper.

Some urban frontiers grew from other causes. San Francisco, and to a lesser extent Los Angeles and Seattle, owed their early prosperity to their admirable natural harbors, and of course to the Gold Rush. Indeed, actual attempts at urban planning occurred in San Francisco even before the Overland Trails started bringing their millions westward. The Mexican authorities had the settlement called Yerba Buena surveyed in 1839, formally laying out streets that remain at the heart of the city a century and a half later. When the Americans took over in 1847 and renamed it San Francisco, they re-surveyed, thoughtfully planning for future growth that came much more rapidly than they expected, thanks to the Gold Fever. In fact, during the height of the first great surge in 1849, the city's population doubled repeatedly in spans of less than two weeks at a time! Even the most thoughtful planning could not have taken this into account, and San Francisco early on suffered an ill that beset most frontier towns, that of outgrowing the services and government immediately available. Whole blocks of the city were nothing more than hastily erected tent 'hotels' and saloons built on either side of muddy streets, with no protection of police or fire brigades equivalent to the task of protecting the citizens. These overnight cities also suffered from the 'boom and bust' phenomenon far more than the plains settlements based on agriculture. Men and women who came to get rich quick either did, or they moved on. They formed little loyalty to the town or city, took little interest in civic affairs and society,

and were prone simply to pull up stakes and move on overnight, creating an unstable and at times troubled local society.[11]

For every growing metropolis like San Francisco, there were hundreds of small hamlets of 2,500 or so, many of which would achieve that size and then remain static for generations, having fulfilled the natural limits of population imposed by what the land and the local economy would support. If not by the railroad, the farm town was more likely to be found beside a river like the Platte, the Kaw, the Columbia, or the Arkansas. Some of the streams were navigable, but the greater concern was the water itself. Moreover, when

spaced out on the immigrant trails or the later established routes connecting larger towns, the rural villages tended to appear at about twenty mile intervals, often with even smaller hamlets in between. The spacing was not accidental. Along the main travel routes, such intervals provided overnight stops at the end of each day's journey, while for the farmers living outside town it meant no more than half a day in the wagon to reach town for supplies or to sell a crop. By the 1880s, when larger towns both on and away from the railroad were erecting grain elevators for storage of cash crops, a traveler could never get lost for no sooner did he leave the limits of one town

THE LIGHT MAIL COACH

The light coach is thought to have originated in Hungary during the fifteenth century, and the English stage wagon also influenced development of this mode of transportation. By the time the configuration known in this country appeared it was similar to the heavy Concord stage but had considerably smaller dimensions and much lighter construction. For these reasons it was obviously faster but not as rugged as the sturdy Concord and was

Above: *Although telegraph lines joined east and west in Salt Lake City by 1861, and effectively did for the Pony Express, Wells Fargo continued as a vital mail and passenger link to the nascent cities.*

Below: *Even as late as 1893, the Concord stagecoach continued to be an essential and robust form of transport, here for miners and their heavily armed escort bound for gold camps in Colorado.*

used primarily for short, easy runs over reasonable terrain, and was further restricted to use only in moderate weather due to the exposed format of the passenger compartment. Some of these lighter wagons were pressed into service by military paymasters who traveled from post to post under guard to deliver pay to military units within a small district. At least four horse teams were used, with a driving crew of two, driver and armed guard. The mail and other valuable cargo were normally carried in a covered or enclosed compartment, known as the boot, under the driver's seat. Passengers were restricted to ten or twelve, almost half the pay load of the larger coaches. Those inside had more comfort, such as it was. Dust was everywhere and only blankets and lap robes protected from the cold and rain. The same type of leather sling suspension was used as was on the heavy Concord but the lightness of the mail wagon accentuated the sometimes violent acrobatics of the passenger cabin, causing acute discomfort to passengers afflicted with motion sickness, a disaster in a confined space. This beautiful stage has been restored in the colors of the Deadwood and Cheyenne Mail Coach. Unfortunately, few examples of such vehicles have survived the rigors of time but they certainly were a hallmark of the American West. Mark Twain described the stagecoach as a 'cradle on wheels'. Most others would not have been so kind. Any one of those horribly sick, terribly cold and totally exhausted passengers probably would not have agreed with him.

than, on the horizon ahead, he could see the tops of the silos in the next.

Almost all such towns, whether in Kansas or New Mexico or Oregon, went through the same phases of development. First was the shabby collection of wooden buildings, devoid of style or symmetry, and designed for shelter and ready utility, nothing more. A few were more than one story for the larger stores or rented quarters and hotels, the rest like law offices and barbers were tiny one level affairs stuffed in between the bigger structures. False fronts rising up to a second story roof level became immensely popular, for no practical purpose, but only to give an impression of greater size and importance. The only building of truly imposing stature would be the principal hotel, and even it probably started out on a smaller scale. A few churches and a school, and some saloons on the outskirts, completed the picture of the unplanned, helter skelter community. Private homes ringed the business section, usually one and two story frame buildings, with perhaps a porch around the street sides, and a stable in the rear. There were animals everywhere in a frontier town, some domestic livestock like chickens and pigs wandering freely in the dirt streets. Most towns never smelled beautiful.

If fortune smiled and the town and its people prospered, the ensuing years saw a gradual attempt to give the place a greater sense of permanence and appearance of solidity. New brick and stone blocks replaced the old

Right: *Freund's gunstore in Laramie, Wyoming Territory, 1868. Although such towns went through a makeshift stage of development, some businesses ensured that everyone knew what they were trading.*

wooden offices and hotels. Houses, too, were built of masonry, and streets were paved with brick or cobblestones. Street lamps went up, an unused block was turned into a park or a town square, and even the saloons took on a more genteel air, with mahogany bars with marble tops, etched glass in the doors and windows, wooden floors and gas lighting. They also grew in number in proportion to the town's growth. Livingston, Montana, had 3,000 people in 1883, and thirty-three taverns, and a mining town like Leadville, Colorado, chiefly populated by men, could have 140 saloons and beer halls, leaving no doubt as to where their priorities lay.

A feature of the larger, more prosperous towns was the considerable size of their transient population, a fact demonstrated by the number and size of hotels in such communities. Many people settling the frontier were on the move, salesmen, 'drummers', speculators, gamblers, and more. Moreover, hotels were looked on not just as overnight stops, but also as 'homes' for thousands of stationary residents either unwilling or unable to rent or buy a proper house. Room rates included all meals, eaten communally in the dining room, which meant that a small society grew up within each establishment, and to many this compact form of community suited them

ideally, especially those who had come from the large urban centers of the East. Young married couples, single professional men, widows and spinsters, often favored such accommodation. Having no other family nearby, and being largely strangers to the community with no established place or social standing, it gave them a place to belong.[12]

Inevitably there were the seamier sides to the growth of towns and cities in the West, and the larger the community, the more there were. Besides the saloons, always the object of loathing from the more respectable side of town, there were the gambling halls, even when they were only in the back room of a

Left: *By 1874, there were traffic jams in main street, Helena, Montana, as prospectors and settlers swarmed into town at news of a gold strike in outlying hills. Thus did towns establish a presence.*

Above: *Hays, Kansas, was one of the main shipping points for Texas longhorns, and an important meat market. Whether it was beef or real estate, such towns generally supplied all that settlers could want.*

Below: *A freighting scene in Nebraska City, c. 1870, indicates the growth of commerce. Freight-wagon caravans continued to supply frontier towns as the country developed after the Civil War.*

GAMBLERS

Faced with all hardships imaginable, westerners desperately needed some form of diversion, and gambling became their favorite pastime. They would gamble on anything and it was socially acceptable to do so. Games of chance, cards, dice, roulette, horse racing, fist fights, cock fights were all considered legitimate gambling affairs. Everyone gambled but professional gamblers were a natural product of this prediliction, and they assumed many guises. Few were the slick dandy with the brocade vest and pomade hair. Most were rough, callous men and nearly all were patently dishonest. Gambling got its start on riverboats heading up western tributaries, but soon every camp, railhead and cow town had some form of game in the saloon or whorehouse. Everyone knew these men were cheats and that the games were probably rigged in their favor, yet people still indulged in any one of different ways to lose money. Another by-product of gambling was the resulting dispute that sometimes led to a gunfight, the ultimate gamble of life. Some of the great Western art depicts this climactic incident, the shootout over cards – N.C. Wyeth's 'Wild Bill Hickok at Cards' famously illustrates the notorious reprobate at one of his favorite occupations – but in most cases retribution of a cardsharp was not so permanent. Regardless, the profession certainly had its pitfalls and has resulted in a rather low perception of the Western gambler today.

1 Sharps Model 1 four shot Pepperbox.
2 Storage case for gaming chips.
3 Holder for gaming chips.
4 Red, white and blue gaming chips, each color indicating a different denomination.
5 Roulette table and wheel.
6 Leather shoulder holster for Colt single-action revolver, .45 caliber.
7 Carpet bag.
8 Leather shoulder holster holding a Colt double-action Lightning revolver, .41 caliber.
9 Fancy vest, white background with blue stripes.
10 Remington double deringer, .41 caliber.
11 Gold and enamel watch and fob.
12 Deck of cards, advertisement for Marlin Firearms.
13 Colt first model deringer, .41 caliber.
14 James Reid knuckle-duster revolver.
15 Silver dollars and pocket purse.
16 Knuckleduster.
17 Josiah Ells third model pocket revolver.
18 Silver-plated, double-doored cigar box.
19 Deck of cards.
20 Unwin and Rodgers knife/pistol combination.
21 Pair of dice.
22 Gaming chips.
23 Minneapolis Firearms Co. palm pistol, 'The Protector', .32 caliber.
24 Brass spittoon.
25 Fur-covered saddlebags.
26 Winchester Model 1873 rifle, .44-40 caliber.

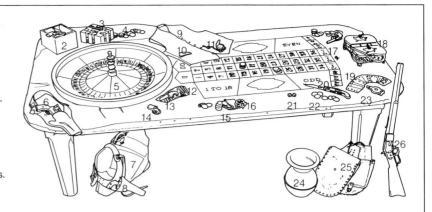

barber shop or in a room over the general merchandise store. Reformers, especially later in the century, would rail on interminably against such enterprises.

Even more did they attack the most inevitable concomitant to a westward push in which most of the settlers were men. Prostitution came west almost as quickly as the first men started to cross the plains and mountains. Indeed, at first many native American women earned trade gifts from lonely trappers, though quite a few eventually became wives instead. When the Overland Trails started to bring single men in greater numbers, and communities started to form with farm laborers or townsmen with no wives, the advent of more traditional prostitution was inevitable, so that, in time, the higher minded would complain of some western towns that 'almost every other house is a drinking saloon, gambling house, or bawdy'. Perhaps as many as 50,000 women earned a tentative living in the West between 1850 and 1900 by selling themselves either in the saloons, or else in rented houses on the outskirts of town. Most worked and lived alone; many operated in 'houses' of up to a dozen or more. All too many languished in 'cribs', the tiny shack in an alley with only a

Above: *Dodge City was a Cow town with Character. Created in 1872, its fortunes rose with the arrival of the railroad. The bartender in one of its many dens of iniquity is Bat Masterson's brother.*

Below: *As it became a railhead for Texas cattle, cowboys poured into Dodge City. Bars considerably less salubrious than this were plentiful, happy to slake the thirst of cowboys with money to burn.*

cot, where a woman usually ended her days as beauty and health wasted away from her profession. It is no wonder that they were called 'daughters of joy' in one breath, and 'sisters of misery' in another.[13]

Hosts of single women came west seeking to make their way, with at first no thought of 'going on the game'. They came as seamstresses, milliners, nurses, teachers, laundresses, and a host of other skilled and unskilled trades, most of which, unfortunately, failed to provide an adequate living. The fortunate ones soon found husbands among the single young men. Those less fortunate were all too often forced to consider the 'oldest profession' as a last resort, preferable to destitution. There was some money to be made in it, especially if there were a military post nearby, or a railroad construction gang, or if she lived in a rail center where the larger cattle herds were brought for transportation to market by the inevitably frolicsome cowboys who herded them. A very few actually earned enough to leave the business, buy substantial homes, and even achieve a measure of social respectability, though their reputations were always looked on as 'colorful' to say the least. But for the rest, it was one long story of run-ins

Above: *'Squirrel Tooth' Alice was one of many Dodge City good-time girls. Saloons and prostitutes followed the hard-living, fast-spending cattlemen. Both contributed fully to the city's seamy reputation.*

with the law and the higher-minded citizenry, drunken, smelly cowhands, and the occasional brute. The innocent farm boy looking for this first taste of worldly pleasure was a rarity, though it is probable that the women's lives were still not as dreary as those of their descendants a century later. They played a useful role on the fringe of frontier society, while the law took a semi-lenient attitude toward them so long as they plied their trade within proscribed limits, and the press, if at all, looked upon them in only a mildly humorous glance.[14]

Yet few should mistake the presence, even the occasional prevalence, of what some called 'sin', as meaning that the frontier West was in any way as wide open and uncivilized as popular culture have suggested. Westerners in the later years of the nineteenth century, and on through the twentieth, enjoyed projecting an image of themselves as a rip-roaring, wide-open population where 'anything goes' was the watchword. The bare fact is much different, and nowhere does it show better than in perhaps the most famous frontier town of all, Dodge City, Kansas. In 1882 one of its newspapermen struck at the heart of the matter when he declared that 'the city's rude and uncouth character is the in-

Below: *Closer to the Rockies, Denver found its early wealth in gold and silver. Prostitutes like the 'Denver Madam' Mattie Silks clearly expected to deal with a more discerning clientele.*

WESTERN WOMEN

Like the other characters of the western frontier, the adventuresome females who traveled West were no shrinking violets. While these women came from all stations in life, socialite to servant, most were tough, hard-bitten people acquainted with hardships of every kind. There were a number of whores and fortune seekers – dance hall girls in western movie parlance – but most of them were hard-working homesteaders and mothers struggling to survive in an inhospitable land. Fashions mirrored social status such as existed. Town women wore clothing more in keeping with eastern fashions; some even managed to obtain classy and expensive pieces of jewelry imported from Europe. The cameo brooch in the plate (30) came from Asprey's, London. Farm or country women more often wore coarse homemade garments or whatever was available: hardly glamorous. Extant period images depict women who would not be considered particularly attractive today.

1 White cotton blouse over brown coarse country skirt and cotton apron with decorative hem.
2 Gingham country sun bonnet.
3 Spectacles with silver wire rims.
4 Beaver fur handbag.
5 Small green and white beaded handbag.
6 Nosegay with small metal holder and decorative artificial flowers.
7 Full length white cotton nightgown.
8 Blue camisole.
9 Silver handled clothes brush and hair comb.
10 Brown muskrat fur hat.
11 Pair of beaver mittens.
12 Black cloth cloak with decorative trim.
13 Chain link handbag with metal clasp closure.
14 Pierced silver nosegay with decorative flowers.

flowers.
15 Silver handled spectacles
16 Child's white silk cap with tassel.
17 Embroidered white hat with decorative pink ribbon and two hat pins.
18 White elbow length formal gloves and black hair net.
19 Green taffeta fancy dress with decorative black trim.
20 Pink ostrich feather hand fan.

21 Pierced white fabric parasol.
22 Umbrella with carved black handle.
23 Black and brown beaded handbag.
24 Gold timepiece with silk carrying bag.
25 Diamond ring with storage case.
26 Cameo brooch with storage box.
27 Black and yellow beaded clutch purse with metal clasps.
28 Silver heart shaped locket and bracelet.

29 Silver and green beaded handbag.
30 Cameo brooch with storage box; European import.
31 Spools of thread and buttons from sewing basket.
32 Round, dyed, dried grass sewing basket with top.
33 Darning tool.
34 Sewing needles.
35 White silk, medium heel shoes.
36 Wood-handled shoe horn.

dication of a polished and established future'. 'As the homely child becomes a handsome man, so will Dodge, born of ugliness and roughness, mature in brightness and smoothness.'[15]

Certainly there could be no doubt about Dodge's rude beginnings. It started with Fort Dodge just after the Civil War, and then Dodge City itself was founded in 1872. It owed its early growth to the rising trade in buffalo hides, becoming quickly the major center for a business that was eventually to slaughter the American bison to the edge of extinction. 'Buffalo City', some called it, but as the herds dwindled to almost nothing by 1876, so the town almost died. Fortunately, the railroad had reached Dodge by then, and the abundant grasslands of western Kansas provided ample sustenance for cattle just at the time that southwestern cattlemen were looking for a newer, closer railhead to drive their herds to for marketing. Thus Dodge quickly went from Buffalo City to 'queen of the cow towns'.

Inevitably, with the still-lingering buffalo hunters and the new influx of cattlemen, Dodge became a rough and tumble town, full of men described as 'fearless as a Bayard, unsavory as a skunk'. Saloons and brothels and gambling houses followed almost instantly as this last outpost of the frontier became to some a virtual Babylon. Whiskey was the only drink sold, and it was made on the premises from casked alcohol mixed and diluted. It could be terrible, and make men mean, and some 300 barrels of it were consumed every year in the 1870s from its sixteen saloons. Across Front

Above: *Dodge City, viewed from Boot Hill, the city's overcrowded cemetery, in the 1870s. It developed considerably from this unprepossessing group of shanties but by 1885 the rowdiness had gone from it.*

Below: *Dodge's Front Street might boast brothels, saloons and dance halls but it also supplied other essentials: clothing, guns, ammunition, liquor, wine, cigars, tobacco, hardware and tinware.*

Above: *Its name probably as commonplace as Front Street in any western town, this timbered hotel stood elegantly among lower-rise stores. Brick was used far more after a destructive fire in 1885.*

Below: *Zimmermann's Hardware Store in about 1885. The name of the owner, at the right of the picture, suggests his European origins. Such stores supplied all needs, including, apparently, buggies.*

Street, on the disreputable 'south side', were the brothels like Rowdy Kate Lowe's Green Front Saloon, and the dance halls that scarcely disguised their real purpose. Inevitably drinking and prostitutes led to arguments, fights, and guns, and at the end of this chain of events came Dodge's most unenviable reputation for lawlessness.

But this period of the city's history, in fact, lasted less than a decade. It was over by 1885, and years earlier a much different sort of civilization was taking hold. Civic pride could take hold even on the raw frontier, and so could the appeal to economic survival of local farmers who saw the cow town image of Dodge and the southwestern herds making it difficult for them to sell their own livestock. Political reform came first, followed by increased attention to law and order, and step-by-step the limitations started to drive the lawless elements out to other cities instead. Saloons and brothels were occasionally closed, the local farmers assumed an ascendancy in civic affairs, and the march of Eastern culture – never entirely abandoned by westerners – stepped forward once more. A terrible fire in 1885 helped clear out some of the shanties and opened lots for newer, nicer buildings to serve a new destiny. A college was built, the number of churches came to dwarf the number of drinking halls, theaters and even an opera house opened their doors. Though the decline of the cow town era brought a general decline in economy, the town survived, and thrived in its own way, reflecting the eventual, inevitable, triumph of the kind of civilization men

BABCOCK PRINTING PRESS

Civilization of the frontier was accomplished by various means. The covered wagon, the plow, the Winchester rifle and the printing press all played an important part in the process. Newspapers did as much to induce migration west as did gold fever, and their promises were sometimes just as fleeting. By 1820 there were some 250 weekly newspapers or gazettes on what was then the frontier. Some fifteen years later, in 1835, the steam-powered press had replaced the tedious hand press and the rotary press cylinder, which came into use by 1861, really made the newspaper available in large quantities to an audience desperate for news. Rolls of newsprint replaced sheets by the close of the Civil War in 1865 and wood pulp replaced good rag paper by 1870. The public was fascinated by illustrations and photo-engraving appeared in 1873, followed by half-tone reproductions in 1880. Richard March Hoe is the man credited with many of the technological innovations which made the newspaper the mass media it is today. 'Buffalo Bill' Cody had grand aspirations for the town he founded, Cody, Wyoming. Part of his effort to develop the site was the purchase of a Babcock steam-driven printing press for the local newspaper, the *Cody Enterprise*. This machine printed the *Enterprise* and is typical of presses used throughout the West. These papers were to become the social conscience of the era and did much to shape public opinion on issues and politics.

Above: *Dodge's prosperous City Drugstore, late 1880s. Its site on the corner of 2nd Avenue and once notorious Front Street suggests the extremely simplistic topography of early American towns.*

Below: *As it grew more prosperous, any town worth its salt needed a newspaper. Such buildings as this would constitute the paper's office and generally housed the printing press.*

and women thought they had left behind, over the once-chaotic and unstructured community that first emerged on the new frontier.[16]

It was to be seen everywhere, this blossoming of culture and civilization in the prairies and mountains. In the final three decades of the century, more colleges and universities were founded west of the Mississippi than had previously existed to the east. Stimulated largely by the 1863 Morrill Act, every state obtained grants of Federal land for the erection of state universities. Indeed, such schools were commenced in places where there was not yet sufficient population to provide students, so great was the confidence in the future of the areas being settled, and almost every frontier state and territory would claim its university town as the new 'Athens of the West'.

Religion spread with even greater speed and penetration, spurred by the vital role of the church as a social center of the frontier community. Almost from the first the churches, too, contributed to the expansion of education. So too, in its way, did a flourishing press. Every town of 1,500 or more had at least one newspaper, and usually two or more, each taking different views of social and political topics of the day and engaging in spirited – and usually intemperate – debate that, while it may have done little for veracity, still stimulated the minds and emotions of the people. Censorship was unknown, and the print gave vent to every kind of opinion conceivable, absolutely unfettered.[17]

Thus the sweep across the continent that began with the wispy tracks of the wanderers and explorers, steadily grew into a more and more deeply rutted road as the opportunists came and went on their way to elusive riches, and the settlers followed in train, coming to put down their roots and stake their lives on their claims. In the short span of less than a century, the West that they had originally imagined was found, realized, conquered, and then lost to legend and myth by the coming of community. And that, after all, is what almost all of them, from prospectors to prostitutes, had wanted all along – simply a place to make a new start, and belong.

REFERENCES

1 Richard A. Bartlett, *The New Country*, pp. 151-2.
2 Carl Wittke, *Refugees of Revolution* (Philadelphia, 1952), p. 120.
3 Bartlett, *The New Country*, pp. 154-69.
4 John Mack Faragher, *Women and Men on the Overland Trail* (New Haven, Conn., 1979), pp. 16-17.
5 Bartlett, *The New Country*, pp. 171-2.
6 Faragher, *Women and Men*, pp. 36-7.
7 Craig Miner, *West of Wichita* (Lawrence, Kans., 1986), pp. 67-9.
8 Bartlett, *The New Country*, pp. 215-18.
9 Miner, *West of Wichita*, pp. 149-50.
10 *Ibid.*, p. 171.
11 *Ibid.*, pp. 92-3; Bartlett, *The New Country*, pp. 406-11.
12 Daniel Boorstin, *The Americans*, pp. 145-7.
13 Anne M. Butler, *Daughters of Joy, Sisters of Misery* (Urbana, Ill., 1985), pp. xv-xix.
14 *Ibid.*, pp. 152-3.
15 Odie Faulk, *Dodge City* (New York, 1977), p. 176.
16 *Ibid.*, pp. 180ff.
17 Boorstin, *The Americans*, pp. 153-5.

VI

CRIME & PUNISHMENT

Below: *Members of the Dalton Gang lined up in death after the failure of their bank raid in Coffeyville, Kansas, 1892.*

INEVITABLY, WHEN SOCIETY and civilization arrived in the West, there were those who could not adapt, could not live by its rules, or those who had come in the first place to escape the restrictions of the East. The West was not, as often pictured, a region teeming with lawlessness and violent crime. But there was enough of it, to be sure, and it should hardly have come as a surprise. Throughout human history, the thinly settled fringes of civilization have always attracted the nonconformists, the more adventurous, the more unscrupulous, those most likely to look upon themselves as a law unto themselves. Violence and criminal activity did not first come to the American west with the rush of immigrants who followed Lewis and Clark. For more than two centuries before, from the first Spanish settlements in the southwest, where there were men separated by long distances from the restraining influences of government and society, there was crime.

Indeed, almost from the first white movement across the Mississippi, these factors encouraged men of lawless tendencies to choose the West as the scene of their careers. An Arizona governor, writing in the midst of one of the worst uprisings of violence in western history, put his finger on the whole course of civil disturbance. 'Crime, everywhere present in our common country, is far more frequent and appalling in the Territories than elsewhere, because of the less regard generally paid to virtue and the rights of property, but more generally because of the fact that criminals – fugitives from justice – from thickly settled sections of the East, flee to the wild and unsettled portions of our Territories.'[1]

Much of it was unavoidable. The mere fact of the presence of hostile Indians and environment led to a virtually universal spread of weapons, and a mentality that looked upon the reflexive use of them as the only means of preserving life. Life was not 'cheap' in the West, but blood was shed far more easily, with

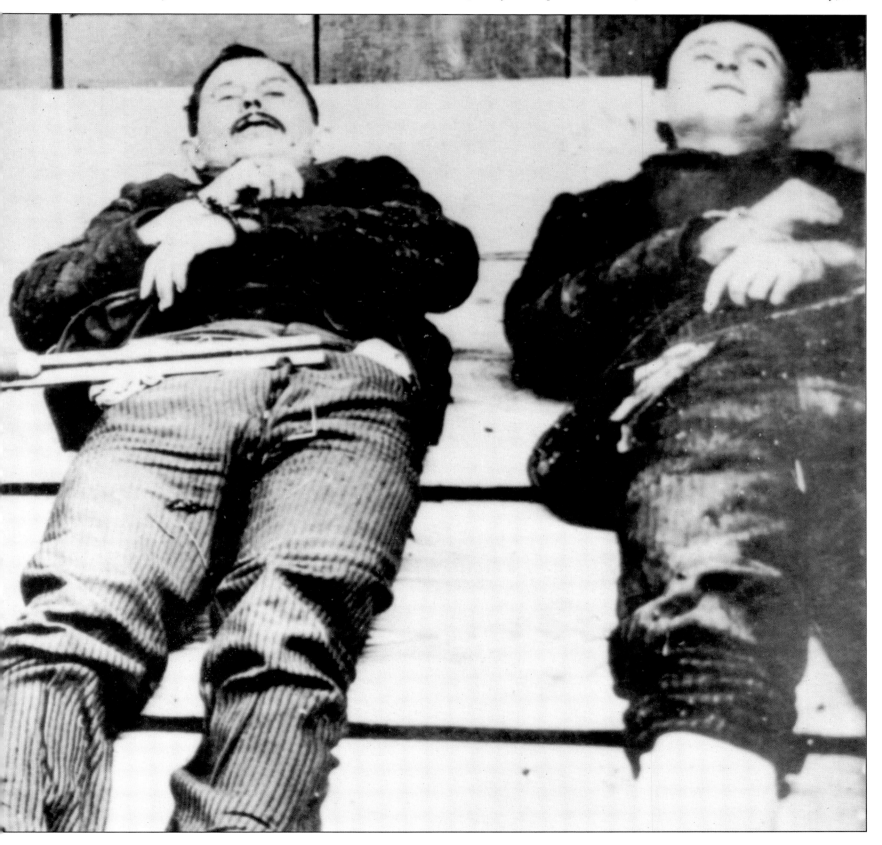

less forethought, and over seemingly lesser matters, than east of the Mississippi. The theft of food or a cow or horse was hardly a capital offense in Ohio; in Arizona or Kansas it could mean starvation, isolation, or death for the victim, and brought about punishment in kind, and swiftly when it was often the victim himself who had the only opportunity of redressing the crime.

Add to this natural situation the influx of abnormal characters who saw in the West their only haven, and what followed was inevitable. Thousands of refugees from the Civil War – draft evaders, deserters, men bitter over the loss of their homes – crossed over during and after 1865. Along with them, both before and after, came the sociopaths who simply could not function in the East. Many of these seized on the excuse of the war as a means to live out their naturally violent and often psychotic natures. Though the war brought an end to Quantrill and Todd and Anderson, it left hundreds of their henchmen looking to ply the only trade they knew.

Crime in the West took on every known hue, and went far beyond the shooting and rustling and robbing so prevalent in the popular mythology. Embezzlement was much more popular than shootouts. Petty thefts far outweighed bank robberies. On the whole, the

Right: *They were hanged with their hats on, too: another unknown unfortunate strung up, a barely acknowledged statistic in a land that, early on, was simply too enormous to police adequately.*

Below: *Much of the West was a legal and jurisdictional nightmare: transgressors met their just deserts if caught. This man's crime is not recorded; he was simply hanged from the nearest tree.*

larger eastern cities saw far more crime than the West, and much of it was more genuinely lurid and dramatic. But, as in all things, the particular romantic appeal of the West shrouded its criminality with an extra aura of violent romance.

In the average frontier community large enough to have some kind of formalized law enforcement, the overwhelming majority of all offenses were of the most petty character. Drunkenness could account for more than forty per cent of arrests, disorderly conduct another twenty, and prostitution – where it was actually outlawed – about ten per cent. In Arapahoe County, Colorado, in 1882, for instance, a total of 780 individuals breached the law sufficiently to find themselves in the county jail. Some 206 of them were petty thieves. Another 114 were accused of grand larceny, with an almost equal number, 112, of vagrancy. Assault and battery, usually as the result of drunkenness, accounted for 74, and carrying illegally concealed weapons added 26 more. 'Mischief', whatever that might entail, resulted in the doors closing on 20, with forgery and arson leading to the arrest, respectively, of 14 and 11. The crime most commonly associated with the frontier, robbery and killing, accounted for just 18 burglars and 14 accused murderers. Moreover, crimes of

Right: *Murderers, robbers, rustlers and rapists met with short shrift. Whatever his crime was, Sanford Duggan was lynched from a cottonwood tree along Cherry Creek, Denver, on 2 December 1868.*

violence against individuals seemed to occur at no greater rate than they did a century later. Of course, given the nature of courts, evidence, and other factors, probably an equal number of crimes were committed for which no one was ever arrested, or for which an arrest could not be sustained, much as in later years, so these numbers should certainly be higher to reflect the true amount of lawbreaking that actually took place.

Besides the fact that a substantial number of people carried arms as a part of their occupation, or had them available at a moment's notice, the looseness of frontier attitudes toward security also provided a tacit encouragement, especially to petty theft. Locks on doors, while not unknown, were often not used in small towns, where everyone knew everyone else, or so they thought. Banks, especially in the early days, had few if any safes, depending simply on a locked box, or even the banker's taking the deposits to his home each night. Livestock, of course, were by definition out in the open, and especially on the larger farms and ranches it was impossible to keep watch over them every hour of the day. Fencing, which came in during the 1870s and onward, could keep cattle in, but it could hardly keep a would-be thief out. With mail coaches often carrying money and valuables

Below: *Barns and livery stables might serve a different purpose from that originally intended. Four men (one is omitted from this photograph) hang from beams. The horse seems quite indifferent.*

in the packages entrusted to them, and being forced to travel long stretches of isolated trail or road between towns, they provided a tempting target as well.

For the rest, the general run of frontier crime assumed an almost banal character. Perjury, incest, contempt of court – usually by the inebriated, bearing false witness – generally the result of some petty feud, writing obscene letters, filled the dockets of every Western court. Mistreatment of the Indian, chiefly by selling him whiskey or trespassing on his land, using tribal reservation grazing for livestock, and more, accounted for a fair proportion of indictments as well. Then there were those who outraged frontier morals by bigamy, adultery, and rape. On a lonely frontier, with far more men than women, sexual offenses were sometimes even more prevalent than drunkenness.[2]

Whatever the nature of frontier crime, the people began early efforts to combat it. In the early mining camps of California and Colorado, for instance, the men met in council and agreed upon codes of conduct and appointed members of the community to see that they were observed. Usually such men received neither pay nor recognition by title, but it was a duty in the interest of all, and few refused to

so act. When genuine statute laws arrived with expanding civilization, more formal and traditional means of law enforcement appeared.

In some of the boom towns that grew so much faster than the ability of civic authorities to keep pace, impromptu interim means had to be found. San Francisco set the precedent with its police force, the first in the West, organized in July 1849. So pressed were they for facilities that an abandoned sailing brig had to be used as a jail, and within two years the extent of lawlessness in the booming city became such that the police could no longer cope. Citizens took a hand and formed two 'vigilance committees' to assume the duties abandoned by policemen who went off to the gold diggings.

Such vigilance or 'vigilante' organizations were soon found in other Western communities, especially where citizens found their officially elected or employed peace officers unequal to the task. Though often accorded a sinister connotation by rumors of lynchings and mob justice, in fact most of such committees worked within their local law and without undue violence. Indeed, they generally worked closely with their courts, leaving trial and punishment to the judges. And even where vigilantes did act as arresting agents, prosecutors, and judges, they did not

Below: *The hanging of 'Big Steve' Long at Laramie City, Wyoming, flanked by satisfied looking townspeople. Although Long warranted a nickname, most did not. They were just run-of-the-mill desperadoes.*

Right: *George Witherell tempted fate once too often. Jailed for murder in 1871, he served sixteen years of a life sentence. On his release he murdered again and was hanged in Canon City, Colorado, in 1888.*

tend to mete out heavier punishments than the courts which, in such cases, were usually too distant, corrupt, or ineffective, to be involved. In short, they operated on the periphery of the formal law enforcement establishment – when there was one – but rarely outside it. Mob rule certainly took over, from time to time, but it was invariably just that – the disorganized, spur of the moment outpouring of frustration, outrage, and crowd mentality. The vigilantes, despite very occasional excesses, were another matter entirely.[3]

Certainly the most popularized of all forms of frontier disorder was the riotous escapades of the trailman come to town after months on the range, with every thirst and hunger a man can have pent up and bursting to be sated. Especially at the railhead cow towns like Ellsworth, Hays City, and Dodge City, Kansas, the arrival of several dozen rowdy cowboys with their herds seemed to be the signal for an orgy of stampeding through town on horseback, Colts blazing, drunken brawls, saloon fights, and behavior that generally drove the peaceful citizens of the town to cover. Such events did, occasionally, occur but they were rare and in any case towns like Dodge suffered through such experiences only as long as the herds kept coming, which was usually no more than two or three years before the local grass gave out or another nearer railhead took away the business. Nevertheless, glowing tales of Wyatt Earp backing down deadly cowboys in Ellsworth, or cowing more would-be brawlers in Wichita, Kansas, continue to capture the im-

Left: *Unless you happened to be the victim, vigilante justice might be short and sweet. Citizens who resented the shortcomings of legally appointed officers often took the law into their own hands.*

Below: *The last public execution to take place in Arapahoe County, Colorado, July 1886, in the bed of Cherry Creek. This photograph shows the gallows, and the numbers a formal hanging might attract.*

THE HANDGUN

Handguns were ever present in the West and on the frontier in almost every model then in production. The most popular and probably the most common was the Colt pistol. Of all the Colts, the single-action Army revolver easily provokes instant recognition as the pistol that won the West. The handgun was a tool for protection and self-defense and was employed as such in the great majority of instances where its use became a necessity.

1 Volcanic lever action no. 1 Navy pistol.
2 Volcanic lever action No. 2, Navy pistol.
3 Colt third model dragoon revolver.
4 Colt Model 1849 pocket revolver, .31 caliber.
5 Colt Model 1855 side hammer pocket revolver, second series.
6 Colt Model 1851 Navy revolver, .36 caliber.
7 Full pack of 6 Hazard's .36 caliber cartridges.
8 Colt Model 1860 Army revolver, .44 caliber.
9 Colt Model 1862 police revolver, .36 caliber.
10 Full pack of 6 Johnson and Dow .44 caliber combustible cartridges.
11 Whitney second model Navy revolver, .36 cal.
12 Colt Model 1861 Navy revolver, factory alteration to cartridge.
13 Colt Model 1860 Army revolver, Richards alteration, .44 caliber.
14 Remington new model Army revolver, factory alteration to cartridge.
15 Starr Arms Company single-action Model 1863 Army revolver.
16 Colt single-action Army revolver, .38-40 caliber.
17 Colt single-action Army revolver, .45 caliber.
18 Full box of 20 rounds of .45 caliber ammunition.
19 Colt single-action Army revolver, .45 caliber.
20 Colt double-action Thunderer revolver.
21 Colt Model 1878 double-action Army revolver.
22 Merwin, Hulbert and Company Army revolver, early model with square butt.
23 Merwin, Hulbert and Company Army revolver, early model with bird's head butt.
24 Hopkins and Allen XL no. 8 Army revolver, .44 caliber.
25 Forehand & Wadsworth new model Army revolver.
26 Smith & Wesson model 3 single-action revolver, .44 S & W caliber.
27 S & W no. 2 Army revolver, .32 caliber.

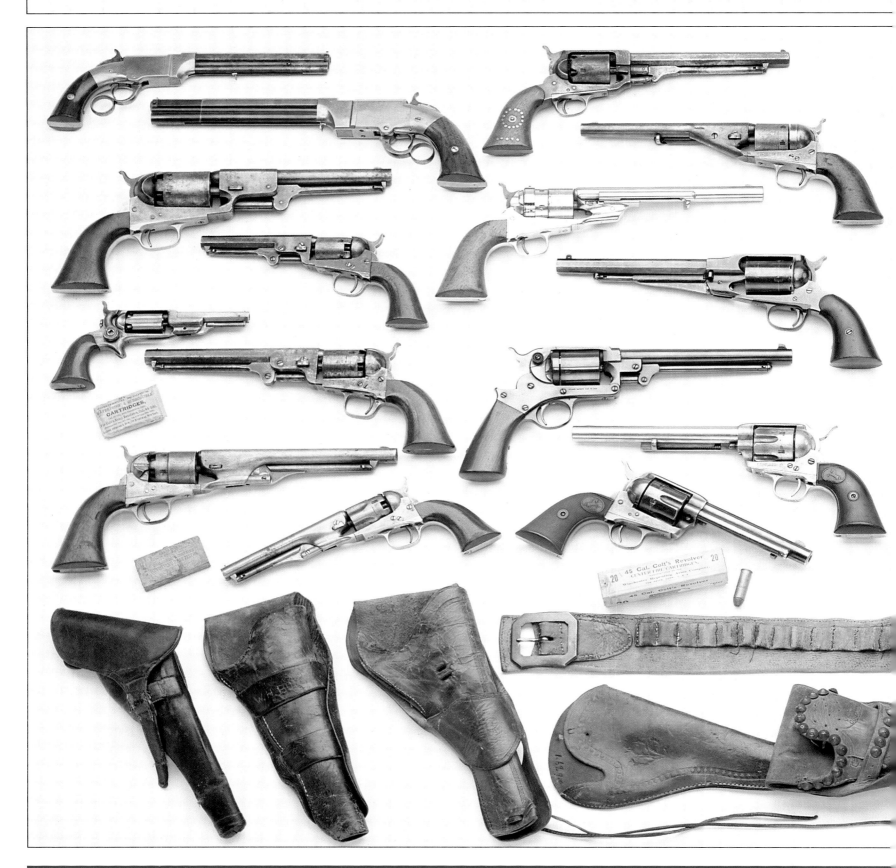

28 S & W first model American single-action revolver, .44 S & W caliber.

29 S & W double-action first model revolver.

30 Manhattan Firearms Co. pocket model revolver, .31 caliber.

31 Full box of 50 rounds .38 caliber Winchester center fire ammunition and five loose rounds of .38 caliber rimfire.

32 Deringer pocket revolver, .32 caliber.

33 Colt Cloverleaf model revolver, .41 caliber.

34 Gutta-percha holster.

35 Double-loop holster for a Colt single-action Army revolver.

36 Single-loop holster for Colt Model 1878 double-action Army revolver.

37 Embossed holster for a Colt single-action Army revolver.

38 Double-loop holster made from a military flap holster for a Colt Model 1861 Navy revolver, altered to cartridge, with belt.

39 Double-loop holster for a Colt single-action Army revolver.

40 Full box of 50 rounds of .44 cal. S & W special ammunition.

41 Military flap holster for a percussion revolver.

42 Hand-made holster with rawhide seam for a Colt single-action Army revolver.

43 Buckskin California or 'Slim Jim' open top holster for Navy size .36 caliber revolver.

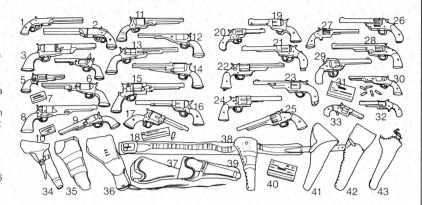

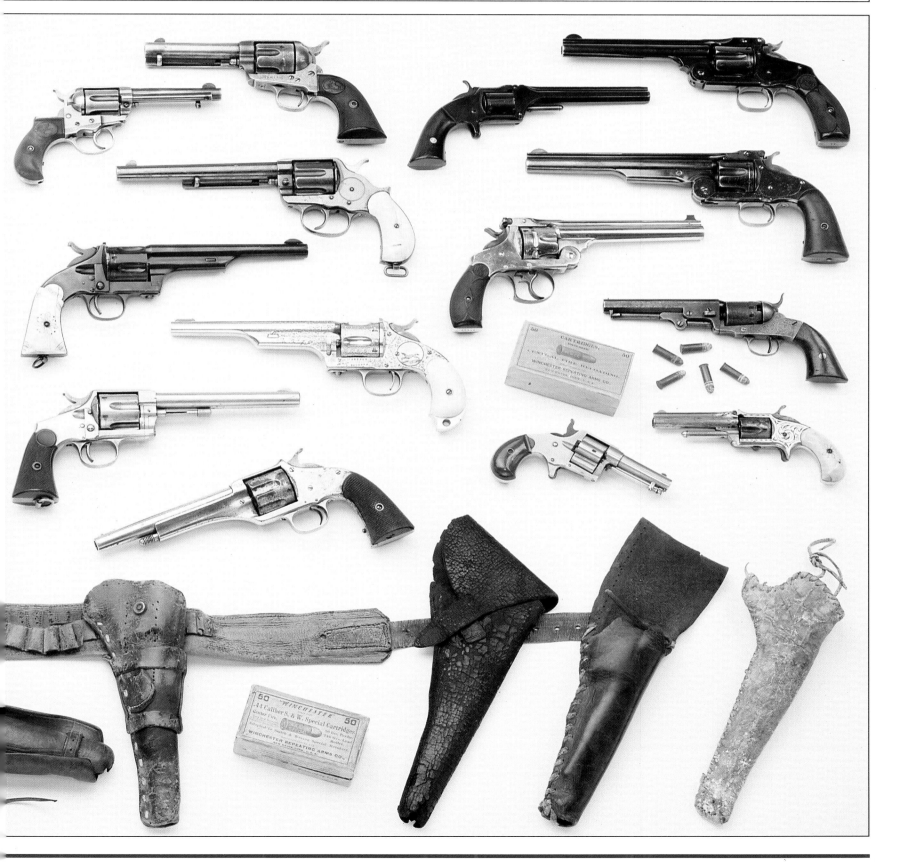

agination. The simple fact is that most of the brawling and rowdyism associated with the trailmen in town was isolated and individual. The small army of frolicking riders terrorizing a town simply never happened.

But of wicked men there were in truth plenty enough to keep the lawmen busy and the presses dripping with lurid tales of violence and daring. Dodge City had its first murder in 1872, when it was barely founded, and fourteen more ensued before its first year was out, enough so that a cemetery called Boot Hill had to be sited outside town. Most of the larger towns in Kansas, Colorado, Texas, and the southwest, experienced similar outbursts of lawlessness in their early years.[4]

However, the first of the sensational crime in the West came at its eastern fringe, in Missouri. It was here that Frank and Jesse James, and their cousins the Youngers, continued the life of robbery and killing begun with Quantrill during the Civil War. Interestingly, too, these early outlaws enjoyed a small measure of support from elements of the local citizenry, for their depredations – it was claimed – merely avenged the wrongs done to Southern sympathizers by the Yankees during the war. The James brothers and their small gang of miscreants preyed only on Yankee bankers, Yankee mails, and later Yankee trains, even being ascribed a kind of Robin Hood status with claims that they shared the proceeds of their robberies with their downtrodden friends and families.

The truth was a far different matter. Jesse James, at least, bore evidence of psychopathic

Above: *At the age of twenty-two, Jesse James was already a seasoned thug, having ridden with Quantrill toward the end of the Civil War. The Jameses later joined forces with their cousins, the Youngers.*

Below: *The James Farm, Kearney, Missouri, 1877, birthplace of Frank and Jesse James and the haven to which they retreated after their exploits in the Civil War – and after numerous bank jobs.*

Above: *Frank, Jesse's older brother, had taken part in the guerrilla raid on Lawrence, Kansas, in 1863. Surviving his sibling into old age, he later charged tourists 50 cents a time to visit the James Farm.*

tendencies, probably exaggerated by a morphine addiction. His brother Frank may have been at best simple minded, and deferred continually to his younger sibling, while those who rode with them were a sorry lot of society's losers and misfits. Their takings were rarely large, and did not last long, most of it squandered on liquor and women, and precious little, if any, ever finding its way to the hands of needy friends. After a 'job', they simply went back home or melted into the rural fastnesses they had used when with Quantrill, emerging again for another robbery when the money ran out or the thirst for another taste of the old days grew too strong. The Youngers seem to have been a cut above, more intelligent, less prone to gratuitous violence. But Jesse James would kill just for the fun of it, even when shooting down an inoffensive and unarmed bank teller. After almost two decades of intermittent outlawry, he was shot down in his home in St Joseph, Missouri, by one with whom he was acquainted. As befits the character of the victim and the men he led, James was shot in the back. His brother Frank later spent some time in the Jackson County jail, and then lived as a small sort of local hero and object of curiosity for years afterward. Their cousins the Youngers, meanwhile, suffered tragedy in one of Jesse's schemes for robbing two banks at once in Northfield, Minnesota. The townspeople fought back for a change, killing one Younger, wounding and capturing two others. One eventually took his own life, while Cole Younger lived through more than twenty

Above: *Jesse James, son of a Baptist minister, was shot dead by Bob Ford at his home in St Joseph, Missouri, on 3 April 1882. By this time, James was living under the pseudonym Howard.*

Above: *Bob Ford was an acquaintance of Jesse James and his guest when the killing took place. At first sentenced to death, then pardoned, Ford himself was shot dead by a James partisan years later.*

Above: *Cole Younger and his brothers joined the James gang in the murderous fiasco at Northfield, Minn., in 1876. Given a life sentence for his exploits, he later became a successful lecturer.*

years of imprisonment to become a lecturer on his release. In the flight from the debacle, the James brothers had simply abandoned the Youngers. So much for honor among thieves, even those tied by blood.

Spurred by the early example set by the Jameses and Youngers, a number of other outlaw gangs began depredations, though none were quite as effective at generating a legend of glamor and almost legitimacy. Operating in bands of five to ten or more had a certain logic to it. A lone gunman or two might not be sufficient to intimidate the bank guard or store-keeper, especially when each probably had a firearm near at hand. But three or four would be far more imposing a threat and deterrent to citizen heroics. Moreover, as banks became a prime target, it meant that robberies had to take place right in the middle of town. That needed three or four inside doing the job, while one or two others held the horses and kept a watchful eye out for police. Several of the gangs also followed the James-Younger lead by being family affairs. The five Daltons operated in Kansas and Nebraska. The two Reno brothers robbed farther west. The Clantons hovered on the fringes of the law in Arizona. Almost to a man they met violent ends. Not one of the Clantons lived to die of old age. One Reno was shot and the other lynched. Two of the Dalton brothers were killed on a single robbery attempt, and only the youngest, Emmett, lived to become an old man. Whatever there might have been of romance and adventure in their early expectations, when these men went into the profession they found it a seedy, unglamorous, inevitably dangerous, and eventually deadly pursuit with little economic compensation, and even less life-expectancy.

In areas particularly remote from established law enforcement, virtual outlaw communities could arise. The southwest saw a small society emerge in Arizona and New Mexico involving not only the Clantons, but also more than a dozen other gunmen and robbers who alternately drifted into and out of the main area of operations, depending on where the pickings were best, where a few cattle might be stolen, a mail coach robbed, and so on. Johnny Ringo, 'Curly Bill' Brocius, and as many as twenty or thirty others worked as satellites around the Clanton nucleus. In the Indian Territory, bands of white renegades lived in uneasy harmony with resentful native Americans, preying on Mexicans across the border, and cattle herders to the north. Such 'Comancheros', as they were called, rarely risked entering established civilization.[5]

Perhaps the best known of such outlaw societies was the notorious but ironically named Wild Bunch, who operated largely in Wyoming and the north central West. Led by colorful figures William 'Butch' Cassidy and Harry 'Sundance Kid' Longbaugh, they brought a far greater element of dash and romance to their 'trade', along with a considerably lesser degree of resort to violence. While twentieth-century novels and films have portrayed them as lovable, happy-go-lucky outlaws plying their craft with almost adolescent innocence and enthusiasm, the fact is that they were among the most wanted and hunted of all Western miscreants.

Above: *Bill Brazelton robbed a number of stagecoaches in Arizona Territory during 1878-9. Killed by a posse while being arrested, he was displayed in death still wearing his highwayman's mask.*

Above: *Men like Bill Cook easily found places in the Who's Who of petty outlaws. Orphaned at fourteen, a whiskey pedlar and train robber, he died of consumption in prison in New York in 1900.*

Above: *Dead outlaws were photographed in semi-lifelike poses for various reasons – often as a memento for the arresting lawman, more generally as grim warning to the fate of other would-be transgressors.*

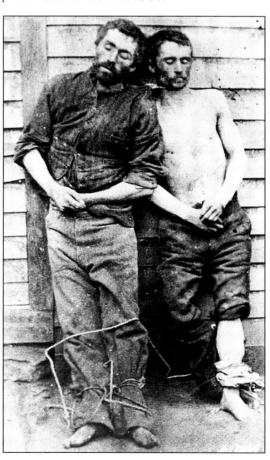

Above: *The brothers Sam and Billy LeRoy had various aliases, none of which could prevent them from being hanged together, for stagecoach robbery, in a Colorado railroad depot in 1881.*

THE GUNFIGHTER

The natural habitat of the gunfighter was the frontier town and, with the line between bad men and good often blurred, they were not always outside the law. Coming from diverse backgrounds (Billy the Kid originally from the slums of New York, while Jesse James was a preacher's son from Missouri), they had one ambition in common – to survive. There was little to admire in this breed of killer and many, such as Wild Bill Hickok, were notorious liars, their distorted reputations instilling fear whenever they rode into town. This man, well armed, carries a Parker shotgun and the equally deadly Peacemaker .45 sidearm housed in a Slim Jim holster.

It may have stemmed in part from their degree of specialization. Most gangs and individual criminals did gravitate toward whatever form of crime suited them best. The Clantons were primarily cattle rustlers. The James-Younger crowd went after banks, though they also brought off the country's first daylight train robbery. The Hole-in-the-Wall gang joined up with the Wild Bunch in 1897 and went after trains with a vengeance, and that earned them the enmity of the Union Pacific, which could afford to hire the best detectives. Stagecoaches, the perennial target of motion picture robbers, suffered very little, and chiefly only in the southwest and California. One colorful, if inept, west coast bandit calling himself Black Bart, picked exclusively on stage coaches. Clearly no run-of-the-mill bandit, he was apparently settling old scores by his actions, for he left behind bits of doggerel complaining of his injustices suffered at the hands of California's establishment, ending with: 'on my corns too long you've tread, you fair-haired sons of bitches.' He got fame for his alliterative name, and a long prison term for his inept robberies.

Above: *As railroad companies offered more stubborn resistance, outlaws like Butch Cassidy used stronger methods. In 1899 the express car of the Overland Flyer was dynamited for the $30,000 it contained.*

Below: *Taking umbrage at the attention given them by the Wild Bunch, the Union Pacific appointed, from left to right (mounted), Messrs Hiatt, Kelliher, Lefors, Davis, Funk, Carr to track them down.*

Above: *Black Bart picked on stagecoaches, those of Wells Fargo in particular, in the late 1870s. Identified as a citizen of the city of San Francisco, he was finally tracked down with the help of a laundry mark.*

Above: *Annie Rogers and Harvey Logan, in a studio photograph. Otherwise known as 'Kid Curry', Logan's Hole-in-the-Wall gang joined up with Butch Cassidy in Utah to form a formidable outlaw band.*

Far more than easterners realized, frontier crime was often wrapped up in more than just mindless outlawry and thieving. It often had intricate political undercurrents behind it, social tensions, and most often of all, economic origins. Nothing illustrates this better than the celebrated Lincoln County War in New Mexico Territory in 1878-9. Its beginnings traced back to two men, one English, one a Scot. John Henry Tunstall arrived in New Mexico in 1876, aged a tender twenty-four, bent on becoming a cattle rancher. His antagonist was lawyer Alexander A. McSween, ten years older than Tunstall. The two were passingly friendly acquaintances at first, and discussed the prospects for land purchased in Lincoln County, not far from Santa Fe. The former was intensely ambitious to make his fortune, the latter a slightly unscrupulous man with a shadowy past.

Tunstall followed McSween's advice and bought in Lincoln County. The county seat, the town of Lincoln, was largely dominated by one overbearing merchant, Lawrence G. Murphy, who owned the main store, and much of the business in the county. The army gave him its contract for beef purchasing, as well as other contracts for agricultural products for nearby Indian reservations. The man was an undisguised bully and cheat, who padded his bills to the government, purchased stolen cattle at cut rate prices for resale, and in the end virtually controlled all manner of farm prices, thus making most of the surrounding settlers in some degree dependent upon his favor. Few dared to cross Lawrence G. Murphy. At his side he often kept the hard-drinking young hothead James J. Dolan, who had no hesitation about using his sidearm.

When Tunstall settled in Lincoln County, he had no intention of bowing to Murphy's rule, in part perhaps because of the natural antipathy of an Englishman for an Irishman. Tunstall formed a small confederacy with McSween, the latter opening influential doors and making introductions, providing Tunstall with vital information, to work around Murphy and find a route to the coveted contracts. Tunstall also attached to his side a few young men of gamecock natures and handy gun hands. The first was Dick Brewer. More would follow.[6]

Tension mounted as Tunstall opened a store of his own in Lincoln, just as Murphy's own enterprises were starting to dissolve thanks to his corruption being suspected in Santa Fe and Washington. Then Tunstall started the Lincoln County Bank, and obtained the business of some of New Mexico's leading citizens. It was too much for Murphy, who decided to leave business, and sold out to Dolan, whom Tunstall would describe, along with his associates, as 'men who need killing very badly'.

But it was the Dolan mob who started the killing. Cocky thanks to the knowledge that the sheriff was an ally, Dolan and a small gang of erstwhile cowboys and rustlers locally called 'the Boys' decided to challenge Tunstall. They stole some of his horses and mules right in front of Brewer, who responded by raising a gang of his own and tracking down the offenders. Shots were exchanged, though no one was hurt, and the horses were recovered. Shortly the sheriff conveniently allowed the rustlers to escape. Soon Tunstall and Dolan almost came to a shoot out themselves, and then each began to augment his staff of gun hands. It required only a spark to ignite a war between two increasingly armed camps, and Dolan provided that on 18 February 1878, when he had Tunstall murdered.

Thus commenced the Lincoln County War. Within hours nearly fifty gunmen were waiting for McSween to decide the next move. He tried legal writs, but the gunmen soon took matters in a direction more to their liking. Two separate and unlawful posses started combing the country for Tunstall's killers. McSween's henchmen became known as the 'Regulators', and before long one of Tunstall's assassins was taken, and quickly killed in mysterious circumstances. Sheriff William Brady threatened to arrest McSween himself, and to prevent that six of the Regulators hid behind a low adobe wall on the morning of 1 April. When Brady walked past, all six rose up and blasted away with rifles and pistols. Brady and a deputy were killed. When two of the Regulators tried to get the arrest warrant from Brady's pocket, other deputies opened fire, wounding two, but the ambushers all escaped to safety.

Two weeks later a party of Regulators including Brewer had a shootout with one of Dolan's people outside town, leaving both the victim and Brewer dead in the dust. Tempers rose in the territory to a fever pitch, and one observer aptly captured the atmosphere. 'They all wanted to kill somebody,' he said. 'Every son-of-a-bitch over there wanted to kill somebody.'

Most of them got the chance. There were more battles between the Boys and the Regulators, who now rode about the county with no goal in sight other than to catch some of their opponents at a disadvantage and get the drop on them. McSween beat the charges against him and was a free man. Soon the local military, the territorial governor, and even

Right: *The eponymously named Blazer's Mill, seen here in 1884, belonged to an Iowa dentist named Joseph Blazer. It was the scene of a shootout between McSween's Regulators and one Buckshot Rogers.*

Above: *John H. Tunstall, an Englishman, tried to oppose the business monopoly imposed on Lincoln County by Lawrence Murphy. After Murphy withdrew, Tunstall was murdered by one of his hired guns.*

Above: *Alexander McSween had initially advised Tunstall. Unwilling to sidestep the violence begun by Tunstall's death, he was himself murdered, running from his burning home into a hail of bullets.*

Above: *In April 1876 Sheriff William Brady was gunned down in Lincoln's main street. A victim of the Regulators, his death escalated the war and brought Billy the Kid a conviction for his murder.*

Above: *Cattle man John Chisum recommended Pat Garrett to Governor Lew Wallace as the man who might bring law and order to Lincoln County. Billy the Kid bore Chisum a grudge, apparently for wages unpaid.*

President Rutherford B. Hays, had been brought into the squabble. Then Dolan managed to select the new sheriff, who immediately went after the Regulators with warrants, and unauthorized posses composed chiefly of the Boys and several outright outlaws. They scoured the county for McSween's men, virtually sacked the small town of San Patricio, and skirmished several times without taking any prisoners or taking more lives. In response McSween collected an army of his own, numbering over fifty. At last the non-violent lawyer rode at the head of his band and led them into Lincoln on 14 July and fortified themselves in his house. Down the street Dolan and his men waited in the old Murphy store. When the first shot rang out that evening, it commenced a sporadic gunfight that would last for five days, and not end before an Army detachment arrived. Soon afterward some of the Boys set fire to the McSween home, and in a desperate attempt to escape after nightfall, many of them slipped off into the darkness. McSween could not, and when he yelled outside about surrendering, 'deputies' approached. McSween and a few others showed themselves, and were cut down in a hail of bullets.

For almost a year after the McSween fight, the two sides continued bushwhacking and stalking one another, often with the nominal leaders like Dolan no longer exercising real control, and even the military powerless to contain the bloodletting. Worse, Lincoln County now became a haven for outlaws from other regions like Texas, who heard of the reign of lawlessness and recognized a place where they might flourish. Murder, torture, rape, theft and plunder, even in Lincoln itself, became commonplace. The county had descended into virtual anarchy.[7]

It was in this atmosphere of chaos that one of the original Boys, who later became an ardent adherent of Tunstall's, emerged as a symbol, and started a legend. William Bonney came out of a past shrouded in mystery. He was born Henry McCarty in the Irish slums of New York sometime in 1859. When his widowed mother remarried to a William H. Antrim in Santa Fe in 1873, young Henry soon adopted his step-father's surname, and soon thereafter fell in with the proverbial bad companions. He stole butter when he was fifteen. A year later he stole clothing from a Chinese laundry. Brought before the local sheriff, he displayed the innate charm that endeared him to many who came to know him, by persuading the lawman to let him have the freedom of a hallway outside his cell. Minutes later he had climbed up a chimney and escaped. He never went home again. He had six years to live.[8]

Antrim turned up again two years later, after a forgettable career as a petty thief, stealing a horse now and then, occasionally holding a regular job on a ranch. He was arrested at least three times, and all three occasions saw him make an escape. By the time he was seventeen he was carrying a revolver in his trouser pocket, and on 17 August 1877 he got in a fight with a local blowhard in Arizona and shot him in the stomach. When brought before a coroner's jury, it decided that 'Henry Antrim alias Kid' should be indicted and tried. The boy who bore that nickname 'Kid' decided not

to wait, and escaped once again, bound for New Mexico.

He was short, slender, with a boyish grin and disarming manners that belied his poverty-stricken background. Unlike most frontier toughs, he read fluently, loved all sorts of music, spoke passable Spanish, and revealed a sparkling wit. Yet he was also restless, undisciplined, hot-tempered, and apparently completely untroubled by matters of law. That is not to say that he had no ethics, for most of the gunmen lived by a loose code of sorts, one that decried murder unless in retribution for an equal act, one that forbade rape, even of Mexican and Indian women. Besides, no one seeing his winning blue eyes and affable nature could imagine him committing such crimes. But then few would have expected him to be capable of what he actually did do, either.

By the fall of 1877 Antrim had joined one of New Mexico's more feared outlaw gangs, the Boys. And shortly he rode under a new name, William H. Bonney, an alias whose origin is entirely lost to history. He was Billy Bonney, or just 'the Kid'. Alias and nickname had not yet combined to produce 'Billy the Kid'.

And thus he rode into the Lincoln County War. Running with friends like Brewer, Charlie Bowdre, 'Doc' Scurlock, Billy soon joined Tunstall's following, though he probably never had a chance to become as lovingly fond of the Englishman as legend has attested. Nevertheless, when Tunstall was murdered, the Kid took a blood oath to 'get some of them before I die'. It was the kind of youthful bravado that many a nineteen-year-old might exhibit. But Billy Bonney meant it. As one of the Regulators, he participated in the mysterious death of some of the Tunstall assassins. He was one of the six who leapt up from behind the wall to murder Sheriff Brady, taking a wound himself. He was one of the daring ones who made it to safety from the flaming McSween home. Thereafter his exploits made him a leader among the Regulators, though for some time they contented themselves with stealing horses and cattle, and holing up at Fort Sumner, where the Kid took to courting local girls, white and Mexican.

Some months later, tired of the intermittent fighting, the Kid sent a peace feeler to Dolan, and the two and their followers met to negotiate. A party ensued, and a man was killed by Dolan and his men. Billy left immediately, and soon afterward offered to turn himself in and testify against Dolan, in return for pardon for his earlier crimes. In fact, he actually met with the territorial governor, General Lew 'Ben Hur' Wallace, and the deal was made. Dolan was never convicted however, and Billy soon returned to his old ways as a rustler. The sputtering out of the Lincoln County War left him largely isolated, without purpose. He got into more trouble, another fatal shooting, and by late 1880 a newspaperman had inadvertently called him 'Billy the Kid'. Before long even the Kid's native New York was reading stories of

Left: *One of the few people to 'shoot' Billy the Kid and survive was a wandering photographer at Fort Sumner in 1879 or 1880. This tintype correctly shows that he* was *not the left-handed gun.*

the exploits of the boy-killer who was the acknowledged leader of legions of outlaws. The legend was on its way.

Meanwhile the reality had less than a year to live, but he would take more with him before he died. With his notoriety came rewards for his capture, up to $500, and the new man charged with bringing him in, Pat Garrett, was good at his job. He almost got him one time, and lost him in a round of gunfire. But two nights before Christmas, Garrett cornered Billy and four others. Charlie Bowdre was killed, but the rest surrendered. Billy was brought to trial for one of the killings in the Lincoln County War, convicted, and sentenced to be hanged in April 1881. Two weeks later he broke out again, and for the last time, killing two deputies in the process, at least one of them a cold murder. Garrett went after him, tracing him to his old haunts at Fort Sumner. There on the night of 14 July 1881, Garrett was waiting in a darkened bedroom when the Kid walked in, sensed a presence, and said in Spanish, 'Quien es? Quien es?' Garrett answered with two shots, and one struck the Kid over the heart, killing him instantly. He was just twenty-one.[9]

He had lived and died by the gun. Indeed, it was the prevalence of firearms, and the general proficiency and willingness to use them, that made young men like Billy so terrible, so much a threat to the frontier community that in places like Lincoln County they could reduce civil order to a shambles. In the Kid's case, his guns of choice were the Winchester 1873 carbine, and a Colt 'Thunderer' .41 caliber double-action revolver. Indeed, those two names, Colt and Winchester, would echo again and again when old-timers talked of the 'helldorado' days of outlaws and the men who tracked them down.[10]

The Colt came west first, chiefly in the same models used in the Civil War, the .36 caliber Model 1851 'Navy' revolver, and the more deadly .44 Model 1860 'Army'. Both were cap and ball firearms, meaning that the six chambers had to be loaded separately with powder and ball, sometimes contained in a single paper wrapped 'cartridge', and then shoved home by a rammer built in below the barrel. Copper percussion caps placed on nipples at the back of the cylinder did the rest. They were single-action weapons, meaning that the trigger performed only one function when pulled. It fired the weapon. The hammer had to be cocked back with the thumb first, turning the cylinder to the next live round in the process. When brass bound rimfire cartridges were developed, many of these cap and ball pieces were 'converted' to use the new ammunition, making for faster loading, but no enhancement of speed in firing.

The so-called 'Peacemaker' came along in 1873, a slightly smaller, more sturdy and refined version of the Colt, built for the new metallic cartridges. It quickly came to dominate Western handguns as the firearm of choice. Offered first in .45 caliber with a

Right: Pat Garrett caught up with the Kid on 14 July 1881 at Old Fort Sumner, putting two bullets into his body in a darkened bedroom. Billy the Kid's death turned him into a folk hero and a legend.

LEVER ACTION LONGARMS

The name Winchester is synonymous with the Wild West, the American frontier and all the romance that Hollywood and generations of writers have attached to it. Less apparent is the growth of an American corporation and the great design and machine shop people that created these legends of iron and wood. The company can be traced back to 1848 but Oliver Winchester did not appear until 1855. The Winchester Repeating Arms Company actually began in 1866 and continued on into the second half of the 20th century. By no coincidence the Winchester firm concentrated their efforts on longarm development and production, leaving the Colt almost unchallenged in the handgun field, a convenient and lucrative business arrangement. The most popular caliber was the .44-40 which was also available in the popular Colt single-action handgun, allowing the same ammunition for use in both arms. Antique Winchester rifles and shotguns are today highly collectable.

1 Volcanic lever action repeating carbine with detachable butt stock. .41 caliber.
2 Box of self-contained cartridges for Volcanic firearms with three rounds.
3 Cleaning rod, very rare, for a Volcanic.
4 Fifty round box of cartridges for Henry repeating rifle.
5 Early iron frame Henry rifle, .44 caliber rimfire.
6 .44 caliber flat nose rimfire cartridges for Henry rifle.
7 Later fifty round box of .44 Henry cartridges.
8 Brass framed Henry rifle, as 5, above.
9 Metal and wood cleaning rod variations encountered with Henry rifles.
10 As 9.
11 Winchester Model 1866 repeating rifle. The brass frame is retained but King's patent loading port

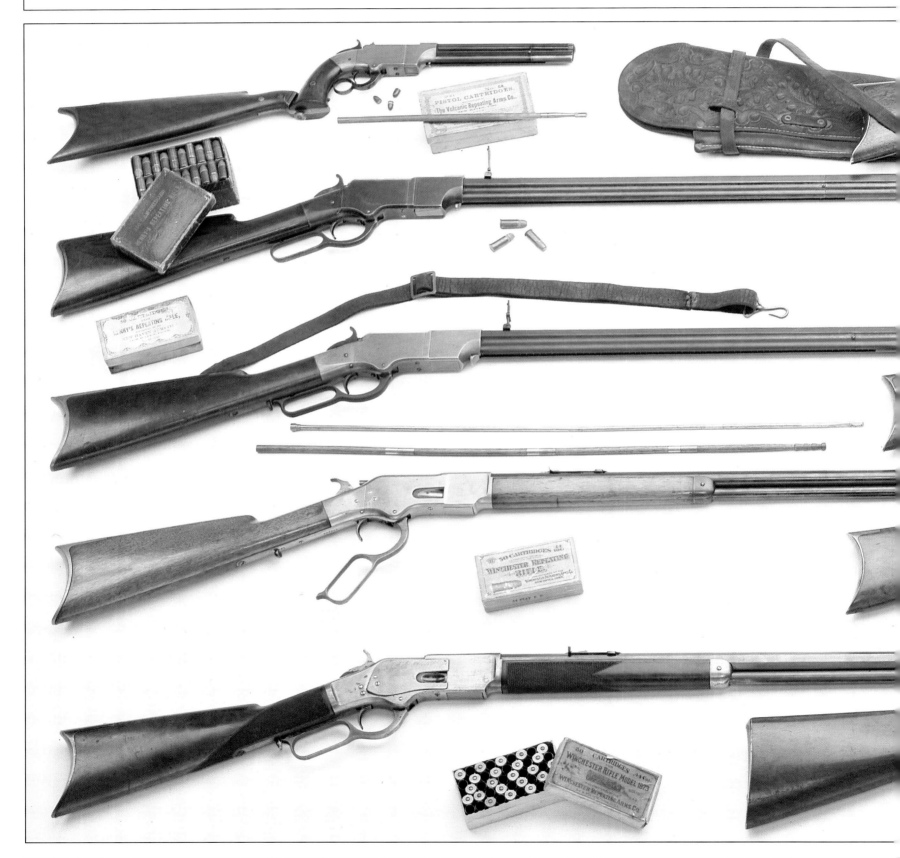

is obvious on right side of the arm.

12 Fifty round box of ammunition for above rifle.

13 Winchester Model 1873 octagonal barrel rifle, most popular model in the West.

14 Fifty round box of .44-40 caliber ammunition for above rifle.

15 Leather saddle scabbard for a long barreled rifle.

16 Winchester Model 1876

octagonal barrel rifle.

17 .45-60 caliber round for above rifle.

18 Winchester Model 1886 rifle with shotgun style butt.

19 Twenty round box of ammunition for above rifle in ever popular .44-40 caliber.

20 Winchester Model 1894 round barrel rifle.

21 Winchester Model 1895 rifle with tang rear sight.

22 .45 Winchester round

for above rifle.

23 Leather ammunition belt with nickel buckle for heavy caliber ammunition.

24 Winchester Model 1887 experimental takedown shotgun. Its quickly detachable barrel assembly did not go into general production.

25 Twelve-gauge shotgun shell for Winchester lever action repeating shotgun.

26 Mills patent shot cartridge belt.

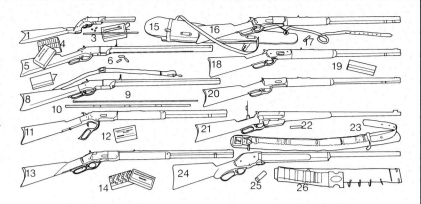

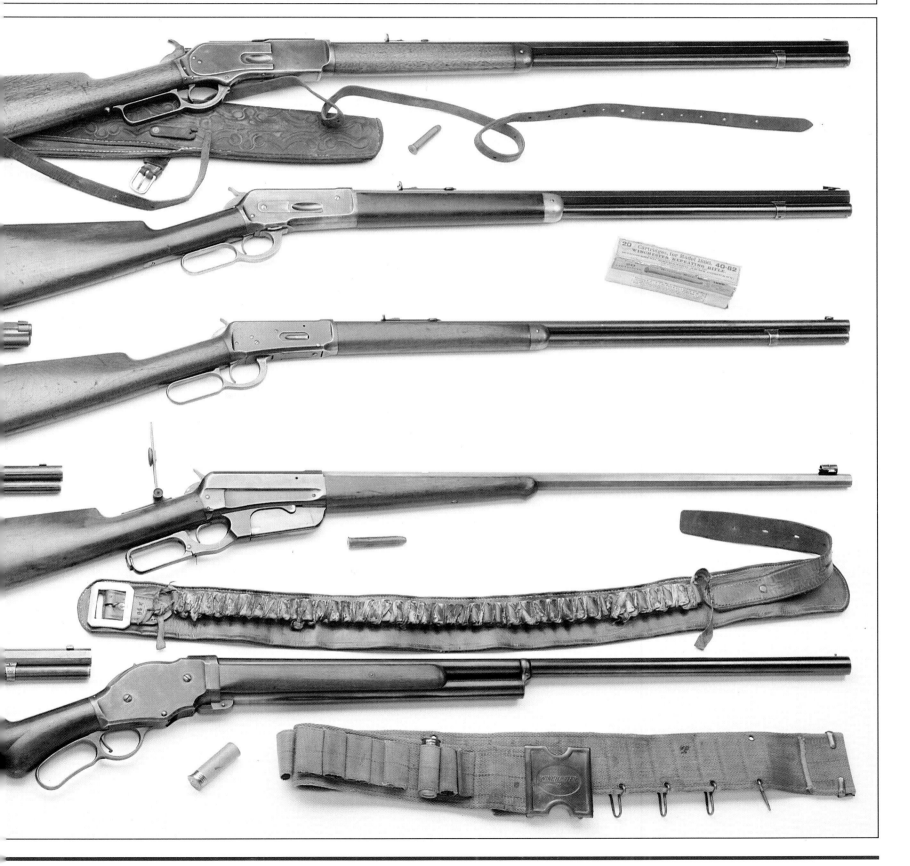

7½-inch barrel, it was later issued in a variety of bores and barrel lengths. So popular was it that the model never went out of production. It was still a single-action weapon, like its predecessors, but then Colt introduced the 'Thunderer' in .41 caliber, and the .38 caliber 'Lightning', both double-action revolvers. This new refinement allowed for greatly increased speed in firing, for the simple pulling of the trigger rotated the cylinder, cocked the hammer, and then fired the piece. The only disadvantage was that the greater pressure necessary on the trigger to perform all those tasks could lead to a shaky aim, but since most men never fired their pistols at something more than a few feet away, precision of aim lost some of its importance.

For accuracy and distance, men who carried guns preferred rifles. A host of them came west after the Civil War, many sold as war surplus. Single-shot breechloaders like the Sharps rifle came in calibers up to .50 and packed such a huge killing force that it became the preferred buffalo gun. Then in 1873 two new developments came into Westerners' hands. The Army adopted the new Model 1873 Springfield 'trap door' rifle, the first official U.S. Infantry arm to use metallic cartridges. A

door on the top of the breech end of the barrel hinged upwards, allowing the bullet to be laid into place. It was single shot, but still could be loaded and fired with considerable speed. Custer's men carried carbine versions at the Little Bighorn, and within a few years of introduction, many were in private hands. Using the massive .45-70 cartridge – a .45 caliber bullet driven by seventy grains of black powder – it briefly replaced the Sharps in the buffalo trade.

But then the Winchester Repeating Arms Company outdid them all. Its precursor, the Henry firm, had made repeating rifles in limited quantities for the military during the war. But now in 1873 it introduced its new Winchester '73, soon to be known as 'the gun that won the West'. It could fire up to fifteen .44 caliber cartridges as fast as the user could jerk a lever beneath the stock down and back up again, pulling the trigger each time. It was simple, durable, powerful, and accurate. Three years later Winchester brought out the Model 1876, basically the same gun, but chambered for the massive .45-70 load, just in time to attract the dwindling attention of buffalo hunters as the herds started finally to die out on the plains.

Below: *Women, as well as men, turned to crime. Pearl Hart earned her place in history as the last stagecoach bandit. In 1899 she held up the stagecoach to Globe and got away, for a short time, with $430.*

Above: *Recorded for posterity. The same Pearl Hart in different guise. This, and the photograph below left, was taken during her shortened five-year sentence in an Arizona prison for the crime.*

Below: *Jennie Metcalf, or the Rose of the Cimarron, was supposedly a member of the Doolin gang which had its hideout on the Cimarron River, not far from Guthrie, in lawless Oklahoma Territory.*

Of course, literally scores of other weapons were carried on the plains and in the deserts. Pistols by Smith and Wesson, Remington, and others, shared space in the outlaws' gear with shotguns, sporting rifles, and old military long-arms of all descriptions. Peaceable citizens used the same weapons as well, though more often owning just a game rifle than a pistol, while law-abiding cowboys usually carried only the handgun, having little need for a rifle except in dangerous times. But the Colts and the Winchesters earned their pre-eminent place in the pantheon of vital tools of the West by becoming the weapons of choice for bad men and good.

And there were good men using them, too, not just the Jameses and Daltons, the 'Curly' Bills and the Billy the Kids. Keeping the peace required a force of staggering size, with perhaps as many as 25,000 men serving in some such capacity during the nineteenth century in the West. Few of them were lifetime professionals; most drifted in to and out of law enforcement as circumstances and opportunity commanded. A few worked both sides of the law, like Tom Horn, one-time lawman later hanged for assassination. Furthermore, the peace was not just maintained by the local

Right: *Tom Horn came to Wyoming in 1894 with a reputation for liquidating cattle thieves. Employed by the big stockmen in the state, he continued to ply his trade until he made an uncharacteristic slip.*

sheriffs and marshals. Private detectives and guards, railroad guards, local, county, and state rangers, and more, all contributed something to the colorful mix of 'lawmen' – and ladies, it should be noted, for at least one community had a 'Lady Deputy Sheriff'.[11]

Many were appointed, especially the deputies. The sheriffs were elected either by town councils or popular ballot, though in all categories political influence and cronyism often entered into the selection. If a man had a good record in the Civil War, it was often considered an excellent qualification. Men were hired because they had a reputation for being tough, fair-minded, brave, good with a gun. The best were smart, fearless, and honest. Ironically, only a few of the best known lived up to all three requirements.

Local authorities told the peace officer what he could and could not do. Almost every lawman was empowered to carry a weapon. But few were given sanction to use it without specific provocation. Moreover, powers of search and seizure were usually severely limited, and governed by the courts and councils. The titles given the lawmen varied according to choice. In some towns they were constables, in others policemen. The man in charge could be either,

Below: *Horn's fatal error was to kill a fourteen-year-old boy; in his cups, he confessed to it. Unlike many of his kind – paid murderers – he did not escape the gallows, hanging in Cheyenne in 1903.*

LESSER KNOWN FIREARMS

'Westerners' arsenals usually boasted at least one cheap shotgun and pistols and rifles made by a host of little known firms.' Colt and Winchester remain household names in the West, but firms such as Remington, Roper and Marlin manufactured comparable weapons that found a ready market out West. Their names may be forgotten by all but collectors, but their products proved just as lethal and effective as those of better-known competitors.

1 Colt Lightning large frame slide action rifle, competitor of the lever action Winchester and Marlin arms, but never as popular.
2 Two .50-95 express caliber cartridges for the above rifle, the largest caliber available for this model.
3 Remington long range Creedmore rifle, once the property of General Custer and one of the finest Remington arms ever made. .44-100 caliber.
4 Mills patent type fabric cartridge belt with nickeled Winchester belt plate.
5 Marlin Model 1881 lever action rifle with half magazine and octagonal barrel. Capable of handling large caliber ammunition, it was a serious competitor of the Winchester Model 1886 arms.
6 Box of .45-70 caliber cartridges of type used by the above rifle, a favorite caliber of hunters and soldiers.
7 Colt Model 1855 half stock percussion sporting rifle, made 1857-64. Revolving cylinder longarms were never entirely successful, always prone to mechanical failure.
8 Six round packet of .44 caliber combustible cartridges for the above firearm.
9 Remington-Keene magazine bolt action rifle. Popular with frontiersmen and issued by the U.S. Dept of the Interior to arm Indian police.
10 Twenty round pack of .45-70 caliber cartridges made at Frankfort Arsenal, Philadelphia.
11 Sharps Model 1874

sporting rifle with part octagonal and part round barrel, one of the most popular rifles of this company.

12 Twenty round box of .40-70 caliber cartridges, one of the more popular calibers available in the above rifle.

13 Roper revolving shotgun, a 12-gauge four shot weapon that utilized a reloadable steel cartridge case.

The fragile mechanism tended to malfunction with hard usage.

14 Whitney-Kennedy lever action repeating rifle. This arm appears to be a special order, as indicated by the fancy wood, checkered stock and flip-up front sight.

15 Leather rifle cartridge belt with nickeled buckle used with appropriate large bore ammunition.

16 Unmarked, inexpensive double barreled percussion shotgun, 12-gauge, typical mid-19th century firearm.

17 Leather shot bag for use with any firearm similar to the above.

18 Ballard single shot sporting rifle, made by the Brown Manufacturing Co; a quality firearm.

19 Twenty round box for .40-70 Ballard cartridges.

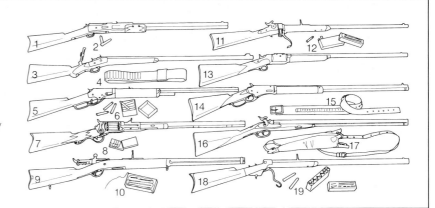

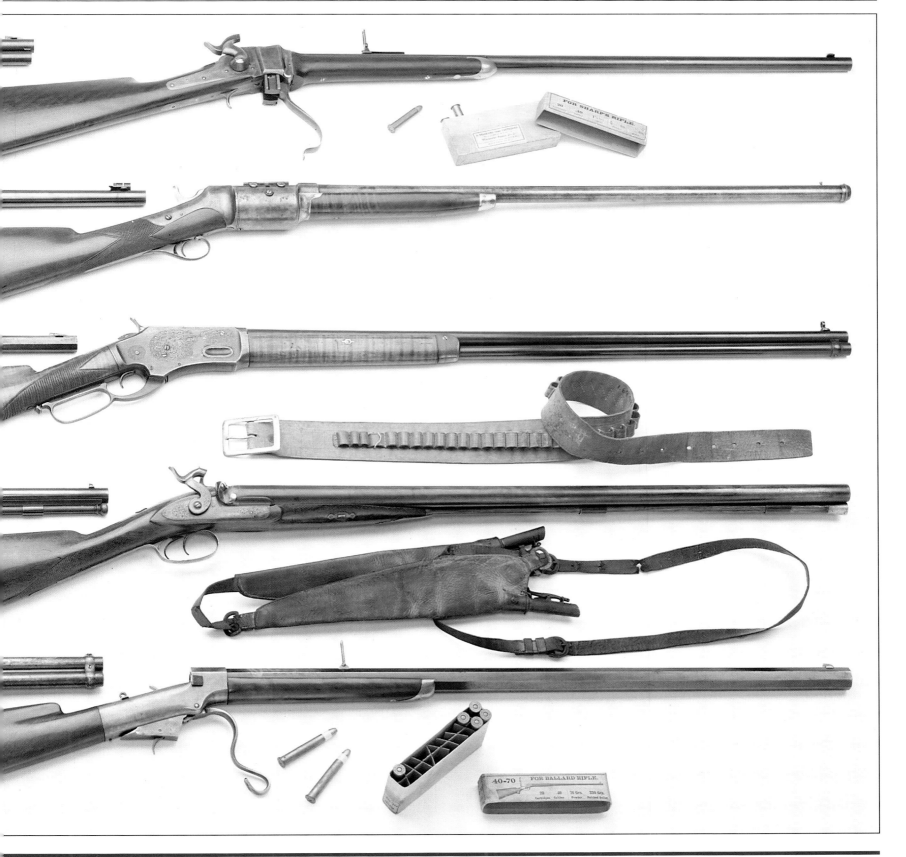

or he could be a sheriff or a marshal, or chief of police. Counties, too would have their sheriffs, while the state forces were such as the Texas Rangers or the New Mexico Mounted Police. In organized territories, United States Marshals were appointed, generally by Washington, acting on recommendation of the territorial governor or legislature. Thus the latter-day confusion of titles by which Western lawmen are known. No hierarchy of authority can definitely be assumed on the basis of title – there was, in a sense, nothing in a name.

Their daily routine differed widely from what the cheap press in the East portrayed. Most lawmen never fired a shot in the line of duty. Rather, they spent their days serving civil and criminal warrants, chasing tax delinquents, putting drunks in the lock-up overnight, and simply being visible in the community as a deterrent and as a reminder that there were rules by which everyone was expected to abide. Often their income was supplemented by small set fees for issuing summons, or by percentages of amounts collected from delinquents. They dressed like everyone else except in the few cases where a town

Above: *Originally formed in 1835 to patrol the young republic's borders, the Texas Rangers did not discriminate between evils. Most here are armed with Colt Burgess or Winchester rifles.*

Below: *Arizona Rangers existed too: Deputy Sheriff Farnsworth and Ranger Foster, right, well armed in rugged country. Arizona Territory was one of the last to achieve statehood, waiting until 1912.*

issued uniforms, and even the shining badge of office – the legendary 'tin star' – was not universal. As for their weapons, they carried them according to individual choice. Some simply tucked their pistol inside the waistband of their trousers. Others stuffed it into a pants or coat pocket. Some dispensed with the pistol and carried a shotgun instead. And for those who wore their handgun in a belted holster, it was almost invariably worn high on the hip, not slung low down on the thigh as in romantic fiction and film. A few like James Butler 'Wild Bill' Hickok affected more colorful attire. He wore two pistols at times, carried in holsters slung from crossbelts, and worn with the butts forward, so that he had to reach across his stomach with either hand to draw. But he was the exception. To most of these men, their weapon was a tool of their job, and they knew that it could be just as dangerous to themselves as to miscreants.

Equally contrary to the myth was the absence of stand-up gunfights. The fact was that the peace officer, whenever possible, confronted a dangerous antagonist with overwhelming force in the form of deputies or posses, and generally by surprise. Nothing

demonstrates the prudence exercised by such men – and the corresponding reluctance of desperadoes to go up against an armed and ready lawman – than the fact that from 1870 to 1885, during the heyday of the worst of the Kansas cow towns, the communities of Abilene, Ellsworth, Caldwell, Dodge City, and Wichita, combined only had sixteen deaths inflicted during the course of challenging or apprehending individuals by peace officers. Most fatalities, in fact, occurred, then as now, as a spontaneous by-product of domestic quarrels and drunken saloon brawls.[12]

Of course there were the dramatic exceptions, the men around whom such an aura and legend arose that they quickly overshadowed the tens of thousands of other forgotten lawmen. Perhaps the most notorious cool hand, fast shot, and dead eye was Hickok, a truly iron-nerved man. A native of Illinois, he moved west after the Civil War, worked as a gambler and earned the nickname 'Wild Bill', then landed in Kansas after some time as an army scout. In 1869 he was elected sheriff of Ellis County, and at Hays City killed two men, one in breaking up fighting drunks, and the other in unexplained circumstances. Defeated

for re-election, he moved on, being arrested in 1870 for assault in Topeka. A few months later he killed a soldier and wounded another, and though not prosecuted he moved on to Abilene where he got an appointment as city marshal. He spent his time gambling in the Alamo Saloon unless there was trouble, and when it arose, he used his guns first and thought afterward. In one shootout, he got his man, but in the darkness and rush he also killed one of his own deputies. He was soon discharged.

Hickok gravitated on to William F. Cody's 'Wild West' Show for a time, then moved to Wyoming for a couple of years, living chiefly by gambling. Then in 1876 he set off for the Black Hills in the new gold rush that saw thousands stream into South Dakota. He ended up in Deadwood Gulch and made a few efforts at mining, but gambling was still his preferred trade. 'Wild Bill' seems to have had premonitions of his own death, or at least a growing paranoia. He had killed many and outraged many more in his life, and in the transient community of gamblers and opportunists of the West, he often came across those he had had run-ins with in the past. It was said that in his last months he slept with his guns, if he slept at

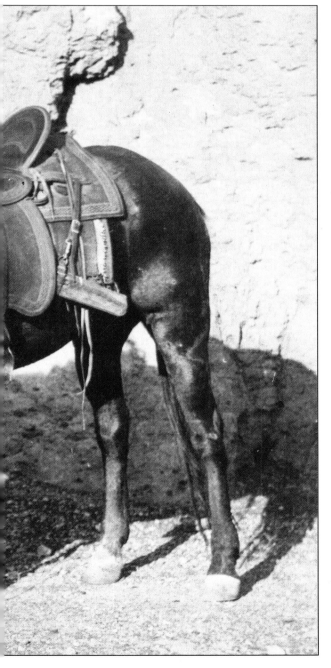

Above: *'Wild Bill' Hickok went to the cow town of Abilene as marshal in 1871 with something of a reputation. A colorful place, and only a few years old, it stood at the northernmost point of the Chisholm Trail.*

Hickok's tenure there was short-lived. Sacked for mistakenly killing one of his own men in a shootout, his wanderings finally took him to Deadwood, where he was shot in the back in a saloon.

LAW AND ORDER

Lawmen . . . marshal, sheriff, constable, peace officers by any name were tough and brutal men. Many had been on the other side of the law in earlier times or other locations. They were as violent as the element they were hired to control. Legend has inaccurately depicted, even distorted, these rugged frontier individuals. In early range wars, peace officers were often little more than hired assassins operating on instructions from the big ranchers. Many were gamblers, pimps, gunfighters and ex-convicts. They did their job because they were good at it, it was usually safer than rustling cattle and they were paid well and regularly. Some among this group were loyal and honorable men but, as a rule, they were an unsavory lot. Regardless, the peace officer of the West was a colorful and feared, if not respected, man. As the frontier receded in the face of progress, so did the individuality of these larger than life men. And as it vanished, so did they.

1 Wombat fur double-breasted overcoat worn by Henry Dahlem, first sheriff of Park County, Wyoming.
2 Colt single-action Army revolver used by Sheriff E.N. Wolf of Lampasas, Texas, 1884-90. Wolf purchased the pistol in 1882 with a 7½ in. barrel and cut it off to 4⅝ in.
3 Coin silver-headed cane engraved 'Col. Cody "Buffalo Bill" to Jack Stilwell, Nov. 14, 1893'. The tip of the cane is a brass .44-40 shell casing.
4-6 Contemporary sensational pulp papers.
7 Nickeled iron handcuffs with key.
8, 9 Legal treatises: *The Compiled Laws of Wyoming*, 1876; *Revised Statutes of Wyoming*, 1887; *Laws of Wyoming*, 1869; and *Session Laws of Wyoming Territory*,

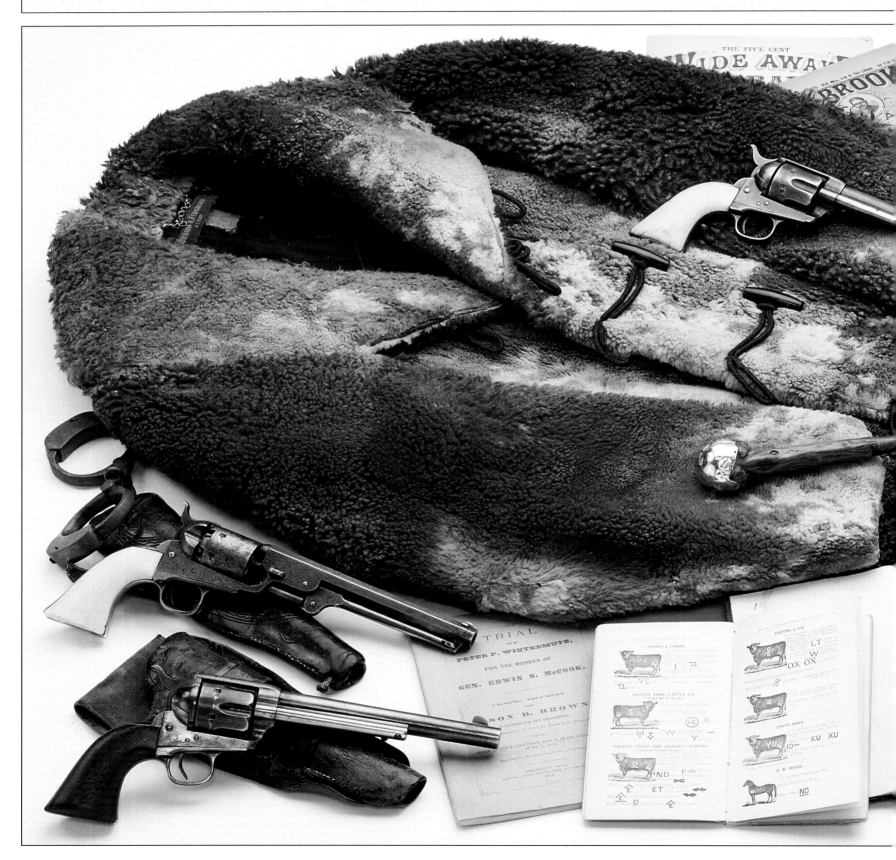

186

1879 and 1886.

10 Pair of metal handcuffs or restraints.

11 Colt Model 1851 Navy revolver, .36 caliber, percussion, engraved with ivory grips.

12 'Slim Jim' style leather holster for revolver above.

13 Colt single-action Army revolver carried by Marshal William Bunt of Emporia, Kansas. Note 7½ in. barrel, .45 caliber.

14 Mexican double loop

leather holster for revolver above.

15 Pamphlet: *Trial of Peter P. Wintermute, Cheyenne, Wyoming, 1874.*

16 Brand book of the Wyoming Stock Growers' Association, 1885.

17 Book: *The Banditti of the Plains, or The Cattlemen's Invasion of Wyoming in 1892*, by A.S. Mercer.

18 Five-pointed nickel silver badge of the Special Police of

Livingston, Montana, made by G.J. Mayer Company, Indianapolis Indiana. (Courtesy of Old West Antiques, Cody, Wyoming.)

19 Pair of patent metal handcuffs.

20 Alligator hide traveling bag of Deputy Sheriff E.S. Hoops, Cody, Wyoming, c.1890.

21 Dime novels of the period: Morrison's Sensational Series.

22 Pair of metal handcuffs or restraints.

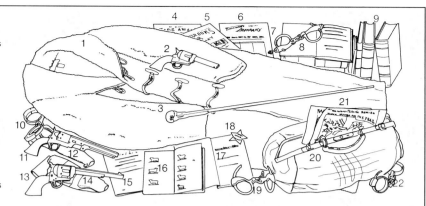

all, and that he littered the floor of his room at night with crumpled pieces of newspaper, so that anyone approaching in the dark would make a noise. On 2 August 1876, he was playing cards in a saloon with his back to the room when he was shot in the back of the head by a local derelict who claimed to have a grudge against him, but who may also have been in the pay of local elements with grudges of their own. It was hardly the end the tabloid press and the legends would give to their public.[13]

Hickok was typical of a very small number, which also included Ben Thompson and Dallas Stoudenmire, both Texas lawmen quick with a gun, both ready killers, and both destined to die in shootings themselves. There was another of equal fame who took quite a different route, yet showed how variable were the fortunes and ethics of some of the men who occasionally stood for the law. Wyatt Earp, like Hickok, came from Illinois. When he was twenty he was living with his family in Lamar, Missouri. He married two years later, but his young wife died in childbirth, and soon thereafter he took to stealing horses in the Indian Territory. When arrested, he posted

bail, then ran off for Kansas, never to return. He became a buffalo hunter, but also plied an avocation as a gambler, even ending up in Hays City for a time, though he may never have known or even met Hickok.

Earp moved on to Ellsworth in 1873, and to Wichita the following year, in a 'progress' almost repeating Hickok's, and paralleling the advance of the railheads and the consequent money to be made relieving cowboys of their pay after the herds sold. Again he gambled, and in Wichita at least he held a job for a time as a city policeman, though not as either marshal or sheriff, as legend has it. In 1876 he was fired and fined for fighting with a candidate for the office of marshal. In April the city council voted against rehiring him, and the next month charged Wyatt and his brother Virgil with vagrancy. The brothers left town and moved on to Dodge City. Earp served as a policeman for a time that year, and again in 1877, meanwhile getting himself fined $1 for fighting with a prostitute. In 1878 he became assistant marshal and served for more than a year, yet made only forty-seven arrests. 'He was an efficient officer if he could surround himself with a bunch of killers,' recalled one

Above: *Virgil Earp accompanied brothers Wyatt and James to the fledgling boomtown in 1879. Once a stage driver and a deputy marshal in Arizona Territory, he hoped to find wealth in the silver-rich hills.*

Above: *Wyatt Earp's reputation was not a wholesome one. He came to Tombstone in 1879 with a busy resumé: horse-thief, policeman, embezzler, assistant marshal, gambler – but always a formidable foe.*

Right: *With men like Earp and Hickok keeping the peace, the presence of a more formal judiciary body was essential. Here, judge, attorney and aids convene in Tombstone's new courthouse in the 1880s.*

Above: *Morgan Earp was the youngest of the four Earps. He joined his brothers in Tombstone in 1880 and was involved in the O.K. Corral fight. In 1882 he was murdered in a pool hall, the motive probably revenge.*

Above: *John 'Doc' Holliday and Wyatt Earp had met in Dodge City. Holliday had all the right attributes for friendship: gambler, sometime dentist, alcoholic, consumptive, he was also a cold-hearted killer.*

citizen. 'He was no lone wolf. He was always the leader of a vicious pack.'

And so he was. In Dodge City, Earp led what he called the 'Peace Commission' in exerting not only law and order, but also pressure on competitors of the saloon that he favored. He also formed an alliance with a consumptive dentist and cold killer named John 'Doc' Holliday. When Earp left Dodge City in 1879 to move on to brighter prospects in the Arizona Territory, so did Holliday, several of Earp's brothers, and his mistress Mattie, whom he would later abandon. Years afterward, reduced to prostitution, she took her own life. Earp, meanwhile, soon settled in Tombstone in December 1879, where there would be gambling pickings from a local silver strike. He worked first as a shotgun guard on local stage coaches, got a job as a deputy sheriff, was fired, then took a job in a local saloon where he soon became a ringleader among a band of unsavory toughs, including Holliday, his brothers, and other flotsam from the Kansas cow towns. They got into a feud with a local faction that included the Clantons and their rustler friends, and which also involved jealousies over Wyatt's new girlfriend,

THE MARSHAL

It was not unusual for gamblers and gunslingers to become lawmen. This dual role was best epitomized by Wild Bill Hickok who, while marshal of Abilene, Kansas, spent much of his time at the poker table in the notorious Alamo bar. A variety of badges of office were worn by these lawmen, ranging in style depending on rank. The plainest, as shown here, generally identified the wearer as a U.S. Marshal, the highest rank and an appointment made direct by the President. In addition to carrying a Parker shotgun and a Smith and Wesson .45 1st Model Schofield sidearm, this man wears early-style boots with two-inch heels and calfskin tops stiffened by the stitched pattern.

the supposed involvement of some of the Earps' cronies in a fatal stage robbery, and the appointment of Wyatt's brother Virgil as city marshal. Quickly matters came to a head, and on 25 October 1881, the Earp faction, operating under the umbrella of Virgil's badge, met with the Clantons and others near the O.K. Corral. In a few seconds one Clanton and two of his comrades lay dead, and the West's most legendary gunfight was over. Many argued that it was little better than murder, others adhered to the heroic version that Wyatt later told to his biographer Stuart Lake. In either case, bloody echoes of the fight continued for months, with Morgan Earp assassinated, Virgil maimed in another attempt, and a host of the opposition waylaid and murdered by Wyatt and friends. He left Arizona, never to return, and later prospected in Alaska, then relocated to California. He was in sporadic trouble with the law for years afterward, charged with fraud, bunco, vagrancy, and even suspected of 'fixing' a prize fight in which he was the referee, and on which he may have bet on the man he adjudged to be the winner. He died in 1929, aged eighty, after having made one of the most enduring of all contributions to western legend by dictating his memoirs to Lake. The book was almost entirely fictional.[14]

Thus was the story of law and order, crime and punishment, good men and bad, reflected to posterity like so much of the rest of the West. It was simply too big to contain mere mortals, whether explorers, mountain men, or gunslingers. Time after time the legend outstripped the reality, and the participants themselves actively contributed to their myth. But beneath the cloud of romanticized nonsense, the real story is just as dramatic, whether it be of blue-eyed Billy gone wrong, a weary aging Hickok fearfully setting out each night's paper traps, or the perpetual con artist Earp in the end conning posterity by inventing his own past. There was law and there was order on the frontier. Only their definitions were often mixed, and their enforcers and violators often had no clearly defined idea of which side they stood on. In a moment, and from any provocation, that side could change, too. Like so many who had come before, the outlaws and the shady lawmen were like all the rest of the Westerners in a way: they were out for opportunity. The men who preserved the peace tried, and largely succeeded, in preventing them from finding their opportunity at the expense of others.

Right: *Dave Mather was typical of a breed of men with a foot in each camp. Itinerant gunfighter, he was also assistant marshal of Dodge City in the 1880s. He was acquitted for killing his successor in 1884.*

REFERENCES

1 Frank Richard Prassel, *The Western Peace Officer* (Norman, Okla., 1972), pp. 4-5.
2 *Ibid.*, pp. 11ff.
3 *Ibid.*, pp. 28ff, 76-8, 130-31.
4 Odie Faulk, *Dodge City*, pp. 150-51.
5 Glenn G. Boyer, ed., *I Married Wyatt Earp* (Tucson, Ariz., 1979), p. 26.
6 Robert Utley, *High Noon in Lincoln* (Albuquerque, NM, 1987), pp. 14-15, 25-6.
7 *Ibid.*, pp. 28, 64-5, 114-16.
8 Robert Utley, *Billy the Kid* (Lincoln, Nebr., 1989), pp; 5-9.
9 *Ibid.*, pp. 14-15, 48, 146, 193.
10 *Ibid.*, p. 33.
11 Prassel, *The Western Peace Officer*, p. 34.
12 *Ibid.*, p. 47.
13 Kent L. Steckmesser, *The Western Hero In Legend and History* (Norman, Okla., 1965), pp. 112-20.
14 Prassel, *The Western Peace Officer*, p. 51; Boyer, *I Married Wyatt Earp*, p. 38n; Frank Waters, *The Earp Brothers of Tombstone* (Lincoln, Nebr., 1960), pp. 37-40 and *passim*.

Below: *More often than not, killings did not involve gunmen. The fatalities here resulted from a squabble over water rights between the Berrys, Kansas farmers, and the Deweys, a prominent ranching family.*

VII

LIFE
ON THE RANGE

Below: *Round-up on a Texas ranch, a later photograph taken after the range was fenced in by the end of the century.*

ALMOST INCREDIBLY, GIVEN the reputation it has in posterity, and the image of itself that it encouraged at the time, the West enjoyed far more of peace than violence, more of building than destruction. For every day of armed conflict between red and white, for every gunfight or robbery, for every catastrophe that man or nature could visit on the land and its inhabitants, there were scores, perhaps hundreds, of days and weeks of quiet. Indeed, though the life of all on the frontier was one of hardship and toil, solitude and monotony characterized their existence far more than the excitements so many expected. Most of all this contrast between image and reality epitomized the most pervasive symbol of all Westerners, the cowboy.

None can say with certainty where the name came from or just when it first appeared. In fact, some claim to find its roots antedating the American West by nearly a millennium, all the way back to Ireland around A.D. 1,000. It appeared sporadically in literature from 1705 onward, when Jonathan Swift used the term, and it is to be found in American colonial references from time to time, applied, appropriately enough, to young men and boys who herded cattle. By the 1830s, however, it began acquiring a distinctive usage on the western frontier. In Texas a 'cow-boy' was a cattle thief who stole beeves from the Mexicans. A few decades later, however, the word evolved into its more conventional usage, to define men who worked cattle. 'If a man works on a salary and rides after the herd,' said the Denver *Republican* in 1883, 'he is called a "cowboy".'[1]

American impressions of the cowboy differed widely, even among the people with whom he lived and worked. 'The cowboy is a fearless animal,' wrote a Texas livestock editor. 'A man wanting in courage would be as much out of place in a cow-camp, as a fish would be on dry land.' The cowboy had to be cool and courageous, which meant in turn that he could not afford to act either the bully or

the troublemaker. Living and working in a dangerous environment, he had to be able to count on the goodwill and cooperation of his fellow cowhands. 'Cowpunchers were square shooters, upright, and honest men,' asserted another. 'I never heard of a cowpuncher insulting a woman. If they were not up to par they were soon run out of the country.' Indeed, some liked to read an almost medieval code of honour and deportment into the cowboy character. 'The cowboy is as chivalrous as the famed knights of old,' claimed one admirer. 'Rough he may be, and it may be that he is not a master in ball-room etiquette, but no set of men have loftier reverence for women.' Completing this picture of the cowboy as a paragon of virtue is the assertion of 'his entire devotion to the interests of his employer. No more faithful employee ever breathed than he.'

Such glowing encomiums may have been overstated to be sure, but they contained elements of truth. More down to earth was the assessment of another observer in 1887. 'He is in the main a loyal, long-enduring, hard-working fellow, grit to the backbone, and tough as whipcord; performing his arduous and often dangerous duties, and living his comfortless life, without a word of complaint about the many privations he has to undergo.' That rang much closer to the truth.[2]

Yet others saw the same cowboys through an altogether different lens. 'Out in the Territories there are only two classes,' said a New Mexico Territory journal in the late 1880s, 'the "cowboys" and the "tenderfeet". Such of the "cowboys" as are not professional thieves, murderers and miscellaneous blacklegs who fled to the frontier for reasons that require no explanation, are men who totally disregard all of the amenities of Eastern civilization.' 'He is the best man who can draw the quickest and kill the surest. A "cowboy" who has not killed his man – or to put it more correctly his score of "tenderfeet" – is without character standing, or respect.'

Another New Mexican was even more harsh. 'They are supposed to be herdsmen employed to watch vast herds of cattle, but they might more properly be known under any name that means desperate criminal. They roam about in sparsely settled villages with revolvers, pistols and knives in their belts, attacking every peaceable citizen met with.' And in 1871 a Texas journalist declared of the cowboy that 'of course he is unlearned and illiterate, with but few wants and meager ambition'. He lived on plug tobacco and cheap whiskey, and dreamed only of gambling and women. 'His dress consists of a flannel shirt with a handkerchief encircling his neck, butternut pants and a pair of long boots, in which are always the legs of his pants. His head is covered by a sombrero, which is a Mexican hat with a high crown and a brim of enormous dimensions. He generally wears a revolver on each side of his person, which he will use with as little hesitation on a man as on a wild animal. Such a character is dangerous and desperate and each one has generally killed his man.'[3]

Such appraisals revealed as much about their writers as about the cowboys, and were highly colored by their time and place. The unflattering New Mexican appraisals came from pens that still heard the echoes of the anarchy of Tombstone and the Lincoln County War, in both of which the lawless elements also happened to be cowboys. The more glowing tributes came from areas like Texas where the cowboy predominated. Perhaps one of the

fairest judgements of the breed came from the hand of one who employed cowboys for a lifetime, a ranch owner, who wrote in 1874:

He lives hard, works hard, has but few comforts and fewer necessities. He has but little, if any, taste for reading. He enjoys a coarse practical joke or a smutty story; loves danger but abhors labor of the common kind; never tires riding, never wants to walk, no matter how short the distance he desires to go. He would rather fight with pistols than pray; loves tobacco, liquor and women better than any trinity. His life borders nearly upon that of an Indian. If he reads anything, it is in most cases a blood and thunder story of a sensational style. He enjoys his pipe, and relishes a practical joke on his comrades, or a corrupt tale, wherein abounds much vulgarity and animal propensity.[4]

Below: *In the early days of the drives, most of the cattle were Texas longhorns, descended from those brought to America by the Spaniards. With horns up to four feet long, longhorns could be fierce customers.*

Above: *Because longhorn meat was lean, stringy and tough, and the cattle took time to mature to their full weight, ranchers crossbred them with European stock to produce new breeds.*

They came almost from everywhere – Civil War veterans of both blue and gray, freed Negroes, immigrants from England and Scandinavia, itinerant laborers from every section of the eastern United States, and thousands of

Mexican-Americans either adopted when the Union assumed control of their homelands, or else migrated up from below the Rio Grande. In the days before the Civil War their activities were largely restricted to the wide prairies of Texas, but in the boom of settlement and new land of the post-war generation, cowboys operated literally everywhere that grass could grow or a cow graze.

Nevertheless, while good men went into the trade from Missouri and Illinois and Mississippi, even, almost from the first the Texan was the acknowledged 'king' of cowboys, with only the ever-present ethnocentrism of the day failing to accord an equal status to the *vaqueros* from both above and below the border. 'The Texans are, as far as true cowboyship goes, unrivaled,' noted one observer, 'the best riders, hardy, and born to the business.'[5] It should hardly have come as a surprise, since it was in Texas that their craft and trade truly emerged and first flourished, even though the appellation of 'cowboy' at first still carried connotations of a low-life nature. And the dislocation and economic upheaval of the Civil War in Texas effectively removed any stigma formerly attaching to men who owned no animals themselves, but minded the herds of others for a wage. Moreover, these rugged, lean men were ideally suited for the strenuous, often dangerous, life of the open range. They had been practically born in the saddle. They grew up knowing the use and lore of the rope and saddle, pistol and rifle. A night alone on the spaceless prairie held few terrors for them, and a whole season of virtual solitude with perhaps only a half dozen other cowboys in some remote extent of a giant rancher's domain, did not give them pause. It was all part of a life they had led since youth.

It was much the same for the *vaquero*. Indeed, the cattle ranching business ran even deeper in his blood than in that of the Anglo-Texan, for it was the Spanish who centuries before had introduced the twin necessities of the cowboy profession to North America, the horse and the cow. The cattle were initially just wild beasts that escaped from their owners, roamed and flourished on the broad ranges, and then bred into hardy species like the longhorn that could survive most effectively on the country. The first 'cowboys' were the Spaniards and Mexicans who were essentially cow-*hunters*, sent out to recover lost stock, and later to round up the wild groups. By the time of the Anglo absorption of Texas and the Southwest, a rich *vaquero* tradition had evolved among the men, mostly half-

Above: *By 1880 thousands of cattle roamed the range. In spring and fall ranchers counted heads and branded new calves. In Texas, springtime meant preparations for driving the herds north to market.*

THE COWBOY

Although the cowboy had a heroic image of himself perpetuated by artists like Frederick Remington, he was actually an overworked laborer, riding miles and fighting the elements. The golden age of the American cowboy ended in the mid-1880s with plummeting cattle market prices halting the romanticized freewheeling days. The cowboys' attire was protective: heavy leather chaps against thorny brush, Mexican sugar-loaf sombrero (back) against the sun, the plainsman style with its low crown (foreground) against the wind. The classic cowboy saddle, evolved to meet their specific needs, could last a working lifetime. The leading cowboy carries a Winchester '73 rifle.

breed Mexican-Indians, that shared many of the same elements that would form a part of the cowboy code, but also some distinctly different features of its own. Unlike the Anglo cowboy, for instance, a *vaquero*, unless 'tainted' by too much association with the Texans, would look with contempt at the big pistol hanging at a *gringo*'s side. It was much more manly, thought they, to defeat an opponent by brains and bluff rather than raw firepower, and if a confrontation must come to blood, then it should be with the knife, eye-to-eye, or a whip or lariat. Most of all, however, these hardy men grew up facing, if possible, even greater hardships and challenges, making them admirably suited to be cowboys. Only their Anglo peers would always be reluctant to admit that it was so, preferring to stigmatize the Mexicans as lazy, shiftless, drunken, and untrustworthy. In spite of this, however, the most jingoistic of Texas cowboys still could not deny that much of his trade and a great deal of his language had evolved out of the much older *vaquero* tradition. The lariat that every cowboy carried began as the Mexican's *la reata*. The herd of horses accompanying a trail drive was still called a *remuda*. The quaint and catchy nickname 'buckaroo' by which so many cowboys referred to one another, and which has characterized their speech down through posterity, began in a mispronunciation of the name *vaquero* itself. Without the Mexican cowboys, however much despised they might have been, American cowboys might never have emerged.[6]

Above: *General Phil Sheridan applauded the extermination of the buffalo that had left the plains to cattle and rancher. He wanted to see the prairies 'covered with speckled cattle and the festive cowboy'.*

The cowboy's heyday was a short one, from the end of the Civil War to the mid-1880s. The quality and dedication of such men as these seen here shooting craps could make or break the rancher or cattle baron.

The Texan or Californian or Coloradoan cowboy also owed a lot to the *vaqueros* for his dress and equipment, and even for his original desire to take up the trade, for the two were inextricably intertwined. By the 1870s the romantic dime-novel lure of being a cowboy was bringing thousands across the Mississippi from the East, the 'tenderfeet' so teased and joked about by the professionals. Newspapermen who had come West for a visit, fallen in love with the superficial romance of the men who lived free on the plains, and then went back home to write of their experiences, influenced countless young men – and women – to pull up stakes and take a chance on finding adventure as cowboys. Unfortunately, the journalists had seen only what they wanted to see, the wide sunsets, the endless vistas, the dashing dress and rough camaraderie of the cowhands. That beneath this veneer lay a cruelly taxing life of labor and solitude with little or no future, the print men either did not see or did not care to see. Their eyes filled with starry visions of sitting around the campfires on the range, the tenderfeet would not have heeded any warnings even if offered.

Almost the very first concern of a new tenderfoot fresh off the railroad or overland coach, and an even greater concern for the experienced cowhand, was what to wear. Primarily it had to be utilitarian, which meant rugged enough to withstand years in the saddle, being dragged through brush and briars, worn thin at the knees from endless hours bent down to brand or tend to calves. It must be warm without being restricting, have plenty of

Above: *A soddy ranch house in grass-rich Kansas, on the W.D. Boyce Cattle Company's spread. Worthy of note is the barbed wire, which was patented by an Illinois farmer, Joseph Glidden, in 1874.*

Below: *The key to a contented crew on a drive or round-up was often the cook, who might prepare up to three meals a day on the range. A cowboy's other essential was his horse, herded in the remuda behind.*

COWBOY ACCOUTERMENTS 1

The image of the American cowboy has been greatly influenced by the motion picture industry, which has found this character a fertile field for countless productions. Major studios portray the cowboy in the guise of Paul Newman, Robert Redford of John Wayne. While entertaining and sometimes based on fact, these cinematic efforts have generally been highly idealized and historically incorrect. Few have made a serious effort to portray the cowboy as he actually was. In reality, the heyday of the cowboy lasted only two decades, 1865-1885, and, at best, the maximum number of cowboys was around 40,000. Nearly one cowboy out of three was either black or Mexican and many were easterners or recent European immigrants. Cowboys were a polyglot group and theirs was not a glamorous profession. Few individuals made a lifetime profession of the job because of the general hardships and physical exertions were prohibitive to older men.

1 Horsehide shotgun chaps, seatless protective leggings, with two front pockets and decorative fringe, made by J.S. Collins and Company, Cheyenne, Wyoming. The nomenclature 'shotgun' is used because of the double barrel appearance of the legs.
2 Gray felt wide brim cowboy hat retailed by Capper and Capper.
3 Floral pattern neckerchief or bandanna.
4 Tanned leather gloves lined with cotton fabric with a white and blue polka dot pattern.
5 White angora wool chaps with leather lining and waist belt from Billings, Montana Territory. Such woollies were more commonplace on the cold northern ranges.
6 Leather wrist cuffs embossed with basket weave design. These cuffs became popular about 1880.

7 Buff felt wide brim hat made by Stetson Company, Philadelphia.

6 Blue silk neckerchief or bandanna with raised rib border decoration.

9 Leather cuffs embossed with daisy pattern, made by Heiser, Denver, Colorado.

10 Doghide shotgun chaps, made by W.B. Ten Eyck, Billings, Montana Territory.

11 'Ten gallon hat', called 'The Denver', marked 'John B. Stetson Co.

No. 1 Quality, Philadelphia'.

12 Printed cotton pink and purple polka dot bandanna.

13 Pair of steel spurs with medium size rowels and leather attachment straps marked 'Star Steel Silver'. Highly practical, spurs were also a vital part of a cowboy's image and were seldom taken off.

14 Pair of silver inlaid spurs with small rowels and leathers embossed with

basket weave design and crossed sabers.

15 Pair of steel spurs with saw-tooth rowels and leathers.

16 Pair of steel spurs with spike rowels and leathers with nickel spots.

17 Pair of patent spurs with zigzag decoration and heart-shaped studs for leathers.

18 Pair of heavy steel spurs with large saw-tooth rowels and silver concho decoration.

pockets, and shield him from rain, wind, sun, dust, and the other natural hazards of the open plains. And ideally it should all fit the idiom of dress that evolved in the trade, one that took pride in a certain sartorial unruliness, color, even flamboyance.

His pants were wool, as was the shirt he wore, the sleeves generally too long so that he kept them up by sporting colorful garters on his upper arms. He wore a high-crowned hat with a wide brim, or else a Mexican-style sombrero. Cotton or wool 'long Johns' were ever-present underneath, with cotton socks on his feet. Around his neck he wore a large scarf or neckerchief, its opposite ends knotted in front of him, and the rest billowing down his back. It was one of the universal trademarks of the trade. In high winds and dust storms, the neckerchief was turned around and brought up over his nose – even his eyes – for protection. And, of course, in the popular press it was also used to hide a face when a crime was being committed.

More important still were the cowboy's leather goods. First came his boots. Like the rest of his clothing, they were manufactured and purchased, though the *vaqueros* sometimes made their own as part of a leather-crafting tradition that dated back for generations. The cowboy liked them with high heels and a deep upward arch. It made them awkward for walking, leading to the ungainly stride that most cowhands acquired first from necessity, and later affected as a sign of their trade. But the high arch and long heel had a much more practical side, for they allowed a man to 'bury' his feet in his stirrups for a firm grip, heel and arch keeping his foot from sliding out at inopportune moments, for to fall from the saddle could mean death.

Gloves, too, were of vital importance. The cowboy handled hemp ropes and leather lariats constantly, often with a several hundred pound beeve at the other end. Buckskin was preferred, though in heavy winter on

Above: *Some cowboys might try to look tougher and tidier in posed photographs such as this than they did on the range, but their choice of clothing is correct, right down to the gloves and chaps.*

Right: *C.A. Kendrick recorded cowboy lore at the turn of the century. Though cattle drives were to become a thing of the past, ranching continued to attract men to the only kind of work they knew.*

the high plains woollen mittens were just as important, and sometimes worn under the leather gloves. Over his legs, from the waist to his boot soles, he wore leather 'chaps', derived from the earlier *vaquero*'s *chaparejos*, and they, in turn, evolved from the earlier *armas* of northern Mexico. The *armas* were wide leather capes hanging down from the saddle horn, then wrapping around the rider's legs and reaching back almost to the horse or mule's hind legs. They provided excellent protection from briars and brush, and rope burns. Gradually they became smaller and less bulky, until the 'chaps' developed as essentially a pair of leather over-trousers, fastened about the

waist, open at the seat, and with legs that either wrapped around the owner's, or else buckled at the back. For some reason, along with the hat, they were regarded as the most romantic of all the cowboy's gear, and were often the first things a tenderfoot bought to start his transformation.[7]

'In the morning a cowboy begins dressing downward,' recalled one old-timer. 'First he puts on his hat, then his shirt, and takes out of his shirt pocket his Bull Durham and cigarette papers and rolls one to start the day.' That done, the fellow donned trousers, socks, and boots. When he turned in for the night, he reversed the process, taking off first boots, then

socks, trousers, and shirt. 'He never goes deeper than that,' noted the cowboy. A man slept in his long John's. Then he took off his hat, set it beside his bedroll, and put his boots on the brim to keep it from being blown away by nighttime prairie breezes. His spurs worn on the boots were never removed, virtually a permanent extension of the footgear. 'This is a habit that usually stays with a cowboy long after his days in the saddle are over,' concluded the old-timer.

Besides the ritual of dressing, there was also cowboy superstition. Many wore vests over their shirts, both for added warmth and to stuff tobacco, cigarette papers, and other oddments

into. But many would never button their vests, believing that to do so would lead to colds and rheumatism. Changing underwear was bad luck – besides being impractical if he only had one set of long underclothes. On those rare occasions when the cowboy was in town and actually slept in a bed, he never put his hat on the bed. More back luck. Indeed, superstition in general played a large role in the cowboy's code, for he lived a rugged life in which almost any act or event could be taken as an omen with hardship, disease, injury, and death, never far behind him.[8]

Leather was an integral part of his life. The animals he herded were born in it. He wore it on his hands and feet. It protected his legs from cactus and branch. It held up his trousers, wide belts sometimes two inches in width being preferred. Some wore hats made of it, though they were impractical in the rain, and heavy. Leather vests were much preferred for their appearance, and not a few men had buckskin coats to match their gloves, though the cowboy would usually only wear it when cold forced him to, for the coat – any coat – restricted movement.

Most of all, though, he rode on leather. The saddle was the premier piece of his equipment, so much so that it was almost an item of apparel, and certainly was chosen with more care and treated with more respect than his attire. A cowhand owned his own saddle; without it he could not take employment. The Western saddle, like so much else, developed based on Mexican roots and the peculiar needs of the country. It weighed about 30 pounds, and its most distinctive feature was the pommel or 'horn' sticking up prominently from the top front. It was a secure hold for the cowhand to

Below: *The range was no place for a man on foot and this Western-style saddle offered a measure of comfort to the rider. Most horses were supplied to cowboys by the rancher they worked for.*

Above: *In Montana and Wyoming, where the northern grass might not be at its best until late spring, cattle were rounded up, branded and allowed to fatten before being driven to shipment centers.*

grip when galloping at high speed or taking a sharp turn. When roping a steer, he could secure his end of the hemp to the horn, thereby making of saddle and horse an anchor to secure an unruly beast. Or, he might give his rope a turn around the horn, holding the end in his hands and allowing enough play to control a steer without necessarily bringing it to a dead stop. *Dar la vuelta* is what the *vaqueros* called this technique, literally to 'take a turn', and it led to the Americanization 'dally' and those who preferred the technique being called 'dally men'.

The Mexican cattlemen had a tradition of building their own saddles, in keeping with their general devotion to leather craft, and in time they produced true works of art far too splendid to risk damaging in actual usage. Far more common was a simple wooden 'tree' not unlike a mule's pack, with thin leather draped over it, and wooden stirrups dangling from leather straps. A leather or canvas belt wrapped around the horse's stomach to hold it in place. It was hard on horse and rider alike, and a more friendly saddle gradually developed, with padding on the underside to spare the horse's back, and padding above to comfort the rider's bottom. Sometimes they added *tapaderas* to the front of the stirrups, leather sheets that blocked the foot from going through the stirrup forward. If a rider fell off his mount and a foot went through a stirrup, he could be dragged to death by a runaway mount. The high arch and heel of the cowboy boot was designed in part to provide the same safety.

By the decade of the Civil War, American saddlers were taking the older *vaquero* saddles and improving and adapting them for use in Texas and elsewhere. Within a few years several distinctive styles of cowboy saddle emerged. Those directly descended from the Mexican saddle – and thereby from old Spanish types – were called 'Brazos' rigs or a 'Brazos tree'. Viewed from the side, it showed a deep curving arch from the pommel in front, down through the seat, then swooping back up to the high 'cantle' at the rear, against which the rider's lower back rested. There was also a 'Texas' saddle with a much more flat cross section; a flatter yet 'Cheyenne' saddle appeared farther north, and even a few 'White River trees' from Canada found their way south to the great cattle ranches. Further refinements appeared beneath the saddles in the belts or 'cinches' used to hold them in place. Some had just one cinch, and were thus called 'single-fire' rigs. Others with two cinches, front and rear, were called 'rim-fires'. Certain manufacturers became famous throughout the West for their products, like the noted 'Mother Hubbard' model that appeared after the Civil War, its name connoting the fact that a cowboy's saddle was literally his 'home' and 'cupboard' for much of his life.

Appointments on this home and hearth on horseback included varieties of hooks, rings, and ties, for attaching saddlebags, rope or lariat, a rifle equipped with a 'saddle ring' such

Above: *Horse and rider working in harmony with the brander in the corral. Flat out in the dust, its front and hind legs held by taut ropes anchored to the saddle horn, no steer could avoid the branding iron.*

Below: *Cattle brands were a form of range heraldry: they identified owners and might discourage rustlers. Evident on the flanks of some of these Herefords and Aberdeen Anguses is the TX brand.*

SADDLES

The saddle was the most important single piece of equipment of the cowboy. On working days he spent most of his waking hours riding on it. At night it might be his pillow. A good saddle could cost as much as $35 or $40, a month's wages, so it was the most expensive item a cowboy ever purchased. With this in mind, it is certain a cowboy's saddle was a very personal piece of equipment. The origin of the Western saddle was the 16th-century Spanish military saddle which was brought to the American continent by conquistadores. While there were intermediate variations, actual use directed the evolution to the form seen in the later years of the 19th century. Each part of the saddle had some specific design function or purpose, primarily comfort and safety because of the long hours of use and the rigorous physical type of work. Military saddles of the period served a different function and had no special equipment for ranching. The Mexican saddle, popular in California, was too heavy for prolonged trail use. Indian adaptations were hardly working saddles at all, but more a means to keep rider on horseback. The ornate parade saddles seen in the 20th century have little practical application. True period Western saddles, particularly those bearing the embossed name of the maker, are avidly sought by collectors of Western memorabilia. Various forms of saddles, military, Indian or otherwise, can be seen on pp. 10/11, 28/9, 84/5, 92/3 and 246/7 of this volume.

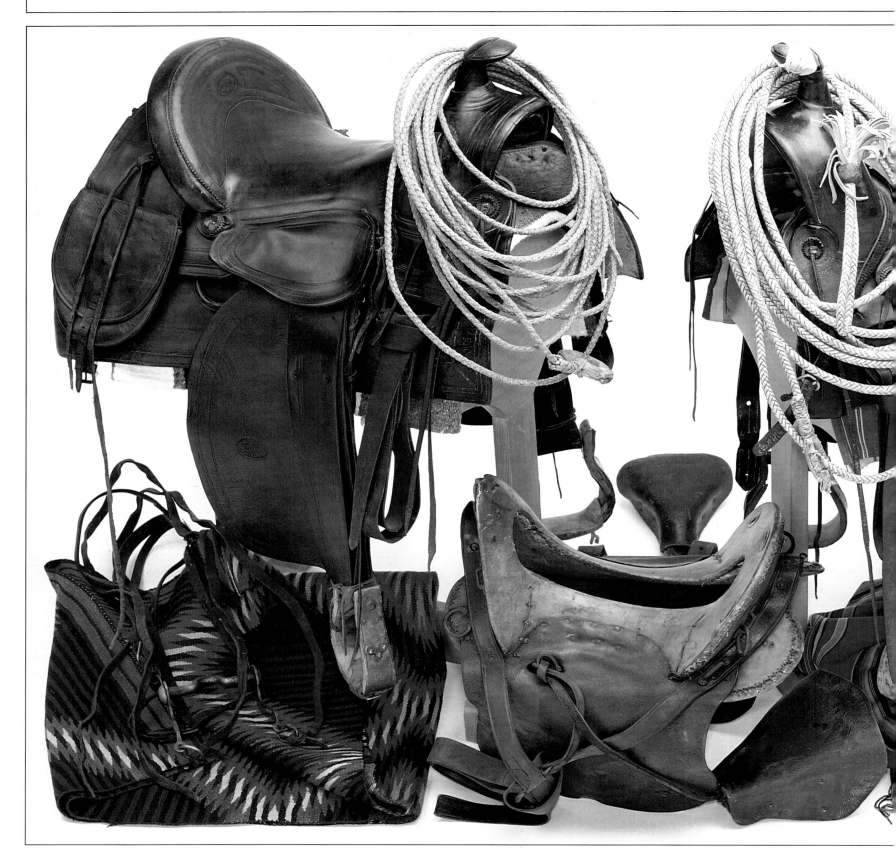

1 'Denver' style full leather saddle, about 1890. Note heavy side jockey or skirt and fenders to protect the rider's legs. Saddle bags are positioned behind the cantle and are used to carry small personal material of the rider.

2 Plaited rawhide lariat, about 1885, usually 30-40 ft long. Lariat, from the Spanish *la reata*.

3 Common leather bridle.

4 Course weave woolen saddle blanket.

5 U.S. military McClellan saddle, Model 1859, with rawhide seat, skirt and hooded stirrups.

6 Plaited rawhide lariat, about 1890, usually 30-40 ft long.

7 'Denver' style work saddle, double cinch rigged, somewhat lighter construction, about 1875, with ring bit and woven rawhide bridle lying behind the cantle.

8 Lightweight saddle blanket.

9 Heavy tooled leather California saddle with tapaderos to protect the rider's feet from thorns and cactus, about 1880.

10 Silver-mounted Mexican saddle with silver inlaid saddle cap and neck.

11 Silver-mounted bridle and reins for above.

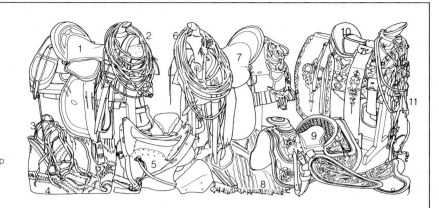

as certain models of Winchesters, and more. A blanket roll might tie onto the back of the cantle. And though separate, the bridle and bit were a constant companion to the saddle, virtually inseparable. A variety of these saw use, from the 'ring bit' popular with the Mexican riders, which could be terribly uncomfortable for an animal, to the variety still in use today.[9]

Contrary to popular mythology, the cowboy rarely if ever rode his own horse, nor did he own one. His employer provided the mount, and only occasionally did a truly long-term sentimental attachment arise, for a hand might work on several horses during the course of a season, and more often than not there was a healthy mistrust in operation. Being fed largely on low protein grass, the horses had to be changed often to rest. They could be mean spirited and temperamental, kicking out without reason or warning, and an iron-shod hoof in the wrong place could maim or even kill. Moreover, they had little reason to love their masters. Some maintained that almost twenty per cent of horses were literally 'ruined' in the act of being broken to the saddle, and one in a hundred would never be

gentled sufficiently to ride. The process of 'breaking' an animal could be brutal to both horse and rider, and involve starving, beating, choking, and almost always exhausting the animal repeatedly until its will to resist was broken down. Sometimes the horse was tripped and made to fall first, then the saddle was put on its back. Or it might be hobbled and blindfolded. Once the 'broncobuster' got in the saddle, the horse invariably reacted by bucking and trying to throw the unfamiliar weight from its back. Holding a quirt or whip weighted with lead shot, the rider would whip the horse's rear flanks each time he jumped. The spurs were not used, nor did he whip him on the shoulders or head. 'Everything in front of the cinch was supposed to belong to the horse,' quipped an old-timer, but in taming the animal, anything behind the cinch could be whipped, gouged, kicked, or whatever other 'technique' the rider preferred. This was another reason that few cowhands owned their horses, for they would be less likely to be stern with them in getting performance on the gruelling trail drives. For ranch owners, when horses were cheap, it was more sensible to

provide mounts, swallow the cost of those lost or ruined in breaking, and have relatively docile working animals left over, while having riders who were not too emotionally attached to them to make heavy demands on the range. The same was true of the donkeys that some rode in preference to horses, especially among the *vaqueros*.[10]

The routine of the cowboy's day quickly dispelled any notions of romance entertained by the tenderfoot. The cattle themselves were obstinate, stupid, inevitably troublesome creatures. They wandered away from the herd constantly. They got themselves stuck in bogs and watering holes and had to be pulled out. They tangled themselves in barbed wire when it began to appear on the range, and had to be untangled. They ate wire, rocks, brush, and anything else designed by man or nature to choke or kill an animal, and had to have it yanked from their uncooperative throats. The cowboy was in the saddle almost all day riding across the trackless grasslands, his only mission to find the cattle in trouble and get them out of it, or to tend the fences that kept the animals contained, or to find the cows who

Above: *An early ranch in Wyoming or Nebraska. The settled appearance suggests a rancher no longer at odds with his surroundings. A gift to nobody, ranching demanded toughness, the will to survive.*

Below: *Driving horses in the high country of the north. Though the West may have seemed like Paradise to the cattlemen, the ordinary cowboy had first-hand experience of the extremes of nature.*

Above: *A proper remuda, or herd of saddle horse and pack stock, kept cowboys on horseback throughout the drive. Horses might be hobbled or kept in with an improvised fence of lariats, as here.*

Below: *Spring round-up on the TDW spread, as indicated by the presence of calves and the leanness of the longhorns after a winter on the range. Cowboys in the background ease their saddle-sore backsides.*

were calving and help them give birth, since they had been domesticated to a degree that, like horses, they could no longer manage it on their own.

During most of the spring, summer, and fall, the cowboys stayed in the saddle much of the day watching after the herd, fattening itself on the lush grasslands of the West. The breeding and calving season came and went, with the endless unbroken routine of daily chores taking their toll on men and animals. Winters could be hard, and the coming of spring would require days of riding the fence lines to mend breaks. Heavy rains of the season would create sink-holes in which the cattle mired themselves, and where they had to be found and rescued before they died. After the rains, the hands roamed over the entire spread gathering the far-flung beeves in a spring roundup designed to take a census of the herd, tend ill or wounded animals, and concentrate them to be fattened through the summer and fall for the drive to the railhead and stock buyers.

A big part of the spring roundup – and a constant headache for the cowboys – was culling

their herd for strays from neighboring ranches. Originally the great western grasslands were entirely unfenced, the animals mixing and intermingling freely. Common law and custom decreed that a calf belonged to the owner of the mother, and it was after the birthing season that the animals were branded to establish final ownership. Cowboys had to learn to 'read' the brands of neighboring ranchers and return them to avoid friction between employers, though out on the range it became common practice for an occasional stray from a neighboring ranch to become steaks for the cowhands' campfire. Indeed, this became almost a part of the cowboys' lore. One never killed and ate one's employer's beeves. The famed Shanghai Pierce, coming across a rival rancher's hands dining on a Pierce beeve, recognized his own brand on the hide, and quipped with barbed cowboy humor that 'the day is coming when every outfit's going to have to eat its own beef'. Unflapped by being caught in the act, the herders neither admitted nor denied, but one said, 'in the meantime this here's mighty good meat'. Pierce sat down and dined with them on his own steer and left without incident, though undoubtedly the cowhands' employer soon provided an unwitting meal or two for Pierce's 'Big D' hands.[11]

During the summer, as ranchers' operations grew larger and more systematic, many harvested hay for the fall, rather than allow the animals to graze indefinitely. A good supply of hay was insurance against a drought, and allowed owners to keep the herd concentrated, which saved time at fall roundup and resulted in fewer lost animals. Of course, laying in the hay fell to the cowboys, and generally they hated it. It was endless, boring

work, and it kept them out of the saddle, where they preferred to be. Worse, in a harsh winter, with snow on the ground, he had to haul the hay out to the animals if the snow was too deep for the cattle to root through it with their noses to reach the winter grass beneath.

Winter, in fact, was the worst season of all, for it meant unemployment for all but a fortunate few. Once the fall roundup and drive to market was concluded, there was little or no work on the ranches until spring. Cowboys were turned loose to fend for themselves, and since few had saved anything from their year's wages, it meant a hardscrabble existence for them. Not a few found their first inducement

to cross to the other side of the law in the necessities of a winter with no money, food, or shelter. Those who did keep their jobs during the cold season spent their time in dreary maintenance chores – repairing cabins, windmills, fences and corrals, chopping wood, digging post holes, building new outbuildings, or whatever else the owner required. 'The Texas Puncher was always sighing for spring,' recalled one, and he was right. For a cowboy the lonesomest place in the world was a 'line shack' in winter, so called because it sat out from anywhere, designed and equipped solely to shelter him for months while he rode the fence lines every day looking for and mending

Above: *One of the perks of riding the range might be fresh beef, though cowboys almost never killed their own employers' cattle. Only in settled territory did the cowboy get a steady, fresh diet.*

Below: *Open-range branding without corrals necessitated closer coordination between cowhands. Note the calf (left) being dragged to the fire and sturdy saddles (foreground) essential for roping.*

breaks. Blizzards, snow blindness, cold, even starvation, all lay in wait for the men out on line for a winter, and the isolation especially could kill them. It is no wonder that a part of the cowboy image soon became a laconic speech that communicated as little as possible, and that in an earthy fashion. Months of seeing no other human hardly encouraged loquacity.[12]

It is no wonder that when the fall roundup came, the cowboys approached it with glee. It was a full season, sometimes weeks long, of doing what they liked best, riding hard over a wide country, disentangling the cattle from the landscape, and gathering them for the arduous, yet sometimes exhilarating trail drive. At the end of the drive, of course, came pay day and a spree in Dodge or Abilene or Wichita.

The roundup began as a community action, each rancher sending several – perhaps all – of his hands to a rendezvous from which they all spread out to cover hundreds of square miles in search of the cattle. They would bring them back, singly and in small groups, to the rendezvous, occupying several weeks in the process, and then start the business of separating them. 'Cutting out', they called it, and the task demanded specially trained horses that could stop, start, and turn literally on a dime to outwit a balky beeve and direct it where the cowboy wanted it to go. The riders of the several ranches worked well together, observing certain rules of conduct, which included not cut-

Top: *Branding irons on an open fire. Branding was an art: too hot, and the irons went too deep and damaged the animal; an even brand that took off the outer layer of skin was reckoned about right.*

Above: *The Becker sisters proved that ranching was not strictly a male occupation. Working here in 1894 at their father's ranch in the San Luis Valley, Colorado, they took it all over after his death.*

Below: *Branding in a corral, without the use of horses. Two cowhands hold the calf down, one by the head, the other by the legs. If the calf were male, such a position might also allow for castration.*

COWBOY ACCOUTERMENTS 2

Because of the special requirements of the avocation, the cowboy developed unique clothing and equipment. There is considerable variation in such items as saddles and chaps, depending upon location or manufacture. One will also discern a decided Indian or Mexican influence on various pieces. Consistently cowboy working equipment is spartan and utilitarian, developed through arduous range use, but there is also a particular appeal to much of this rough material. While Indian and more recently cowboy memorabilia has always been collectible, only really in the last twenty years have these objects become highly desirable. In recent years a proliferation of books on cowboy and Indian collectibles has become evident and interest in the field in general is growing rapidly. The modern cowboy may ride in a pick-up truck or helicopter but the image of the lone cowboy on horseback has become an American icon, a symbol of the West.

1 Hand wrought branding iron with head in form of an L.
2 Hand wrought branding iron, head in form of a U.
3 Braided leather quirt with shot loaded handle.
4 Quirt with red willow root handle.
5 Hand wrought branding iron with twisted shaft and socket for wooden handle, of probable Mexican origin.
6 Braided rawhide lariat.
7 Iron curry comb.
8 Grass rope or hemp *reata.*
9 One-piece twisted rawhide horse hobbles.
10 As above, but from the Remington Collection.
11 Farrier's heavy smooth leather apron used when shoeing horses.
12 Double bladed pocket knife with mother-of-pearl grips.
13 Steel leather punch. The revolving head has various diameter punches.

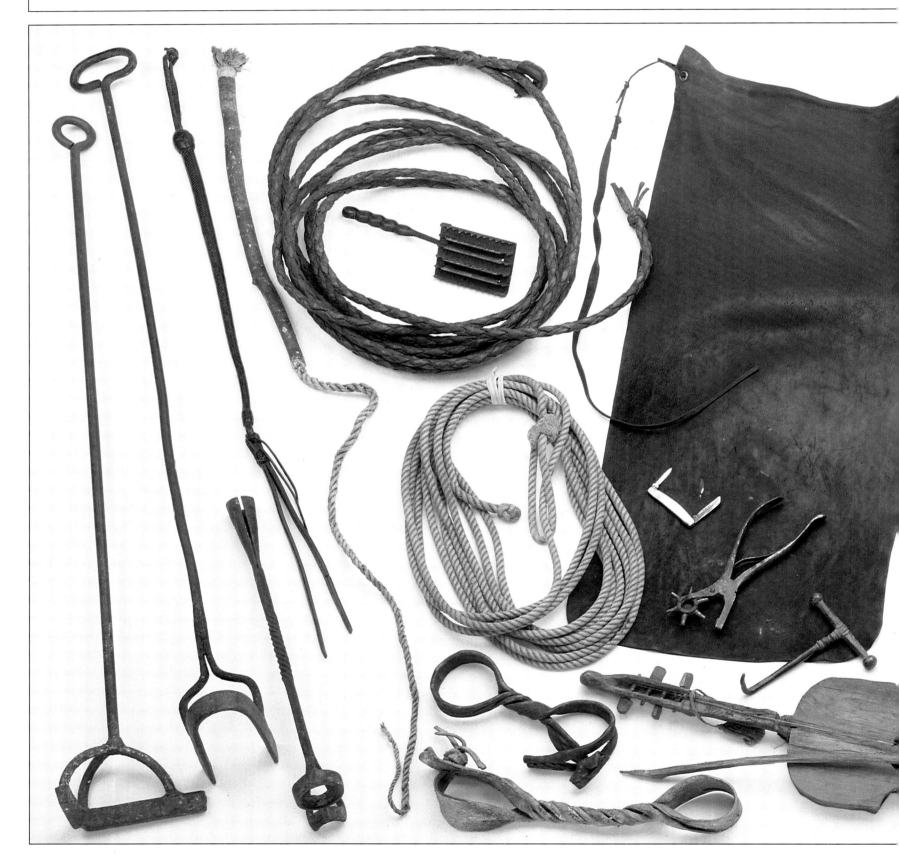

14 Farrier's pick for cleaning hooves.
15 Hand made wooden fiddle and bow, from Remington Collection.
16 Iron horse hoof nippers.
17 Cut horseshoe nails.
18 Various iron horseshoes.
19 Long braided rawhide *reata*.
20 Knife, fork and spoon with beaded decorative handles.
21 Tin pie or eating plate.
22 Copper and brass handled quirt.
23 Barbed wire, Brinkerhoff-Martelle patent, 1885.
24 C.A. Hodge 10 point spur rowel patent, 1887.
25 Crandal's Champion patent, 1879.
26 Stubbe plate patent, 1890.
27 Deckers Two Inch Spread, Huffman's patent, 1883.
28 A.J. Upham's two line 'snail barb' patent, 1883.
29 Kelly's Diamond Point patent, 1868.
30 C.A. Vosburgh 'Clinch Wire' patent, 1876.
31 Crandal's Chain Link patent, 1876.
32 Fork and spoon with leather carrying case.
33 Braided rawhide quirt.
34 Braided rawhide quirt with shorter leather popper.
35 Hand wrought branding iron, head in the form of a pitchfork.
36 Hand wrought branding iron.
37 Hand wrought branding iron, head in shape of wavy M.

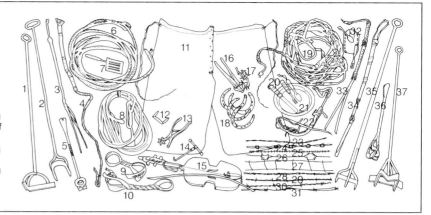

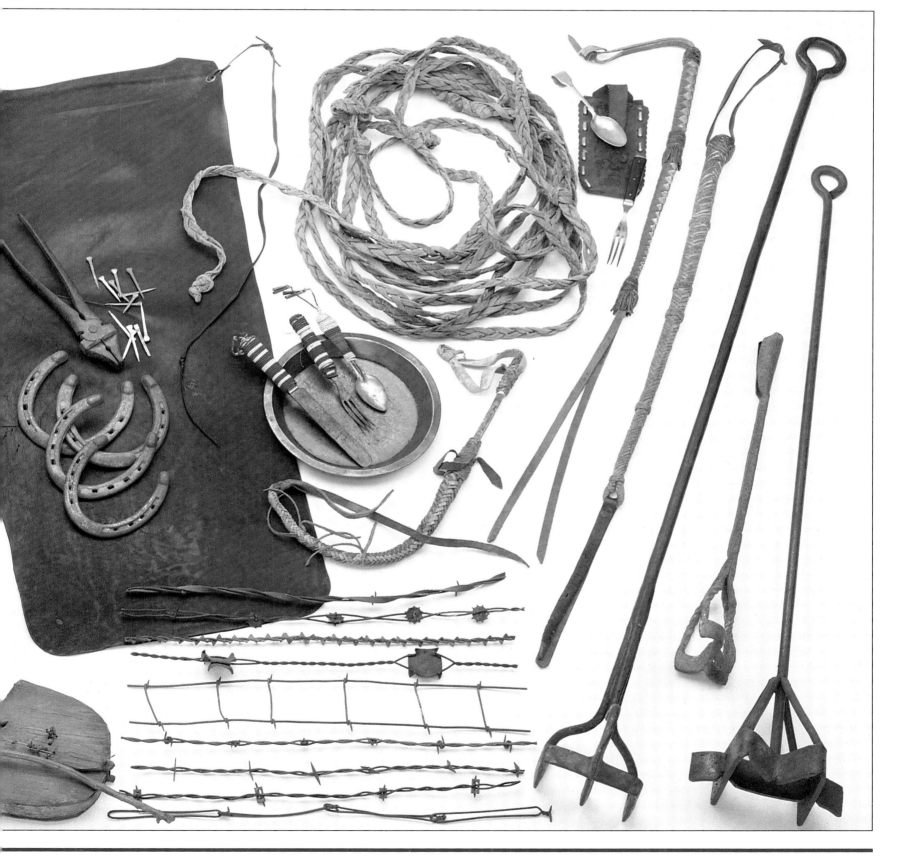

ting in front of another rider when he was cutting out an animal. A dozen fires kept branding irons at near-red heat for branding the calves that followed their mothers in the cutting. Knives castrated the bulls selected for sale rather than breeding, and many animals had to be dehorned to keep them from injuring others, as well as the cowboys and their horses.

The men managed the cattle with their lariats and lassos, slapping the animals to get them to move, roping one that refused to budge, and most frequently just slapping the coiled rope against their chaps to make a constant noise that kept the beeves attention. More than a hundred men and a thousand horses could be in almost constant motion during the weeks of the roundup, with the greatest activity in the first days, when as much as two-thirds – the easy to find two-thirds – of the scattered herds were concentrated at the rendezvous. After that, day after day the small parties of riders set off to different points of the compass to ferret out the more remote and isolated pockets of cattle. A cowboy could count on having days when he spent twenty hours or more in the saddle almost constantly. They learned to sleep sitting upright.

As the cattle were brought back to the rendezvous, more hands had to keep a constant watch on the growing herd to keep beeves from wandering off, and to keep them quiet. Cattle were notoriously spooky in mass num-

Above: *A cattle ranch on the Cimarron River. The ranch remuda (center) compares with the range version on page 209. A permanent corral was both ideal and essential for the breaking of horses.*

Below: *Branding calves on the W.D. Boyce Cattle Company spread, Point Rocks, Kansas, along the Cimarron River. The Cimarron ran through both Colorado and Kansas, and cattle might graze in both states.*

bers. A rifle shot, a clap of thunder, the hiss of a rattlesnake – anything, it seemed – could set off a local panic that spread quickly through the herd. That could mean a stampede, or 'stompede' as some Texans called it. 'One jump to their feet and another jump to hell', one old hand described it. In an instant a quiet herd could become a massive tidal wave of tons of horned beef rushing in an uncontrollable panic. The cowboy caught on his feet in its path was a dead man, and even men on horses knew better than to try to ride into the herd or get in its way. In Idaho in 1889, one stampeding herd literally ran over and killed 341 of its own cattle, and one poor cowboy and his horse. 'Mangled to sausage meat', was how his friends described him and his mount afterward. The cowboys either let the herd run out its fear, or else tried to surround them, waving arms and lariats, firing their pistols, to turn the herd back upon itself and exhaust it. Then came the trying chore of finding once more the scores who had wandered off singly and in small groups. Once they were back under some semblance of control, the herd could calm with remarkable speed, and the riders went to extra lengths to keep them calm. Many tried singing.[13]

Men who shared dangers such as the stampede, and the hardship and loneliness of the rest of the roundup, quickly formed a camaraderie and a rough sort of society based on trust, dependence, and a rugged frontier sense of fun, especially considering that on average

Above: *A sign of the times: a Dakota spread shows that smaller ranchers could grow rich from cattle. The house boasts a side porch and a second story, as well as a mechanical hayrake and a mowing machine.*

Below: *Round-up cowboys outside their bunkhouse, which was usually a separate building. Just as well too: the smell was generally unspeakable – sweat, tobacco, horses and manure making a heady aroma.*

the cowboy's working career expectancy was less than ten years. Enduring all that required a close bond among the men, and a rough and tumble sense of humor for blowing off pent up steam. As a result, no one and nothing was immune from being the object of the drover's fun. Tenderfeet, especially, were the universal object of derision, scorn, and pranks. Anyone caught wearing new clothes and boots was taken for a tenderfoot, and treated in the manner he deserved.

Indeed, even one of their own, a veteran, could be the butt of rough jokes when he appeared in something new or pretentious. One cattleman visiting a cow camp made the mistake of wearing a silk top hat. When he bedded down that night, he set his hat, obviously a source of some pride, on the ground beside him.

'What is it?' asked a nearby cowboy.

'It's a bear,' suggested another.

'It's a venomous kypoote,' suggested a third. 'It's one of those things that flee up and down the creek and hollow "walo wahoo" in the night time.'

The joking continued until one old timer yelled at the owner, 'Look out there, mister, that thing will bite you!' In an instant, as the hapless, and hatless, cattleman jumped aside, the rest ventillated the hat with their pistols until it fell to pieces. Wisely he took it well, laughed – perhaps nervously – at the joke, and then one of the others loaned him a proper hat. They next time they were in town, the shooters pooled their money and bought him a new 'regular cow-man's hat'. The important thing was that he took his kidding in good humor. Soon, said one of the pranksters, 'he hadn't been in that outfit three days until every man on the ranch, even the cook, would have fought his battles for him'.[14]

Laziness brought swift retribution from a cowboy's peers, and it could be brutal. One hand noted in his outfit for spending too much time sleeping under the chuck wagon while

Above: *Cowboys packing bedding before the day's work. On summer drives and round-ups it was probably a pleasure to forsake the bunkhouse – described by some as a rural slum – for the open air.*

Below: *Ranch hands of the W.D. Boyce Cattle Company bedding out for the night in Kansas. Sleeping out under the stars rather than under a roof could be a pleasurable change for cowhands.*

Right: *Round-up outfit in camp, Montana, 1886, shows a pleasant, relaxed scene. However, that year everything changed for cattleman and cowboy. The summer was bone dry but the winter of 1886-87 was the most devastating ever recorded on the northern plains. Storms broke up herds; snow buried them; sixty per cent of the cattle in Montana alone died. Many ranchers lost all that they owned and thereafter gave up altogether.*

the others worked, found himself paying a heavy price. While one man found and killed a large desert tarantula, another fastened a pin to the end of a long stick. Approaching the sleeping layabout, they set the dead spider beside his leg, and then from a distance jabbed him with the pin. When he awoke, one cowboy shammed stamping the tarantula to death, while others assured the stricken man that he had, indeed, been bitten. The spider was not deadly to humans, but many cowboys did not know that, and a 'friend' now prescribed a sure life-saving remedy to the 'bitten' man. First he drank a pint of bear oil, followed that with a package of baking soda, then half a tea-

cup of vinegar, then a quart of water in which a plug of tobacco had been steeping, all of it turning him into 'about as sick a boy as ever lived to tell'. Presumably the 'cure' and the fear of another bite encouraged the boy to spend less time under the chuck wagon, and more in the saddle.

Telling tall tales also became a part of the cowboy's idiom, and pretending to believe him was expected as a courtesy, even in the face of such bald-faced improbabilities as the story of one hand ordered to go out in the frozen cold of winter to find fence poles for stringing wire. Wood for posts was scarce, the weather frigid, and one hand topped a slope to

see several score frozen rattlesnakes strung out. He drove them into the ground, stapled the wire to them and went back to camp, only to be fired the next day when the weather – and snakes – thawed, and the fence slithered away into the brush.[15]

Pranks and tall tales went a long way to break the monotony of the cowhand's life. Indeed, everything was monotonous about it, even the food, though the cattleman ate well. There was just little or no variety. Beef was the staple of his diet, not surprisingly. He ate it three meals a day, generally as steaks fried in grease in a skillet, or else cut into chunks in what he called 'son-of-a-bitch-stew', a con-

ROUND-UP CHUCK WAGON

The chuck wagon was the nerve center or headquarters of any ranch crew on the range. While its origin is unsure, Charles Goodnight, one of the most famous trail bosses and cattlemen, is credited with making modifications to a surplus military wagon, picked primarily for its extra-durable iron axle, to the basic configuration shown. Goodnight added a water barrel and heavy tool box to either side of the wagon bed and a substantial chuck box to the rear of the wagon. Bentwood bows on top accommodated a canvas covering for protection against rain or sun. The chuck box contained numerous drawers and cubbyholes that stored everything including medicinal whiskey, foodstuffs, bedrolls and replacement gear. The wagon shown is actually a round-up wagon which was basically a stationary facility on the range during round-up; it tended to be more prestigious and better equipped than the trail wagon. The trail wagon used on a long cattle drive would be a much more spartan rig, lacking any stove and any such luxuries. This vehicle, actually made in the 1930s, is typical of such generic rigs used during the second half of the 19th century and up until the middle of the 20th century. As crude as it appears, it must have looked like heaven to an exhausted cowboy at the end of the day, for many of whom sociable gatherings at mealtimes offered the closest approximation to a family he might have during his working life. The cowboy had reason to be grateful to Charles Goodnight.

1 Wood folding leg
   camp table.
2 Tin eating or pie
   plate.
3 Tin eating utensil.
4 Condiment and tooth-
   pick containers.
5 Bread dough pan.
6 Folding leg of item 1.
7 Leather chaps.
8 Wooden bench for
   table.
9 Wood and tin wash
   board.
10 Wash tub.
11 Fat or lard storage
    can.

12 Large tin coffee pot.
13 Cast-iron cooking
    skillet.
14 Large iron skillet.
15 Portable iron stove,
    brand name 'The Great
    Majestic'.
16 Milk can.
17 Metal frying rack.
18 Sugar box which also
    serves as a seat.
19 Wooden mixing or
    washing tub.
20 Metal all-purpose
    pan.
21 Canvas cover for
    chuck wagon.

22 Wood and metal
    wagon bed.
23 Metal all-purpose
    pan.
24 As above.
25 Group of branding
    irons.
26 Storage container.
27 Leather harness collar
    for team.
28 Wood storage box.
29 Leather harness for
    team.
30 Tongue of wagon to
    which team of two or
    four horses would be
    attached.

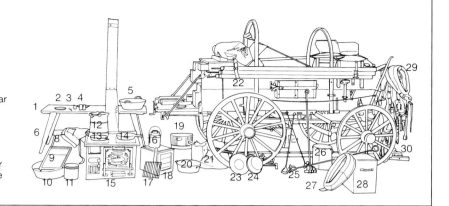

coction of offal, sweetbreads, tongue, other tough parts not suitable for steaks, and flour, and onions, water, and some local chili peppers or other seasonings. It was hearty, nourishing, and an acquired taste. Away from camp on the trail, however, the cow hands ate dried or jerked meat, bacon and other smoked meats, and lots of beans, corn meal, and local game, everything being seasoned with a lot of salt and molasses. Small groups could not kill a beeve for fresh meat because the meat would not keep, and as they moved on they hated to waste what could not be consumed by a small group. And no matter where he was, or what his fare, the cowboy washed it all down with gallons of coffee, morning, noon, and night. They liked it strong and black. There were some variations in diet according to locality, but fruit was always a rarity, and even vegetables other than onions hard to come by. What fruit and vegetables they did get were canned. And ironically, since they were surrounded by cattle, they almost never used milk or butter.

There was an interesting mix of men gathering at the chuck wagon, around the fire, or often as not huddled in the line shack, eating those beans, sourdough biscuits, and drinking all that black coffee. Being thrown together so closely, so dependent upon each other, encouraged a kind of equality among the men that overrode difference of age, education, or background. It also in many instances took precedence over race. While estimates are inevitably untrustworthy, it seems likely that as many as 5,000 Negro cowboys worked the herds alongside their white counterparts. They came by a variety of means. Many were ex-slaves freed in Texas and Arkansas by the Civil War. Others were displaced blacks, free

and former slaves, from the eastern states of the old Confederacy, where they were not wanted and where hard economic times made work scarce. Others came from the North, following the same lure that brought the other tenderfeet.

In some camps, the blacks numbered fully one-fourth of the hands present, especially on the Chisholm Trail drives. In the early days they faced surprisingly little discrimination, especially out on the trail, or in the bunkhouse. Indeed, it appears that blacks encountered less true discrimination as cowboys than in any other profession open to them after the Civil War. Several reasons offer themselves.

For one thing, they were generally hired to perform the most difficult tasks, especially breaking horses, which was both exhausting and dangerous. As a result, those good at their trade won admiration for their strength and manhood that transcended any strong racial resentments. It also helped that the cowboys lived and worked far from civilization, in an almost exclusively male environment. Only the coming of population, more urban conditions, and the presence of numbers of white women, began to result in the imposition of racial barriers. They did not 'get ahead' in the ranch hierarchy; only a few became foremen or trail bosses, much less ranch owners. But

Below: *Suppertime on round-up. The chuck wagon was vital to any trail outfit, essential to a cowboy's comfort, whether on round-up or drive. The tentlike tarpaulin (left) suggests a more permanent campsite.*

Above: *An old-time chuckwagon, c. 1885. Said to have been perfected by Charles Goodnight, it had to be durable enough to survive the trail. The chuck box at the rear was Goodnight's special innovation.*

Right: *A large proportion of cowboys were black, from a variety of backgrounds. Though some might be former slaves, they experienced little or no prejudice from fellow white cowhands on the range.*

they made the same wage as whites and shared the same food and bunkhouses. Even when in town, they ran into only marginal discrimination so long as they were careful. Most saloons required that blacks drink at one end of the bar, whites at the other. And, of course, the age-old sexual taboos of black men and white women precluded the sable cowboys from patronizing white brothels.

Otherwise, so long as they showed good judgement and tact, the black cowhands had little to fear. They encountered some pranks and taunting, but if they took it well, it usually stopped. Many found themselves dubbed with nicknames like 'Nigger Bob' or 'Nigger Newt',

but so long as they took no offense they had no trouble, and in that era the word possessed nothing like the insulting connotations it would later acquire. Fights between white and black were few, and most of the blacks knew well enough not to beat a white man too bad, or not at all. It preserved the peace and did not upset the balance that made the whites comfortable, and tolerant.

They were trusted and respected. Charles Goodnight employed a Bose Ikard on his spread, calling him 'my detective, banker, and everything else'. 'I have trusted him farther than any living man.' Another, Bill Pickett, was called by his employer 'the greatest sweat

and dirt cowhand that ever lived – bar none'. Pickett was one of the few who eventually wound up working for himself, having performed in rodeos for years, saved his money, and bought a ranch of his own. For most of the others, they faced the same long-term hazards as their white peers, working until they were no longer up to the strains of the job, then being let go to try to find something else to do. Many made the trasition from cowboy to cook, riding with the chuckwagon well into old age, earning their $30 a month the same as the cowhands.[17]

Whether white or black or Mexican – more than a tenth of cowboys were Mexican-

---

The first transcontinental rail line ran across central Nebraska, and offered little lure to the growing number of cattle ranchers in Texas by the 1870s. They had beeves to get to hungry markets in the east but the distance to Nebraska was

too great. At the end of the Civil War, their state back in the Union, Texas ranchers looked first at central Missouri. In 1866 the Sedalia Trail picked up the old Shawnee Trail from San Antonio across the Red River up to Sedalia and a railhead on

CATTLE TRAILS 1840s-1880s

the Missouri Pacific RR. Drives later changed direction to the greater stockyards and facilities at Kansas City. In 1866 Goodnight and Loving cut their long trail from central Texas along the

eastern slopes of the Rockies, north through New Mexico Territory and Denver to the railroad at Cheyenne. The trail grew shorter over the years as the Kansas Pacific reached

Denver, then the Atchison, Topeka & Santa Fe cut across southern Colorado. The Kansas Pacific line, snaking across southern Kansas, attracted the Chisholm Trail, first opened in 1867. It followed the rails west,

terminating first in Abilene, then Ellsworth. In 1876 the Western Trail opened west of and parallel to the Chisholm, moving directly to Dodge City. The coming of rails to Texas was to make cattle trails a thing of the past.

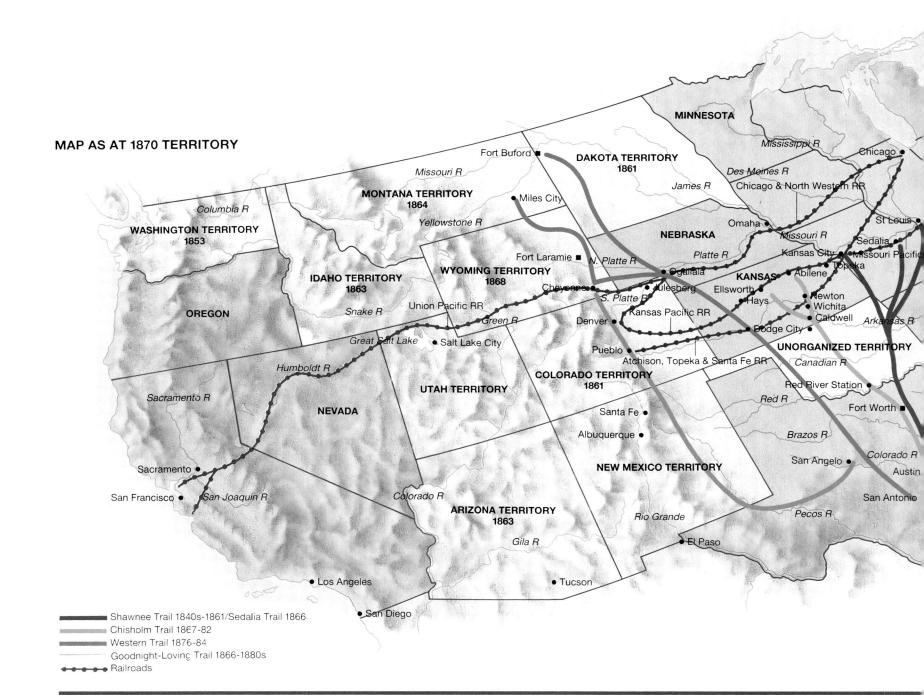

MAP AS AT 1870 TERRITORY

Shawnee Trail 1840s-1861/Sedalia Trail 1866

Chisholm Trail 1867-82

Western Trail 1876-84

Goodnight-Loving Trail 1866-1880s

Railroads

American – the one event that culminated all of their efforts during the year past was the trail drive, the long overland trek from the ranches to the railhead where the beeves could be shipped to the eastern markets. The great trail drives started in Texas in the years after the Civil War, when trails like the Goodnight-Loving and others were opened. Kansas was the first and always the primary goal, for it lay directly north of Texas, across the Indian Territory that later became Oklahoma, and the railroad pushed steadily across it, closer to the source and shortening the distance of the drives. Only Kansas' ban on Texas cattle in 1884, enacted to protect its own growing

herds, and then the building of rail lines directly south into the cattle country itself, finally put an end to the trail drive by about 1895.

But they were impressive while they lasted. In 1871 alone some 600,000-700,000 cattle were driven northward. Every 2,000-3,000 cattle required from eight to twenty cowboys to manage it on the drive, along with a cook, a wrangler to take care of the remuda, and perhaps a foreman. When the drive commenced, a man rode at the 'point' or ahead of the column to act as guide and watch for obstacles. 'Swing' riders flanked the herd on either side some distance back, then 'flank' men further

back still, while the 'drag' rider(s) brought up the rear, followed by the wrangler and the remuda. As the day wore on, the herd strung out into a long, thin line of beef twisting and turning its way along the trail, grazing often, stopping for water, and usually covering little more than twelve miles a day. A host of hazards awaited, from maurauding parties of Indians, to river crossings where the cattle bogged or drowned in swollen streams. Gophers and prairie dogs dotted the countryside with holes that an unwary horse could break a leg in. A stampede could cost days of delay, as could bad weather or floods. Wolves and coyotes hovered on the fringes of the herd

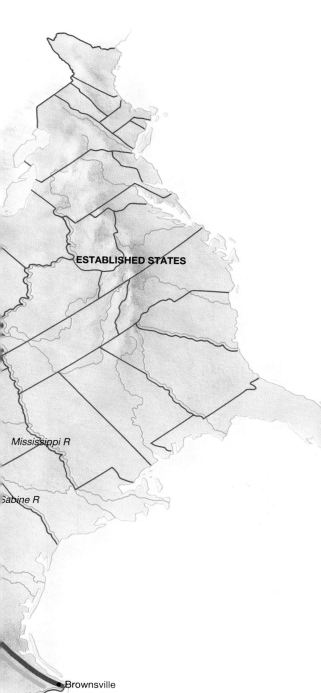

ESTABLISHED STATES

Mississippi R

Sabine R

Brownsville

Above: *Even at the height of the cattle boom, sheep were farmed in numbers in the West: by the 1880s southern Montana had one ranch in five running sheep. Wichita, Kansas, traded in sheep in 1873.*

Below: *Sheep in the Powder River Badlands of Montana/Wyoming. Billings, Montana, became a major wool shipping depot in the 1890s; by the end of the century sheep ranching rivaled that of cattle.*

hoping for a meal. 'For the benefit of those who have not tried it,' wrote one veteran, 'I may say that driving refractory cattle on a tired horse is very poor fun.'[18]

But the cowboys stayed with it, and in a few weeks had their reward when they reached Wichita, or Ellsworth, or Abilene, or Dodge City. The drive could take months, however, if the trail conditions were against them. In either case, when the men hit town and were relieved of their bawling, quarrelsome burdens, it was no wonder that they sought relief in an outburst of energy and high spirits. They got a bath, a shave, bought new clothes, and headed off for the dance halls, bordellos, saloons, and the streets, to spend the rest of their pay and have as much fun as they could pack into the few days before they had to ride back to Texas. If they never actually 'took over' towns as legend has it, still they could fill a railhead with enough drunken, brawling cowboys to give the citizens pause about crossing their paths. Usually the hands confined their activities to the underbelly of the cow towns, mixing little if at all on the respectable streets of Western communities. That done, they gazed into their empty wallets, rubbed their bruised jaws and cracked ribs, held their throbbing heads, and mounted their ponies, heading south once more in little bands of subdued cowpunchers, armed with stories they would tell and exaggerate when their heads felt better, and full of resolution not to squander it all next year, which, of course, they would not remember when the time came. Ahead of them lay the well-worn cattle trails south, and another year of the

Above: *Driving cattle down in Texas, the true cradle of the cattle boom. In the north, the killer winter of 1886-87 had ended the adventure for the big investors, many of whom left, never to return.*

Below: *A trail herd watering. The trail chuckwagon in the background observed the daily routine of moving out mid-afternoon some miles ahead of the herd to set up the next camp site.*

same grinding routine and backbreaking labor. Of all of those who went Westering looking for opportunity, that fickle dream's blessing stuck least of all to these lonely men who, most of all, came to symbolize the West itself.

REFERENCES

1 Richard W. Slatta, *Cowboys of the Americas* (New Haven, Conn., 1991), p. 4.
2 *Ibid.*, p. 47.
3 Douglas Branch, *The Cowboy and His Interpreters* (New York, 1926), pp. 11-12; Slatta, *Cowboys of the Americas*, p. 46.
4 Slatta, *Cowboys*, p. 48.
5 *Ibid.*
6 Odie Faulk, *Dodge City*, p. 62; Slatta, *Cowboys of the Americas*, pp. 41, 43.
7 Faulk, *Dodge City*, pp. 62-4; Jose Cicneros, *Riders Across the Centuries* (El Paso, Tex., 1984), p. 192
8 Slatta, *Cowboys of the Americas*, pp. 48-9.
9 *Ibid.*, pp. 44, 87, 90-91.
10 *Ibid.*, pp. 77-8; Faulk, *Dodge City*, p. 65
11 Dee Brown, *Wondrous Times on the Frontier* (Little Rock, Ark., 1991), p. 222.
12 Slatta, *Cowboys of the Americas*, pp. 81-2; Faulk, *Dodge City*, p. 64.
13 Slatta, *Cowboys of the Americas*, pp. 81-2; J. Frank Dobie, *The Longhorns* (Boston, 1941), p. 88.
14 Brown, *Wondrous Times on the Frontier*, pp. 217-18.
15 *Ibid.*, p. 219.
16 Slatta, *Cowboys of the Americas*, p. 113.
17 William L. Katz, *The Black West* (New York, 1971), pp. 146-8, 160; Slatta, *Cowboys of the Americas*, p. 168; Faulk, *Dodge City*, p. 66.
18 Slatta, *Cowboys of the Americas*, pp. 78-9; Dobie, *The Longhorns*, p. 88.

Above: *The climate could be the cowman's biggest enemy. Winter blizzards could sweep from the north into Texas as late as May. Hailstorms were a hazard too: men spoke of hailstones as big as eggs some years.*

Below: *The long trail drive culminated in stockyards such as these in East St Louis, Missouri, the like of which handled more than half a million head of cattle in the 1880s and made the cattle barons rich.*

VIII

THE END
OF THE OLD WEST

Below: *Buffalo Bill's Wild West Show, 1902. Show Indians play ping-pong to while away the time. By then, most people knew the score.*

THE END OF THE OLD WEST

EVERY TEN YEARS the Bureau of the Census compiled and published population and statistical figures for the United States and its territories, as it still does. Though the Bureau's reports have often stirred controversy, none would exert a more profound psychological impact on the nation than that for the year 1890. It surveyed the spread of towns and cities throughout the West, the diffusion of population through the once-impenetrable vastness, and concluded that 'up to and including 1880 [the last census] the country had a frontier of settlement, but at present the unsettled area has been so broken into by isolated bodies of settlement that there

can hardly be said to be a frontier line'. For decades the reports had discussed the extent of that line of frontier, decade by decade tracking its steady spread westward. But by 1890 it had reached the Pacific, turned inward upon itself to the most remote reaches of the mountains and deserts, and then disappeared. 'It can not,' concluded the head of the Bureau, 'any longer have a place in the census reports.' In effect, Washington was declaring that the frontier was over.[1]

In just the brief span of seventy-seven years – the life expectancy of a man – the West had gone from the wilderness that almost swallowed Lewis and Clark, to a virtual empire of

half a continent. It took the breath away from hosts of Americans, reared on the *idea* of the frontier as a goal, a challenge, as something so great that it could absorb millions and still be fresh, untamed, ready for more teeming adventures looking to better themselves.

It was now composed not of a vast territory, but almost wholly of new states, almost as many as those east of the Mississippi. The work of state making had started with Louisiana, then in 1820 came Missouri, and in the years immediately following, Arkansas, Iowa, and Texas. In the boom of new land after the Mexican War came California in 1850, but then the lull brought about by the sectional

crisis. Not until 1858 was Minnesota added to the Union and then the next year, almost a thousand miles to the west, Oregon, the troubled territory that almost caused conflict with Great Britain, became a state. In 1861 Kansas became the first state born of Civil War. In 1867 its other half of the old Nebraska Territory became a state in its own name.

The boom years began now, as the blanks in the map between California and Kansas, Canada and Mexico, started gradually to fill in. Colorado was admitted to statehood in 1876. Along the way Nevada also moved up from territorial status, and then came the great state-making years. North Dakota, South Dakota, Montana and Washington, all joined the fraternity in 1889, and the next year Congress passed on admitting Idaho and Wyoming.

The frontier was, indeed, coming to an end when that census report went out. In 1893 the old Indian Territory was reorganized into the Oklahoma Territory, and with that act, every square inch of the West finally stood under some form of official governmental organization. Besides Oklahoma, only Utah, New Mexico, and Arizona, still awaited statehood among the contiguous continental lands. Alaska, too, was a territory. By 1909 all but the last would be states.

The effect dazzled many in the East and around the world, and even shook some of the Westerners, not accustomed to being easily upset. Men and women began to ask if the so-called American dream had come to an end. Where would there be room to keep accommodating the hopeful immigrants from the Old World? Where and how would settlers with an itch to move on again as they had in the past find to go? In 1890 the government also moved against the host of unscrupulous land speculators who filed false claims under the various Homestead acts, and then held the land expecting to resell when development could mean great profits, rather than putting it

---

By the closing months of the century, the United States stood virtually complete, and the West of the entrepreneurs, exploiters, opportunists, settlers and scavengers was almost closed. The frontier had ceased to exist; in its place was a thriving agricultural and industrial region poised for ever-increasing civilization and settlement. The business of state-making had progressed relentlessly, beginning, before the Civil War, with California. The question

STATES OF AMERICA 1899

of control of these new western states had helped to precipitate the war, which for a time saw other states try to leave the Union. Afterward, those states, including Arkansas and Texas, were readmitted, joining others like Kansas and Nevada that had been admitted in their 'absence'. Thereafter it was only a question of population, territorial organization and politics, as the great western pie was steadily carved into smaller and smaller pieces. By the turn of the century only Arizona, New Mexico and Oklahoma remained as territories within the contiguous Western states. Sadly and inevitably, the clash of red and white cultures saw one man's progress and another's devastation. The opening and 'conquest' of the American West was an epic of heroic yet bittersweet proportions: an American 'original'.

STATES OF AMERICA AS AT 1899

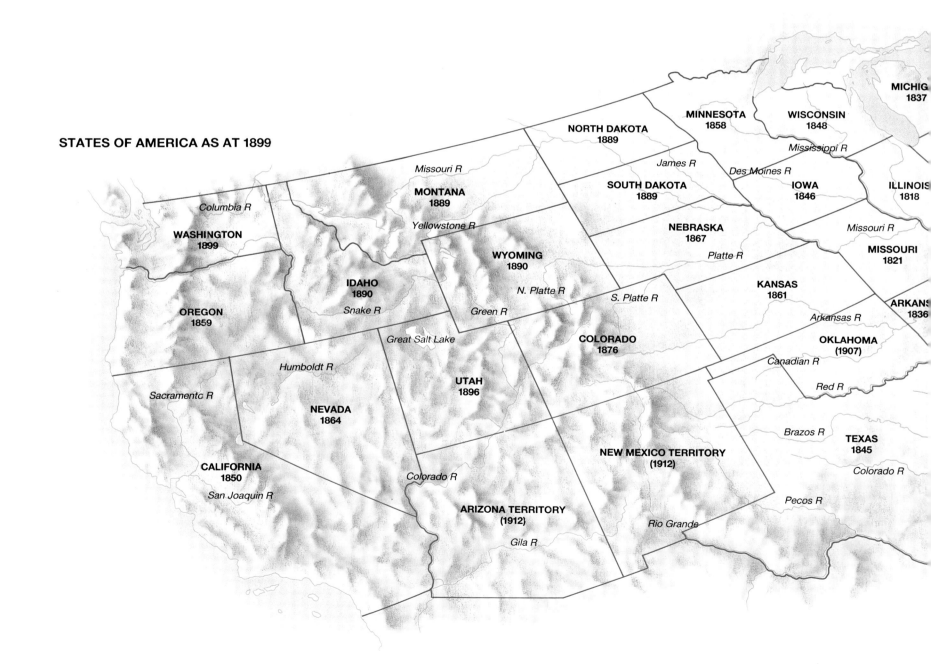

MICHIG 1837
MINNESOTA 1858
WISCONSIN 1848
NORTH DAKOTA 1889
Missouri R
James R
Des Moines R
Mississippi R
IOWA 1846
ILLINOIS 1818
Columbia R
MONTANA 1889
SOUTH DAKOTA 1889
Yellowstone R
NEBRASKA 1867
Missouri R
WASHINGTON 1899
WYOMING 1890
Platte R
MISSOURI 1821
IDAHO 1890
N. Platte R
S. Platte R
KANSAS 1861
ARKANS 1836
OREGON 1859
Snake R
Green R
Arkansas R
Great Salt Lake
COLORADO 1876
OKLAHOMA (1907)
Humboldt R
Canadian R
UTAH 1896
Red R
Sacramento R
NEVADA 1864
NEW MEXICO TERRITORY (1912)
Brazos R
TEXAS 1845
CALIFORNIA 1850
Colorado R
Colorado R
San Joaquin R
Pecos R
ARIZONA TERRITORY (1912)
Rio Grande
Gila R

under the plow and settling it as the law intended. To combat this, and entirely co-incidental with the announcement of the close of the frontier, Washington declared all public domain lands remaining in its hands off limits. Homesteading was to be postponed indefinitely until proper surveys and safeguards could re-open the land for the purposes intended.

The dual effect of these announcements cannot be overestimated. Since 1607 and the first permanent settlement on these shores, there had always been more land available. There had always been a 'West', whether that meant the Shenandoah Valley of Virginia in

the 1700s or the San Joaquin of California a century later. How could Americans now readjust their thinking, their view of their country and of themselves, to the idea that they were at last citizens of a closed system for which any future expansion would be internal rather than external?[2]

In part, the answer was that they simply would not accept it. Expansionism had been a part of the American mind for more than half a century, and in the 1840s it was given both a name and a sense of almost holy mission. It was America's 'manifest destiny' to occupy and settle all of the continent west to the Pacific, argued the men who pushed for war

with Mexico. They were largely the same ones who argued intermittently for the acquisition of Cuba by peaceful means or otherwise, and some even put words into action by leading 'filibustering' expeditions to the island in unsuccessful attempts to claim it for the United States. At the end of the war, they also pressed for not settling with the line of the Rio Grande, but for taking advantage of the presence of Yankee armies in Mexico City to annex all of Mexico itself. Even beyond that, some cast loving eyes toward South America, especially Nicaragua and Panama. Geographically such territory may have lain far to the south, but in the emotional and intellectual cast of the era, it

MAINE
1820

OHIO
1803

IANA
316

ESTABLISHED STATES BEFORE
1800

ALABAMA
1819

FLORIDA
1845

MISSISSIPPI
1817

Mississippi R

bine R LOUISIANA
1812

Above: *In 1880, riverboats continued to carry supplies to still remote places such as this depot sixty miles from Fort Benton, Montana Territory. By 1889, the territory had been awarded statehood.*

Below: *. . . and the railways continued on their inexorable way, carving through landscape and wilderness that only decades ago had threatened to swallow up men like Frémont, who gave his name to this pass.*

was all really just the West with jungles. Even Canada occasionally became the object of covetous eyes, and when Alaska came on the market in 1867, Washington rushed to make the purchase.

By 1890, Americans were still looking for more of the West, and starting to see it in the Pacific. Hawaii, the Philippines, and other remote islands could be turned into the outposts of empire, bases for an expanding American Navy that was coming to look on the Pacific as a part of its rightful hegemony. Islands in the Caribbean, too, resumed their old attraction. All of the old impulses came into play again – the lure of new and strange lands, the opportunity for daring opportunists to move in early, displace the native peoples, and take the best ground, or the resources out of the ground. And with the growing climate of global politics, the government in Washington became one of the opportunists as well, looking not so much for profits, as for bases of influence and continental defense, essentially a way of extending America's borders hundreds, even thousands, of miles beyond its continental boundaries. Somehow, the 'West' would go on.

Indeed, in time the land would open up once more to homesteading, under newer and better regulation, but the boom days were over. Thus it was all the more fitting that the last grab for acreage took place in true opportunistic, and egalitarian, western style. As Oklahoma approached territorial status, powerful politicians in Washington, backed by railroad interests, pressed for opening the last of its non-Indian public lands. The Creek and Seminole tribes had taken sides with the South during the Civil War, and at its conclusion the government exacted a penalty from them by reclaiming nearly two million acres of the land once given to them 'in perpetuity', the only genuine case of large scale reparations being exacted upon Confederates. It had always

been assumed that the huge tract would be turned over to other Indians once the offenders were resettled, but Washington never did anything about it. In such a state of affairs, whites demanded that the land be made available. Some did not wait for government action, and simply squatted illegally on the property, earning themselves the nickname of 'boomers'.

In 1889 Washington finally came to a decision. It would not take back the land without compensation, paying the tribes the same $1.25 per acre that homesteaders had been paying for a generation. But it would take the land back, and then it immediately conducted

a survey to divide it into quarter-section tracts. The announcement went out that on 22 April 1889, the huge area would be opened up for those wishing to stake their claims, on a first come basis. The cry went out across much of the Midwest that once more there would be virtually free land for the taking. As many as 50,000 showed up on the designated day and place. A gun would be fired, and they would rush across a line to race each other for the lots. The first to drive his stakes into a tract, marking it as his own, would have the title.

It was an incredible scene. Men and women showed up in everything from horse-drawn wagons to bicycles and even wheelbarrows.

Above: *It was all about land. Americans saw the acquisition of property as a cultural imperative. When part of Oklahoma was made available in 1889, some 50,000 raced to stake their claims.*

Below: *Opening the Cherokee strip in Guthrie, Oklahoma Territory, 1889, where a makeshift town quickly grew in anticipation of business to come. Speculators, land attorneys and surveyors had a field day.*

They surrounded the surveyed area on three sides, and when the pistol was fired, they hurled off on a stampede the like of which the West never saw before or after. Not a few literally 'jumped the gun' by sneaking into the tract the night before to stake their claims first. They soon earned the sobriquet by which all Oklahomans would one day be known, 'sooners'. In less than a day it was all over.

It was politics that had opened up Oklahoma to the 'sooners' and the rest, just as it had always been political leaders who created the opportunity for others to invade the prairies and mountains. But where leaders in Washington in earlier times had acted in the

West mainly to see it settled and made safe for its white inhabitants, now they increasingly came to change their focus. Like everyone else, politicians felt a sort of trauma at the realization that the frontier was disappearing. They had always made opportunity for their constituents – and themselves – by opening new lands as the older ones filled. Now that there was nowhere else to go, they turned increasingly to the same profiteering frenzy that hit much of the rest of the nation. Through loopholes in statutes and manipulation of the lawmaking process, they managed to force more of the Indians of Oklahoma and other reservation areas out of their land – not entirely,

but greatly restricting them. The reclaimed land went to more of the voracious whites anxious to get a last piece of the Western pie before it was all gone.

In fact, since the days of Reconstruction, Western politics had gotten more and more into the mainstream of the Gilded Age, especially as the growing number of western states acquired more and more votes in Congress, especially the Senate. Politicians became increasingly intimate with the great railroad interests, encouraging the real estate booms that were largely manipulated to sell of the vast domains of right of way land granted to the roads when first built. In the same regions

Above: *A land office established at Hollister, Idaho, prior to the 'rush' on 22 April 1889. In the clear absence of vehicles for a quick dash, the philosophy here seemed to be that there was one appropriate way to treat land – divide it, distribute it and register it. Upon registration, lots would be drawn for possession of the available land. Thus was America to be portioned out.*

Below: *Guthrie was a phenomenon that sprang up almost overnight. Within a month it could boast a hotel, newspapers, stores, numerous restaurants and more saloons than all of them put together.*

'CONQUEST OF THE PRAIRIE'

This oil painting by Irving R. Bacon hangs in the Whitney Gallery of Western Art, Cody, Wyoming. Painted after the end of the 19th century, it is the quintessential allegory of the conquest and civilization of the American West. If it glorifies the West, it pays homage too to 'Buffalo Bill' Cody as civilization's guide and one of the most remarkable figures of the age. At the left of the painting, Buffalo Bill leads a wagon train across the prairie. Opposite, Plains Indians watch his progress with apprehension from their village; before them, their lifeblood flowing away, a herd of buffalo passes, to become just as the Indian another part of the history of the Great Plains. Behind Buffalo Bill are seen the towers and skyscrapers of the modern industrial city, the shape of the future. Behind the advancing wagon train appears another powerful symbol of progress, the railway, which, by the last third of the century, had successfully linked east and west. As the following letter from the artist makes clear, Bacon painted two versions of 'The Conquest of the Prairie'. The original hangs in the C.M. Russell Museum, Great Falls, Montana. Before it was purchased for the Whitney, the second version shown here could be seen at the Irma Hotel, Cody, which Buffalo Bill built in 1902 for, and named after, his daughter. Of the two paintings he produced, the artist wrote in September 1928: 'The writer Irving R. Bacon,

artist-painter of Detroit, Michigan, completed the 10 × 4 ft oil painting entitled 'The Conquest of the Prairie' in the city of Munich, Germany, in the spring of 1908. Before this picture was finished, the writer decided to paint a duplicate canvass of the same dimensions on which to carry out experiments and changes in the composition, which if worked out successfully, were to be incorporated in the original painting. After the completion of the original painting was accomplished, the writer decided to perfect the second canvass, so in the end I had two paintings of the same subject and the same size. However, the original painting was painted more carefully and represented the full extent of my ability at the time. Therefore, the original painting of 'The Conquest of the Prairie', being considered by me the better of the two, was submitted to the Summer Exhibition [in] Munich where it was accepted by the jury and exhibited during the summer of 1908 . . . The following spring this same canvass was submitted to the jury of the Paris Salon, accepted by it and displayed during the summer of 1909 . . . Later, this same painting was exhibited in the Winter Exhibition of the Chicago Art Institute, the Spring exhibition of the Pennsylvania Academy of Fine Arts and on the circuit of the Western Artists' Association . . . The original painting was purchased by C. Harold Wills and the duplicate canvass by Col. William F. Cody, who placed it in his permanent collection at the Irma Hotel, Cody, Wyoming.'

where once prospectors quarreled over rights to a digging, and settlers argued about access to a stream, growing corporations and even conglomerates did battle in court rooms and legislative halls for water rights to whole regions, and mineral rights to ranges of mountains. Where once the individual had come with opportunity in his eyes and hope in his heart, the industrialists, and speculators now roamed with writs in their hands and lawyers in their pockets. Trade unions began to form to combat onerous conditions and unfair wages. There were miners' strikes, and violence when scabs and professional breakers were brought in. Over-production and declining markets led to depressions in several of the Western industries, but especially agriculture and silver.

All of the old ills of the East seemed to descend upon the West in the last two decades of the frontier, and with them the nation, and world-wide problems of the late century. In twenty years, the batting of an eye historically speaking, the frontier had gone through an abrupt about face. The only recourse was the ballot box. Westerners tended to bring west with them their politics pretty much intact, but with the Republican Party holding almost unbroken power through the last four decades of the century, the vested interests with which its leaders kept company could hardly be

Right: *Comanches in a studio portrait taken at Fort Sill, Oklahoma Territory. In 1875 Quanah Parker had led the last diehard Comanches onto the reservation to begin the process of assimilation.*

Below: *Indian 'loafers' outside their shack near Fort Laramie. Probably mixed bloods of Oglala and Brulé stock, they were so called because they spent much of their time loafing around Fort Laramie . . .*

contained, much less stopped. Incipient movements like the Populist Party grew up in response to the increasingly unmet needs of the small farmers and cattlemen, and in the 1890s the new platform of direct election of Senators – instead of having them chosen by state legislatures – conversion from the gold standard to silver to stabilize the currency, and other reforms, saw several Populists win Western governorships and legislatures, especially in the farm belt. Nationally they hardly made a ripple, but it was the West's first attempt to stand up to the East with its own voice. In 1894 when an army of the unemployed mustered from all over the nation

to march on Washington and demand reform, the West contributed the majority of the 'soldiers'. Two years later the Populists, having shot their bolt, merged with the Democratic Party and the West offered up its first Presidential candidate from a major party, William Jennings Bryan. That 'voice' was being heard.[3]

And by then other voices were being heard as well, for not all of the story of the growing politicization of the West was a tale of setback and loss. There were significant 'firsts' out here, as well, none of greater impact than female suffrage. The first women to vote in America did not do so in Massachusetts or

New York, but in Wyoming, which enacted the legislation in 1869, and the next year Utah Territory did the same. It came about for many reasons, some having nothing at all to do with granting women their natural rights, but it came about just the same, setting a precedent that it took much of the rest of the nation decades to follow.[4]

More signs of the coming of modern America appeared in the dying gasps of the old ways of life as the frontier closed. In 1883 General William T. Sherman had declared that 'I now regard the Indians as substantially eliminated from the problem of the Army.' Virtually every tribe had been confined to a reservation, with only a few isolated hold-outs, chiefly in the mountains of northern California, still trying to cling in small groups to their Stone Age way of life. The reservation system, with its persistent and insistent diversion of the red man to the white's civilization, steadily broke down many of the remaining vestiges of their centuries-old culture. The acts of the politicians and the speculators to reclaim their reservation land only further eroded their pride and sense of place.

Many of the tribes took refuge in a return to their earliest religious beliefs, shamanism, and messianic cults. One such prophet was a Paiute named Wovoka, who quickly gathered a following throughout the central and northern

Above: *As they were assimilated, bands of Brulé Sioux established farming settlements. The government provided free doors and sash windows for the rude log cabins they built. Most cabins had bare earth floors.*

Below: *By 1910, when this photograph of a Crow family home in Montana was taken, the Crow of the northern plains had long forsaken their 'war psychology' of the past. The photograph speaks for itself.*

The last stand of the Lakota at Wounded Knee in December 1890 signalled the final death knell of the nomadic buffalo hunting plains Indian. Confined now to designated areas, the reservations, it would be more than a generation before the 'Indian problem' would again be considered. These people – once supreme lords of the bountiful plains – became dependent on almost everything of white manufacture, such as woven fabrics for clothing, Sibley tents, metal cups and kettles; army issue boots even replace the moccasins of the standing warrior who, in his traditional eagle feather headdress, clings to a vestige of a proud past.

plains in 1889. He practised what he called the Ghost Dance, prophecying that his followers would be together again with all of their kin lost to white bullets and treachery. In the euphoria of the dance, he could see to that better world briefly, and so could his followers. He even sent out missionaries to other tribes, preaching both the dance and peace. His was essentially a Christian message adapted to Indian ceremonies.

The Ghost Dance took especial hold among the Sioux, where the bitterness against the whites was strongest, and in a short time the peaceful message of Wovoka was twisted into a new cult of resistance and revenge. Instead of doing the dance to see the next world, these tribes saw in it visions of their oppressors' destruction. They took to wearing garments called 'ghost shirts' that they came to believe possessed supernatural powers, and could not be penetrated by an enemy's bullets. Emotionally, psychologically, and most of all spiritually, as the Ghost Dance swept their reservations in 1890, the Sioux were preparing themselves for war, for one last bid to reclaim their land and their honor.

In November 1890, 600 Regulars were sent to the Pine Ridge and Rosebud reservations as fears mounted of an Indian breakout. The appearance of the soldiers immediately subdued some of the less committed warriors, while the rest pulled back to the farthest reaches of their lands and danced with renewed vigor and frenzy. Several hundred then joined and fortified themselves in a rocky fastness, while elsewhere, old Sitting Bull of the Hunkpapa encouraged the dance on his reservation as well, and Big Foot of the Miniconjous did the same.

The Army sent in General Nelson Miles, who had earlier overseen the taking of the Nez Perce and other fugitive tribes, to end the incipient uprising. He ordered the two chiefs arrested. Sitting Bull was taken on 15 December, and when Ghost Dancers rushed to rescue him, shooting ensued, and the old chief was murdered by his captors. The Hunkpapa were outraged, and left their reservation to join the Miniconjou. Two days before Christmas,

Above: *Photographed in 1895 after the death of Sitting Bull and the suppression of the Ghost Dance, Wovoka was the Paiute shaman whose vision reflected an immense yearning among Indians for a past life.*

Below: *The 8th Infantry moved from Fort Robinson to Pine Ridge in November 1890, in response to a paranoid Indian agent's request. The weather was unseasonably warm; there was no trouble at the agency.*

under the leadership of Big Foot, the 350 people of the united tribes left their reservation and set out to join the Oglala Sioux. Gradually their numbers were increasing, and there were fears that they would unite with the Oglalas and Brulés in their high stronghold. Miles sent out regiments to block their route.

The soldiers of the old 7th Cavalry – Custer's regiment – first encountered the fugitives, who quickly lost their fight and allowed the troopers to conduct them back toward Nebraska, from whence it had been decided they should be relocated to Omaha, far from their reservations and their ancestral lands. On 28 December 1890, the combined party made camp on Wounded Knee Creek, as more troopers arrived, along with artillery. Virtually surrounded by 500 or more soldiers, the Sioux had little choice but to do what they were told the next morning when the paltry 120 men were ordered to surrender their arms.

Then it all went wrong. The proud men refused to give up their guns. The soldiers forcibly began searching their belongings to find them. Yellow Bird, a shaman, started the Ghost Dance. His fervor spread to others. With the situation already explosive, one brave refused to yield his rifle when a soldier found it, and in the argument and tugging the gun went off. The sound sent a shock through both camps. The Sioux, who had been concealing their rifles inside the blankets they wore to keep out the winter cold, took them out and began firing at the bluecoats.

A savage hand-to-hand fight ensued, shooting, clubbing, knifing, and in the confusion the soldiers could not or did not differentiate between Indian man or woman, young or old. Then the soldiers withdrew quickly and their artillery on the hills surrounding the camp opened fire. In a matter only of minutes, 150

Below: *'I did not know then how much was ended. When I look back now from this high hill of my old age, I can still see the butchered women and children lying heaped and scattered . . .'*

Above: *Before the battle. Pine Ridge Agency, S. Dakota. After cavalry rounded up and disarmed Ghost Dance believers on Wounded Knee Creek, four Hotchkiss guns were directed onto the Sioux camp.*

Below: *Some of the dispossessed at Pine Ridge. Numbered among the Indians are American Horse, Young-Man-Afraid-of-his-Horses, Crow Dog and Kicking Bear. Buffalo Bill stands fourth from right.*

Above: *Some of the troopers sent to Pine Ridge before Wounded Knee, alerted by fears that trouble would follow the Ghost Dance. Soldiers remained idle; horses were even tethered to the field guns.*

Below: *Lieutenant John J. Pershing, 6th Cavalry, commanded local Indian police and troops who remained at Pine Ridge the year following the tragedy, trying to keep the pot from boiling over again.*

Indians and 25 soldiers lay dead, with another 89 wounded. Big Foot was among the dead, who lay on the ground that night as a blanket of white snow covered the bloody scene.

It was not, as later described, a 'massacre'. It was a spontaneous eruption of violence born of the uneasiness of the soldiers and the inflamed emotions of the Indians. The Army itself led an investigation, concluding that there had not been any intention of violence on the part of the soldiers, as indeed there had not. It was all a sad, needless, tragedy. It was also the last, pathetic, resistance of the Indian. The rest of the Ghost Dancers gave themselves up within two weeks.[5]

The red man was not the only vestige of the old days and ways to be disappearing in 1890. The range wars of decades before, when cattlemen and sheep herders fought over grass and water, seemed long past, as did the rivalries between livestockmen and homesteaders. If such controversies arose now, they were settled in courts. Resort to violence was a thing of the past. Almost.

In Johnson County, Wyoming, cattlemen and settlers quickly came into conflict with each other when the removal of the Sioux opened new land. The livestock men had organization and political influence on their side, especially when they formed the Wyoming Stock Growers' Association. It had its good sides, including management of the annual collection of the herds, registering brands, protecting the herds from infection, and lobbying in Laramie and Washington.

But the Association also fomented conflict. From earliest days on the Western range, common acceptance dictated that cattle found loose without brands, called 'mavericks', were the property of whomever found them. A number of herders took to starting their own small herds by such serendipity, even though

Below: *'. . . And I can see that something else died there in the bloody mud, and was buried in the blizzard. A people's dream died there.' Black Elk, survivor of Wounded Knee, December 1890.*

REMINGTON'S STUDIO

From these surroundings originated some of the most celebrated Western art of the 19th and early 20th centuries. This was the studio, originally situated in New Rochelle, New York, where Frederic Sackrider Remington produced some 2700 paintings and drawings, 22 bronzes, 2 novels and dozens of magazine articles. The studio is now housed in the Whitney Gallery of Western Art, one of the four major museums at the Buffalo Bill Historical Center, in Cody, Wyoming.

Even as the frontier was closing, Remington was an avid collector of Western memorabilia – cavalry sabers, rifles, hats, animal heads, skulls, Indian baskets, tomahawks, blankets, saddles, clothing – all of which filled his studio and which he used for reference in his paintings as he sought to 'define the West' through his art.

Born in 1861 in Canton, New York, he studied for a year and a half at Yale art school. At the age of nineteen he made a

trip to Montana which was to open his eyes and sow the seeds of inspiration which would turn him back to the art he had abandoned so abruptly. Of that trip and its repercussions he later wrote: 'Without knowing exactly how to do it, I began to record some facts around me, and the more I looked the more the panorama unfolded.' At twenty-one he came into an inheritance and headed for the frontier, buying a sheep ranch near the Flint Hills outside Peabody, Kansas. That venture – one of too much discomfort and hard work

for his liking – lasted about a year. After another business failure in Kansas City, he set out for the Southwest and, on his return, sold two sketches to *Harper's Weekly*, the first works to appear over his signature as a professional illustrator. In 1866 he persuaded *Harper's* to commission him to cover Geronimo's escapades between the San Carlos reservation and the Mexican border. Firmly ensconced in a Tucson hotel away from the action, Remington was to put into pictures first-hand reports from soldiers in the field.

With one exception, that was to be very much his style in the future.

Following Geronimo's capture, *Harper's* sent Remington to the Dakotas to record the Ghost Dance and the unrest in the Standing Rock Agency following Sitting Bull's assassination on 15 December 1890. He was close to Wounded Knee when the massacre took place in late December and, although he turned down the opportunity to join the burial party, his ultimate portrayal of the event as a glorious moment for the Army was to do him little credit.

Emerson Hough, the western writer, attributed the 'discovery' of the West to three rugged individuals: Buffalo Bill Cody, pulp magazine writer Ned Buntline, and Remington. Hough was referring to the West created in the minds of Easterners by these giants. Remington died in 1909, never fully accepted by the art establishment. However, works such as 'A Dash for the Timber', 'The Old Stage Coach of the Plains', and 'The Stampede' represent masterpieces of one of the finest artists of the genre.

their employers offered bonuses for returning any mavericks found for branding. Soon the larger members of the Association feared a growing threat to their hegemony over the range from these small holders and took steps to curb them. Cowboys not returning mavericks were fired. New law decreed that all mavericks belonged to the Association itself, and were to be sold to raise money to meet the Association's expenses. But these measures only spurred the small would-be stockmen to continue, and to start stealing calves as well, or else altering brands to cloud ownership. Local farmers, largely European immigrants, also stole an occasional steer, not for profit, but to feed a family. With thousands of animals roaming the unfenced range, a few surely would not be missed. Besides, the farmers had a grudge of their own as the stockmen tried steadily to erode their pastures for more grazing.

The cattlemen finally lashed out, and on their own without involving law enforcement. In July 1889 they lynched a storekeeper believed to be purchasing stolen cattle, and also a local prostitute who took cattle in payment. The Association denied involvement, but few believed it. Now it hired detectives and professional gunmen to patrol the range, scouring the prairies for thieves. Since there was little way to tell an honest small herder from a rustler, abuse and excess naturally followed. In 1890 and again the next year, more people died in isolated shootings. The farmers and small cattle raisers formed their own asso-

Left: *One of the victims of Wyoming's Johnson County War of 1892 was Nathan D. Champion (right), so-called king of the cattle thieves. Champion was murdered by hired guns brought in by cattle barons.*

Below: *Champion, standing against wheel, second from right, worked for the Bar C ranch in 1884. As a cowboy working small spreads on the grass-rich plains, he had reason to oppose the 'law' of the barons.*

ciation to fight back. Seeing the threat to them-selves and their herds growing, the large cattlemen finally lashed out viciously. In April 1892 they formed a group calling itself the Re-gulators – reminiscent of Billy the Kid's old bunch – and hired twenty-five Texan gunmen to come north to Wyoming. There they were given a 'hit list' of seventy presumed rustlers, and told to go get them, by any means neces-sary. The Johnson County War had begun.

It was a brief conflict. The Regulators bush-whacked here and there, and then cornered two presumed rustlers in a cabin. One was killed straight out, and the other died when they set fire to the house and he ran from the flames. But a friend had gotten word to Buffalo, the county seat, and soon more than 100 deputized farmers and small stock raisers, led by a friendly sheriff, were on the road. A few miles from Buffalo they took the Regula-tors by surprise and besieged them in a ranch-house, only to be rescued the next day by U.S. cavalry. For months afterward county offi-cials, sympathetic to the farmers, tried to pro-secute the Regulators, but without success, and the whole controversy gradually died out. The Stock Growers' Association retained its dominance of the range, and most of the small-time rustlers finally withdrew into the famed Hole-in-the-Wall country, from which they occasionally emerged to take a steer or two, and into which few lawmen or cattlemen dared try to enter.[6]

Not only did the Johnson County War sig-nal the virtual end to the old ways of vigilante

Right: *Poor Ella 'Cattle Kate' Watson had been lynched by rich cattlemen in 1889, along with her onetime lover Jim Averell in Natrona County, Wyoming. She paid the price for being implicated in rustling.*

Below: *The hired guns from Texas posed at Fort Russell in May 1892, after their ignominious defeat in northern Wyoming. Pinned down at the TA ranch house, they had to be rescued by Federal troops.*

'justice', it also played a role in the last groans of the old outlawry that had so distinguished the West in world eyes. Those small time rustlers retreating into the Hole-in-the-Wall were practically the last of their kind. Professional outlawry had almost disappeared by 1890, and the Butch Cassidy bunch were among the last trying to make it pay. It did not, and only their fortress-like refuge in the 'Hole' protected them for a time from apprehension. In the early 1890s the Union Pacific and other train lines, the chief targets of Cassidy's depredations, formed their own special guard forces, specially hired trackers and gunmen who rode with their horses in special cars on the trains and were ready to set out after bandits almost at once. They made things so hot for Cassidy that he gave up on Wyoming and went to South America.[7]

A few lone criminals still tried to make a go of it, but the 'trade' had lost all its glamor in the public eye. Most who tried to take the outlaw trail soon found themselves apprehended, and as the end of the century approached, the only ones who were actually making a living from their wicked ways were the reformed ones like Frank James and Cole Younger, who lectured following his release from a Minnesota prison. Others made rather sad spectacles of themselves being exhibited at 'Wild West' shows and carnivals, recounting their exaggerated exploits in true dime novel fashion. In the end, Westerners preferred to remember them the way they were in their heyday.

A few made their way to the new strikes in the Klondike in the 1890s. Wyatt Earp went there for a time, ever the hopeful prospector looking for easy riches, but he soon returned none the better off for it, and getting arrested for saloon fights in the bargain. The rush

Above: *William F. 'Buffalo Bill' Cody cracked the whip literally and metaphorically during his lifetime. Scout, hunter, Indian fighter and showman, he symbolized the winning of the West.*

Below: *The first official Buffalo Bill's Wild West Show opened in Omaha, Nebraska, in May 1883. Real cowboys and Indians took part in all subsequent shows; this group was photographed in Chicago in 1893.*

PAWNEE BILL

The career of Pawnee Bill (Gordon William Lillie) was closely intertwined with that of Buffalo Bill. Born in 1860, he was initially hired by Buffalo Bill as an interpreter for Pawnee scouts, a star attraction in 1883. His first season as an independent western showman was in 1888 with Annie Oakley and by 1890 Pawnee Bill's Wild West show was on the road, continuing with varied success until it merged with Buffalo Bill's in 1908. It folded mid-season in 1913 with financial problems. Pawnee Bill's fringed buckskin jacket and leggings are heavily garnished with beadwork; he carries a .40 caliber Bulliard repeating rifle such as he used in the circus acts.

W.F. CODY (1846-1917)

Occupations: Express rider, soldier, scout, Medal of Honor recipient, buffalo hunter, showman, entrepreneur. Later advocate of Indians, women, and management of natural resources.

Acquaintances: Included Presidents Grant, Roosevelt, Wilson; Annie Oakley, Wild Bill Hickok, Sitting Bull, George Armstrong Custer, Frederick Remington, Mark Twain.

Qualification: Champion of the West.

1 Tanned leather long coat with buffalo calf hide trim and fringe on sleeves, with colored beadwork and trade cloth decoration.

2 Gray felt wide brim hat with silk hatband marked in sweatband 'Stetson Co. 1224 Chestnut St, Philadelphia.'

3,4 Pair of Colt single-action Army revolvers with 7½ inch barrels, .44 caliber, nickeled finish with ivory grips, together with leather flap holsters lined with deer skin. The handguns were given by William F. Cody to W.F. Schneider in 1880.

5 Pair of Mexican silver-mounted spurs engraved 'Wild West'. The leather straps were embossed 'Morrow & Thomas Hdwe. Co. Amarillo, Texas'.

6 Winchester Model 1873 deluxe rifle, .44 caliber, factory engraved with select wood and gold-plated receiver.

7 Silver-mounted side knife and sheath made by William Rose, New York. Ivory handle is inlaid with two silver escutcheons engraved 'W.F.Cody' and 'Hays City, 1869'.

8 Pair of percussion single-shot deringers, .41 caliber. Silver escutcheons on each pistol are engraved 'W.F. Cody 1865'.

9 Beaded white buckskin gauntlets, probably of Sioux origin.

10 Silver-mounted deluxe saddle, 'Hon. W.F. Cody' inlaid in silver in the cantle. A silver plaque under the saddle horn is engraved 'Collins & Morrison Makers, Omaha, Neb'.

11 Silk top hat.

12 Masonic sword of Knights Templar, blade etched with Cody's name; and leather storage case for above, bearing legend 'W.F. Cody North Platte, Nebr.'.

13 Brown leather cigar

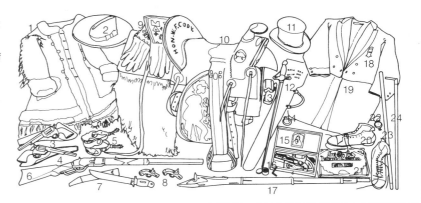

case with ink inscription on reverse 'From Chief Bull to Buffalo Bill'.

14 Gold watch made by the Elgin National Watch Co. The reverse is engraved 'Presented to Edward Z.C. Judson by his friend William F. Cody May 1885'.

15 Cased, engraved Colt Model 1849 pocket revolver, .31 caliber.

16 Tin of caps and gun wrench from cased set, item (15).

17 Relic Springfield Model

1866 Allin Alteration rifle, .58 caliber, named 'Lucretia Borgia' by Cody and used by him to hunt buffalo for the railroad.

18 Medal of Honor, 1862 Pattern. The reverse of the medal is engraved 'The Congress to William F. Cody, Guide, for Gallantry at Platte River, Nebr. April 26, 1872'.

19 Formal black tailcoat.

20 Pair of black high top tie shoes.

21 Stock certificate of Buffalo Bill's Wild West Show.

22 Gold watch with silver squirrel inlaid in front of case. The reverse is engraved 'Buffalo Bill (Hon. W.F. Cody) to White Beaver (D. Frank Powell, MD) Life Long Pards 1884'.

23 Gold-headed wooden cane, head engraved.

24 Chased gold-handled cane, engraved 'Compliments of Jos. H. Horton to Buffalo Bill'.

lacked what the Gold Rush of 1849 had had, somehow. Certainly, 100,000 or more headed for the new bonanza, but all were inexperienced either at mining or Yukon winters. The freezing cold, the killer mountain passes like the Chilkoot, the isolation – none of this had been encountered in 1849. Only a handful got rich, and most of the rest just drifted back home, disappointed. The West could no longer muster a good bonanza, it seemed. It was all disappearing. Where could the young blood of the nation go for the adventure, and excitement, that had once been synonymous with the American West?

It may be more than coincidence that just at this moment, the growing tensions with Spain over Cuba came to a head. The commencement of the 'splendid little war' of 1898 provided a vent for an outpouring of the pent-up national confusion and frustration over what was happening in the continent. To be sure, the Spanish-American War was chiefly a last imperialist land grab on the march of 'manifest destiny'. It cleared the Caribbean of a foreign power, allowed the establishment of an important naval base, and also gained American hegemony over the Philippines for a time. It also allowed the American Navy to exercise and demonstrate new muscle on the world stage, though admittedly against a crumbling old world nation that was outclassed in every way. It was America crowing its new strength and status on the dawn of a new century.

It also saw an overwhelming response from the West. Tens of thousands rushed to volunteer to carry the flag to new lands. Unsuccessful Klondike prospectors returned to take uniforms. Cowboys, tired of the now tedious range, volunteered. Theodore Roosevelt raised regiments of cavalry among these Western cowhands, leading them to Cuba as the famed Rough Riders. In Roosevelt's own word, it was a last chance for a 'bully' adventure. Meanwhile, for those looking to reap large profits from land, with the West filling up, this war offered new prospects. Puerto Rico became an American territory, and soon so would Hawaii. By using their imaginations, and their guns, Americans could make the 'West' go on a little longer. Indeed, in their minds, they might make it last forever.

But at the rate they were consuming and altering their environment, the physical West might not last so long. By 1890 they had changed the landscape irrevocably, and continued to do so at an ever-expanding rate. The forests were rapidly being denuded for the lumber and firewood to provide and heat homes and businesses. Northern California had once boasted the world's tallest forests, mighty redwoods hundreds of years old and measuring forty feet around. Now they were almost all gone, and large lumbering interests were spreading their influence to claim other primeval domains for the axe and saw, even paying derelicts to apply for homestead and pre-emption tracts in order to turn around and sell them to lumber companies who sometimes bought a whole acre for less than the worth of the wood in a single tree. What they did not cut down they burned accidentally through forest fires that swept huge tracts clear. By 1890, even as the first tentative conservation measures were starting to be felt, more than half of the West's forest was gone forever.

The impact on the wildlife, of course, hardly needs retelling. Whole species like the passenger pigeon became extinct as a result of wasteful, pointless slaughter. Even the bison, which once made the prairie thunder to the hooves of literally millions of the shaggy beasts, even the bison approached extinction. By 1900 many did believe them to be gone forever, not knowing that a mere 1,000

Below: *The legacy of the slaughter. Bones of millions of dead buffalo were gathered from the plains and shipped to Eastern processing plants in the 1870s and 1880s to be turned into fertilizer and china.*

Right: *The mark of the beast. Now that the buffalo had all but gone from the prairies, little remained but their bones and wallows such as this, where they would take mud or dust baths.*

animals had been kept alive in the hills by a few sympathetic men, red and white. A whole generation of young Americans at the turn of the century would grow up without ever seeing one except on the back of a five cent piece. The long-suffering beaver came close to suffering the same fate.

Beneath the ground they had changed things forever as well. Wherever gold, silver, copper, tin, lead, and other precious and semi-precious ores were found, the energetic prospectors, and then the large mining companies, honeycombed the earth. They levelled small mountains with high pressure jets of water to wash more ore out quicker, leaving other mountains of slag and rubble bleaching like bones in the sun. They changed the course of rivers to get at the precious metal, and thereby changed the ecology of much of the landscape, turning arid regions into near deserts, while eroding badly the land in the vicinity of the diggings with the run-off water. They dug

Left: *Hydraulic mining such as occurred on the American River in California wreaked untold damage on the terrain. What had begun in 1849 as a relatively innocent adventure became avarice personified.*

thousands of miles of ditches and canals, built the first western dams, and inundated the farm land of others in the process, without heed. Not until 1884 was hydraulic mining legally brought to a halt in California, and only after hundreds of thousands of acres of once-fertile farms were literally washed away.

No longer were there scenic vistas unmarked by the coming of the westerners. Roads criss-crossed the prairies and snaked through the mountains. They were still just worn paths on the ground, to be sure, but closer to the larger towns they were going through gravelling and the other first stages of evolution into hard-surfaced arteries. The railroads made an even more imposing scar across the country. Mountains were sliced by pick and dynamite to cut pathways, or else punched through with tunnels. Built-up grades appeared all along the track, making barriers where there had been none before. The tranquility of a misty dawn in Nebraska or Nevada was shattered now by the shriek of steam whistles, and dirtied by the belching smoke that left a fine layer of cinders along the way. Prairie grass choked by the roadbed in a covering of oil. The automobile lay barely a decade in the future.[8]

Yet not everything presented a picture of unremitting despoliation. As far back as 1866 Californians had realized the unique beauty of the Yosemite Valley, not far from San Francisco, and state legislators set it aside as a park, to remain untouched by the ravages of advancing economy and society. Six years later the National Park Service saw its historic origins in the Federal legislation designating the Yellowstone country a parkland for the benefit and enjoyment of all Americans. Happily, just as the frontier was closing, more and more of its natural and scenic wonders were about to be preserved under the kindly hand of the Park Service. And oddly enough, even some of the local municipalities and individuals began to see the need to hang on to what they still had left of the older West, before it was lost forever. John Muir and others in California strove to protect forest land from complete annihilation, and succeeded in getting legislation through Congress that slowed the rapacious appetites of the lumbermen. He would soon build on this to found the Sierra Club, dedicated to preserving and appreciating the Western environment. Even booming, bustling, San Francisco led the way in the fight for what later became known as 'air quality'. Sensing that the new automobile, barely yet seen on Western streets, presented a threat to the pure Pacific air its inhabitants so enjoyed, the city passed an ordinance prohibiting the operation of vehicles powered by internal combustion engines on its streets. Forgotten before long, the law remained on the books well into the 1960s.

There were not a few old-timers now who could look back in wonder, having lived through nearly the whole spread of the opening and closing of the West. They had seen all of them come, flourish, and eventually wane. The explorers, the Mountain Men, the '49ers, the Boys, the Wild Bunch, the Regulators, the squatters and 'sooners'. Even the cavalryman was virtually a thing of the past now, though he would survive into the next century thanks

Above: *Even as artists like Thomas Moran and Albert Bierstadt were painting their majestic views of the West, photographers continued to record other images; here, progress of the Colorado Midland Railroad.*

Below: *'Mountains were sliced by pick and dynamite . . . or else punched through with tunnels.' Here, passengers rest beside the euphoniously named Tunnel No 10, on 11 Mile Canyon, Colorado.*

to the military's perennial reluctance to abandon something that is already outmoded. The Indian survived, but only in an almost token vestige, like the bluecoated trooper. Only the land continued, eternal as always, and only those who came to settle and work it – the farmers, the livestock men, the cowboys – continued to grow and flourish. And, of course, the businessmen. They and the politicians, the statebuilders, built ever more and more on the foundations of the early town founders and city planners. San Francisco, Los Angeles, Seattle, Denver, Kansas City, Houston, were all well on their way to becoming among the largest metropolises in the United States. In the next century growth would see California alone rise to such population and richness that, if independent, it would rank among the wealthiest nations on Earth. Presidents and great statesmen would come from the West in that next century, men who would steer America on its course to becoming one of the leading superpowers in the world.

Below: *Painting it as it wasn't: Charles Schreyvogel at work on the roof of his Hoboken, NJ, apartment building in 1903. Favorite models were the local handyman and the son of a champagne salesman.*

As the West went into the next century, it gave more than just wealth and brilliant sons. It also leavened the American culture and mind with its own story, a story that was already a legend. However much it may have been fictionalized in the press, exaggerated and sanitized in the recollections of participants, still that legend exerted a powerful influence on coming generations. It was a legend of struggle, of individual and collective men and women fighting hostile elements to create a place for themselves, the very essence of the American ethic of self-reliance, hard work, egalitarianism – of the rewards available to those who had Horatio Alger's 'luck, pluck, and virtue'. No matter that it all came at the expense of the land and its original peoples; that was the West of reality. Americans came to love the West of the legend, as did the world. It stood for what men could do. It stood for never giving up. It stood for the limitless potential awaiting those who kept pressing on into the unknown. In books, songs, films, and art, that ethic would permeate the next century to such an extent that no amount of revelation about the real Wyatt Earp, the true treatment of the red man, or the cynicism and venality of a host of early 'pioneers', could dent the shining armor of the Western ex-

perience. As the great film director John Ford said in all sincerity, when the truth conflicts with the legend, 'print the legend'.

In the summer of 1969, two months short of a century from that moment when the last spike was driven to link Atlantic and Pacific with the iron horse, another equally ungainly vehicle completed another epic journey. One of the three passengers emerged, climbed down a short ladder, and uttered some words about a giant leap for mankind. To those who heard him, those with no poetry in their souls, it was Neil Armstrong announcing that Man had reached the Moon. But old-timers would have known better.

It was just another American, heading West.

REFERENCES

1 Richard A. Bartlett, *The New Country*, p. 114.
2 David Lavender, *The Great West*, p.388-9.
3 *Ibid.*, pp. 389-90.
4 Bartlett, *The New Country*, pp. 357-9.
5 Robert Utley, *Frontier Regulars*, pp. 402-7.
6 Bartlett, *The New Country*, p. 232; Lavender, *The Great West*, pp. 385-7.
7 Frank Richard Prassel, *The Western Peace Officer*, pp. 140-41.
8 Bartlett, *The New Country*, pp. 240-42, 270-72, 339-40.

INDEX

Page numbers in **bold** indicate illustrations or mentions in captions.

Photograph: *The stagecoach from Harlem, Montana.*

Photograph: *Crossing the Missouri River at Wilder's Landing (also called Rocky Point), Montana Territory.*

PICTURE CREDITS

The publisher wishes to thank the following organizations and individuals who have supplied photographs, credited here by page number and position. For reasons of space, some references are abbreviated as follows: **AHC,** American Heritage Center, University of Wyoming, Laramie; **AHS,** Arizona Historical Society, Tucson; **BBHC,** Buffalo Bill Historical Center, Cody, Wyoming; **CFT,** Colin F. Taylor collection, Hastings; **CHS,** Colorado Historical Society, Denver; **CJCLDS,** Church Archives, The Church of Jesus Christ of Latter-Day Saints, Salt Lake City; **CSCSL,** California Section, California State Library, Sacramento; **DPLWHD,** Denver Public Library, Western History Department, Denver; **ISHS,** Idaho State Historical Society, Library and Archives, Boise; **KSHS,** Kansas State Historical Society, Topeka; **MinnHS,** Minnesota Historical Society, St Paul; **MontHS,** Montana Historical Society, Helena; **NA,** National Archives; **NSHS,** Nebraska State Historical Society, Lincoln; **OMHD,** Oakland Museum Historical Department; **SHSW,** State Historical Society of Wisconsin, Madison; **SI,** Smithsonian Institution, Washington, DC; **TSL,** Archives Division, Texas State Library, Austin; **UAL,** University of Arizona Library, Tucson; **UPR,** Union Pacific Railroad, Omaha; **WFB,** History Department, Wells Fargo Bank, San Francisco; **WHCUOL,** Western History Collections, University of Oklahoma Library, Norman. All illustrations have been supplied courtesy of the above collections.

Positions: a, Above; b, Below; l, Left; r, Right; t, Top; m, Middle; al, Above left; ar, Above right; bl, Below left.

The editor offers additional thanks to the following:

Bob and Terry Edgar of Old Trail Town, Cody, Wyoming, who not only allowed us to photograph the hearse on pages 142-143 from their fine and original collection of Western memorabilia, but welcomed us, summer and winter.

The C.M. Russell Museum, Great Falls, Montana, for permission to quote substantially from the letter by Irving R. Bacon on pages 232-233.

The University of Nebraska Press, Lincoln, Nebraska, for permission to quote from *Black Elk Speaks* in the captions on pages 238 and 239.

John Carter of the Nebraska State Historical Society, for advice on photographs concerning the conflict at Wounded Knee.

Eric Paddock and Rebecca Lintz of the Colorado Historical Society, Denver, Colorado.

Colin and Betty Taylor, Hastings, England. Dr Taylor wrote captions for the sixteen pieces of artwork, advised the artist on their authenticity, loaned illustrations and pieces from his personal collection (the C.F. Taylor collection), and acted in an advisory capacity throughout.

Mark Holt for photographs of Bent's Fort and the covered wagon on pages 52-53 and 70-71.

pp. 28-9 No. 3, gift of Nick Eggenhoffer; No. 7, gift of Sanford Beecher; No. 9, gift of Franklin Farnsworth, Nos 11, 14, R.G. Bowman collection. pp. 36-7 gift of Olive and Glenn Nielson; BBHC photo by Robert Weiglein. pp 84-5 No. 15, gift of Lillian Hackett. pp. 104-5 Nos 17, 22, John W. Painter collection. pp. 122-3 Firearms, Dr Kenneth O. Leonard collection. p. 147, gift of Olive and Glenn Nielson. pp. 150-51 No. 5, gift of Quin Blair family. p. 158 gift of Mr and Mrs George Abrahamson and Mr Bruce Kennedy. pp. 186-7 No. 1, Mr and Mrs Stanley Siggins collection; No. 11, D. L. Becker family collection. pp. 218-19, roundup outfit, gift of Harvey W. Willcutt family.

Note on the endpapers. Both maps were photographed from books in the McCracken Library, BBHC. The front endpaper map, constructed from surveys of Lewis and Clark and Pike, dates to 1822. The back endpaper map shows Indian reservations in the United States in 1899.

Endpaper maps, BBHC; **1,** Wadsworth Atheneum. The Ella Gallup Sumner and Mary Catlin Sumner Collection; **2-3,** OMHD; **4-5** CHS; **6-7,** USGS; **9** (a) USGS, (b) SI; **12** (b) SI, (a) Corcoran Gallery of Art, Gift of William Wilson Corcoran; **13** (a) as **12** (a); **16** SI; **17** (a) SI, (b) DPLWHD; **18** (b) SHSW, (l) TSL; **21** (a) USGS, (b) Santa Barbara Mission/Library; **22** DPLWHD; **23** (t) ISHS; **26** KSHS; **27** (a) MontHS, (b) KSHS; **30** (a) St Joseph Museum, (b) OMHD; **34** (b) CJCLDS, (a) St Joseph Museum; **35** BBHC; **36-37** BBHC; **39** (r) CFT, (a) ISHS, (b) KSHS; **40** (a) Burlington Northern Inc., (b) KSHS; **41** (a) DPLWHD, (b) OMHD; **43** (b) OMHD, (a) KSHS; **44-45** DPLWHD; **50** (a) CHS, (b) BBHC; **51** (b) SHSW, (a) KSHS, (b) CHS; **54** (a) BBHC, (b) MontHS; **58** (a) CSCSL, (b) WFB; **59** (a) CSCSL, (b) WFB; **62-63** all CSCSL; **65** (a) WFB, (b) CSCSL; **66** (a) DPLWHD, (b) CSCSL; **67** DPLWHD; **68** NA; **69** DPLWHD; **72** DPLWHD; **73** (a) NSHS, (b) NA; **74-75** all CJSLDS; **76** (t,a) CJCLDS, (b) DPLWHD; **77** (a) CJCLDS, (b) KSHS; **78-79** KSHS; **80-81** WHCUOL, **82** (a) NA, (b) WHCUOL; **83** National Portrait Gallery, Smithsonian Institution; **86** (a) CHS, (b) CSCSL; **88-89** (r) Hayes Otoupalik Collection; **90** KSHS; **91** (b) KSHS; **94-95** all Salamander Books; **97** State Historical Society of Missouri; **98-99** Beinecke Rare Book and Manuscript Library, Yale University; **100-101** (b) SI, (ar) NA; **102** WHCUOL; **106** SI,

107 (l,a) SI, (m,b) TSL; **108** NA; **109** SI; **112** MinnHS; **113** (a) SI, (b) MinnHS; **114** (r) Salamander Books, (b) DPLWHD; **115** (b) MontHS; **118** (a) DPLWHD, (b) SI; **119** (a) Peter Palmquist; **120** (ar) SI, (am, b) NA; **121** (a) SI, (b) CFT; **125** (t) AHS; (m, b) DPLWHD; **126-127** NSHS; **128** (a) UPR, (b) Burlington Northern Inc.; **129** (a) CHS, (b) ISHS; **131** (t) CSCSL, (m, b) DPLWHD; **132** KSHS; **133** (t, b) NSHS; (m) CFT; **136** (a) KSHS, (b) NSHS; **137**; (a) NSHS, (b) CFT; **138** (a) KSHS, (b) US Dept of Agriculture; **140-141** all NSHS; **142** KSHS; **144-145** all KSHS except **145** (m) MontHS; **146** (t) BBHC, (b) DPLWHD; **148** (t) MontHS, (b) UPR; **149** (t) KSHS, (b) NSHS; **152** (t) KSHS, (b) Boot Hill Museum; **153** (a) KSHS, (b) BBHC; **156-157** all Boot Hill Museum; **159** (a) Boot Hill Museum, (b) CFT; **160-161** BBHC; **162** (r) BBHC, (b) DPLWHD; **163** (r) CHS, (b) BBHC; **164** (b) BBHC, (r) DPLWHD; **165** (l) AHC, (b) CHS; **168-169** all Jesse James Farm Museum; **170** (tl) BBHC, (tr) WFB, (bl) DPLWHD, (br) CHS; **172-173** all UPR except **172** (l) WFB; **174-175** all UAL; **176** Lincoln County Heritage Trust; **177** DPLWHD; **180** (bl, al) AHS, (br) DPLWHD; **181** both AHS; **184** (a) DPLWHD, (b) AHS; **185** KSHS; **188-189** all AHS except **189** (tr) BBHC; **191** KSHS; **192-193** CHS; **194** BBHC; **195** CHS; **196** CHS; **198** CHS; **199** (a) CHS, (b) DPLWHD; **202** MontHS; **203** CHS; **204-205** all CHS; **208** (a) Brown Brothers, (b) BBHC; **209** CHS; **210**, **211** all CHS; **214** CHS; **215** (a) Library of Congress, (b) CHS; **216** CHS; **217** MontHS; **220** (a) MontHS, (b) CHS; **221** KSHS; **223** (a) KSHS, (b) MontHS; **224** CHS; **225** (a) BBHC, (b) Brown Brothers; **226** BBHC; **229** (a) MontHS, (b) CHS; **230** (a) Dept of Interior, (b) NA; **231** (a) DPLWHD, (b) WHCUOL; **232-233** BBHC, bequest in memory of Houx and Newell families; **234** (a) TSL, (b) CFT; **235** (a) CFT, (b) SI; **237** (a) SI, (b) DPLWHD; **238-239** all DPLWHD except **239** (b) Henry E. Huntington Library and Art Gallery; **242** all AHC; **244** BBHC; **248** KSHS; **249** (a) CSCSL, (b) KSHS; **250** CHS; **251** National Cowboy Hall of Fame; **252-253** CHS; **254-255** MontHS; **256** ISHS.

Photograph:
Street scene, Bellevue, Idaho, 1885.